Time for a Change of Hemisphere

By Shelby Simpson

Published by

DRUNK
PUBLISHING

Oklahoma City

Drunk Publishing, Inc.
Oklahoma City, Oklahoma
P.O. Box 75734
Oklahoma City, OK 73147
Editing by Ryann Gordon
Cover design by Jenkin Hammond

To my mom, Cate.
You are the best mom in the galaxy.
Thank you is not enough.

To my wonderful partner Chad, my amazing colleagues Mary and Jake, my awesome friends in the USA and around the world, the MPW Program professors at the University of Oklahoma, the staff at World Literature Today, my waxer, and every person that ever heard me say, "I want to be a writer," and replied, "You should."

THANK YOU, THANK YOU, THANK YOU, THANK YOU (repeat into infinity).

Author's Note

Events in this book may be out of sequence. Many conversations are recreated and names changed. It is written from my perspective as a traveler, a flawed human, and a learner. It is drawn from my memory and the memory of certain others who shared some of the events. Others may tell the tales differently, but all the tales are true.

Table of Contents

Prologue

"The biggest adventure you can take is to live the life of your dreams."
Oprah Winfrey

Grey Goose vodka led the conversation. I jiggled my glass to get one last clink out of my melting ice cubes, re-crossed my legs, and kicked off one flip-flop. My tanned foot dangled free and bare in the breeze, just the way I like it. If I'm in shoes, I'm overdressed.

I was sitting with two people—work acquaintances. We encircled a patio table in the fading nine p.m. sun. It was the late August, night sun of Oklahoma that's still hot but not stinging. It's my favorite, but the people I was sitting with were not.

They weren't bad people or not my type, at least one of them wasn't. It's just that they were part of my work life, not my after work life. These days, I try not to blur the lines. I treat my workplace like Superman treats Clark Kent—separate. Work is the stage show. Friends and family have backstage passes.

The ladies I sat with on that brick patio were part of the decorative language reserved for use between nine and five. They were the posturing, politically correct, and metacognition part of my existence, not the *Cards Against Humanity*, Eazy-E, bowl-cut wigs, and keg ball part.

But there I was, after five p.m., smoking a cigarette in front of them and failing big time on my Superman / Clark Kent dichotomy. Blame it on the alcohol. It had my tongue wagging. I had accidently moved from an articulate conversation about higher education to explaining how I'd shown my panties to my elderly neighbor earlier that day.

"Poor gardening-wardrobe choice," I clarified, pointing to my salmon and turquoise baby doll dress and chugging the rest of my drink.

Relax. It will be over soon.

My colleagues smiled and nodded, probably taking mental notes to remove me from their "possible candidates" list for project lead.

I reminded myself to watch my mouth. *Do not mention last year's Halloween costume, or any of them for that matter. I repeat—no John Hancock Blocker stories.*

But it was too late.

With warm, eighty-proof cockles, my storytelling rolled downhill. I moved from panty flashing tales to complaining about people who don't tell you when you have lettuce stuck in your tooth, and then to providing private details of my life. Family details. Things my colleagues didn't need to know, like stories about my ill relationship with a certain family member.

The Goose was fully loose—honking around the field with spread wings and crossed eyes, after-work drinks gone wild. And that's when she said it.

The girl I didn't really like in the first place certified my aversion to her. She knew I'd traveled around the world. Sometimes she slid sideways comments in about me being privileged for doing so. Sometimes she acted like something was off about all the traveling I'd done over the last ten years. This time, she really dug her nails in.

"Ahhhhhhhhh. I get it. You have family problems. You wanted to get away from your life here, so you've been staying busy trying to fill a gap. That's why you move around the world all the time," she oozed through a half smirk.

I stared at her. She lifted her martini in slow motion and inserted the tiny straw into the corner of her puckered mouth. *Slurp.*

I thought, *What a cheese nug for brains, be-atch.*

Then, I considered giving her an old-fashioned choke-out for funsies. Instead I took a long draw on my ciggie and exhaled a dragon plume inches above her head.

Not a word—none were needed.

It wasn't my first rodeo.

XXX

Wanting to scale the globe and not own a house or have a permanent address is something that your friends and family may not understand. When I first started talking about living overseas long-term, some people treated me like I was talking about making a spaceship out of Doritos and flying it into a black hole. Without mad money, a secured job overseas, issued camouflage, or secret Mormon underwear—I was talking nonsense. Besides that, they thought traveling to the places I wanted to go sounded like a death trap, especially if I went without a group or company. Going alone, as a girl, was silly and dangerous.

At age twenty-four when I finally said, "I'm moving to Indonesia for a year," most people looked at me like I'd lit my hair on fire.

"Really?" some would ask with a squeak of skepticism, ending their thought with a pregnant, "Huh…"

Others would just grin at me—*yeah, sure you are.*

It wasn't the sparklers and ass slaps reception I'd wanted. It actually kind of shocked and hurt me.

After I left the United States, my year overseas turned into two, then five, and then many more. With only a few stopovers in the States, my global movement became an even bigger head shaker to some people.

"I think she's moving to Taiwan or somewhere."

"Who knows what she's doing."

"Shelby, oh she's in Guata-Scande-Austra-Phili-andria making out with a guy who uses a stick for a toothbrush."

Dismissive wave of the hand and a flippant flutter of the eyelashes, *She's crazy.*

The longer I moved around, the more my traveling seemed to be considered a high wire act that teetered between interesting and irresponsible.

Now, years down the line, I better understand that the things in life that are different are always scrutinized. I don't think my traveling is unprecedented. It's not. Millions do it. It doesn't make me unique. It doesn't mean I'm unable to hold still, or that I'm smarter, richer, suffering from Peter Pan syndrome, or anything at all. It's just what I choose to do, but it is a different path than the one most Americans walk, hence its dubious acceptance at times.

I've found that a lot of Americans don't like foreign chat, or at least many don't seem to. My lifestyle is sometimes seen as "weird". At times I've been treated like a mystery blob that's washed up out of nowhere on the beach—poked with sharp comments to figure out which box I fit into. I've had labels thrown at me from a safe distance. If one stuck, then I could be filed away nicely into the "that makes sense" cabinet, under H for Hippie or maybe T for Trustafarian, but most likely R—Running from something.

In other countries, long-term travel is understood. People like to talk about life outside of their borders, and not just in a highbrow manner or for political banter.

They shoot the shit about Brazilian titties, cars in Cuba, Ibizan dance parties, or an orangutan in Borneo that helped them hang their laundry. It's not status conversation. It's life. It's everyday talk—for the rich, the poor, and everyone in between. Life in new places is relevant, and if you move around forever, it's no biggie.

Some countries consider long-term travel a rite of passage. New Zealanders even have a name for world travel built into their vocabulary—O.E. It means "overseas experience", and it's dropped into causal conversation a lot.

"He's on his O.E.," says a mom between coffee sips.

"Oh lovely, for a year?" asks the woman across from her, spreading a thin layer of butter onto her toast.

"He thinks maybe two. It depends on where he finds work and when his savings runs dry, but right now he's surfing in Turkey," the mom says with pride.

"Excellent. Good on him," the friend says with just as much pride.

The conversation is barely a blip in their brunch gossip—cool, but not shocking.

Americans don't pass down a tradition of living overseas. The majority doesn't ever live in another country or travel overseas long-term. American parents might not be so chuffed about their kid going away for two years on a vague, worldwide trip straight out of high school, college, or ever. Living overseas isn't necessarily encouraged or believed to be within reach, unless it is accomplished through a company, the military, academia, or church. I have my own beliefs about why Americans stay within their red, white, and blue borders. There are many legitimate and good reasons, but that's a whole other ball of wax I won't go into.

Here's what I want to emphasize: leaving the U.S. to try a new culture is a super healthy and positive move.

People know stuff out there. Other countries and cultures are just as smart, fun, inspiring, supportive, inventive, philosophical, amazing, and correct as America. Sometimes, even more. Learning this does not make you anti-American and it does not mean you have no U.S.A. love or ability to make it here.

Living in a new country will help you gain the depth to understanding America and loving it for what it is and for what it isn't. When/if you come back, your place of birth will be fresh, exotic, and probably more lovable due to your time apart. You'll appreciate and take advantage of the life this incredible country offers. In the U.S.A. there are still wide-open pastures waiting to host the blueprints to your dream.

Also, leaving for a few years does not hinder your career or academic progress. If anything, it will enhance this aspect of your life when you dial into it with harder focus and deeper dedication later on. You'll have real life experience under your belt—super diverse experiences. Pretty sure that's valuable.

If you've been thinking about moving overseas without a plan and you've caught some flack, I'm not surprised.

Ignore it. Follow your dreams. If you haven't, that's awesome. Carry on.

XXX

I'm thirty-eight years old. I've been to thirty-nine countries. I've lived in seven of them. I did most of my traveling over the span of a decade and a bit. When I left on my adventure overseas, I was happy. My life was magnificent. Fun. Funny. I'd just started my first job out of college and it was ah-ite, but I wanted more.

I simply had a raging desire to investigate the planet. It burned in my blood, so I made up my mind to go. Then I did. I didn't know anyone who had traveled internationally long-term. No one recommended it to me. I just figured it out.

So…how does one accomplish long-term world travel?

For me, I didn't get around the world by having a secure job waiting on the other end, nor did I live off a dollar a day, rely on others' charity, or use abandoned buildings as my home-away-from-home. I didn't volunteer, join the military, use only an academic exchange program, church, or any other existing entity. Those platforms are great, but if you don't have or want one of those options, you don't need them.

I was able to go overseas by earning and saving money at home, and then buying work visas for other countries. I worked hard to save money and I saved harder. I didn't make a lot of money, but I stretched each dollar ten thousand miles.

I'm the definition of middle class. I've never made under thirty thousand annually or over a hundred thousand. I've been on both ends of that spectrum, and when I first decided to move overseas I was making thirty thousand dollars in the Bay Area of California. There, that salary is not middle class—it's poor. Yet, I still had enough money to get overseas, because I sacrificed.

I had roommates. I ate at home. I got drunk in my living room before going to the bar. No shopping; no splurging. If you really want something, you can make it happen. It's a sacrifice.

There are trade-ins for your dream becoming a reality, but sacrifices and hard choices exist no matter what you're doing in life. Happiness depends on recognizing the sacrifices you can swallow and the ones that will suffocate you into a zombie existence. Choose wisely and make changes when needed.

You can get working holiday visas for many other countries when you're younger than thirty years old, sometimes even when you're older. I got those visas by researching, calling embassies, filling out paperwork, paying for work clearance, and then getting on a plane without worrying myself into analysis paralysis. The rest I figured out once I got to my destination.

There are many ways to go about saving for travel and affording life in a foreign country. You just have to figure out the way that will work for you. There are even books to teach you, *Life Nomadic*, *The Secrets of a Savvy Traveler*, and many more.

You can travel in groups, with someone else, or on your own.

Sometimes I traveled alone. Sometimes I was with friends. You don't have to have someone with you to move overseas because you're never alone in new lands. The world is full of people who are trying out new soil. You will meet new and amazing people everywhere you go. I recommend going on your own at least once—the experience is invaluable.

I could go on and on, but this book isn't going to teach you how to travel long-term internationally. What this book will do, I hope, is give you the nudge needed to actually get going. I just want to make sure that before you get nudged, you clearly recognize that YOU CAN DO IT, even if you don't have much money or understanding of international life.

If you want to go but you don't know how, don't worry—you'll learn. Just go.

Do it before globalization kills authenticity. Go before ecosystems shrivel and rare environments disappear. Get out before you fill your life with a million reasons that will stop you. Live like you would have if no one ever showed you patterns to follow or footsteps to walk in.

Tell fear to fuck off.

Embrace change.

I dare say that a nationality shake-up could calm down the world—maybe get us closer to understanding each other. Get a new address that ends in Zone Eleven-teenth, Galaxy Blue, B.P. 732 Antananarivo 101—Republic of Madagascar. I double dog dare you.

If you do, you'll see what I'm talking about.

The day I booked my ticket to move overseas for the first time, I was ecstatic. I couldn't sleep. It felt like Christmas Eve, my first time watching Freddy Krueger, and pre-game jitters all balled into one.

During the nights leading up to my actual departure, my mind crawled with a ton of assumptions. I assumed my brass balls would grow bigger and brassier. I thought I'd have my ideals confirmed, my fantasies heightened, and figure out my life. I was sure I'd have my mind blown by nature and my soul touched by humans who would be so much and so nothing like me.

I was right and wrong.

Life is complicated—layered. There is no one view or answer. I didn't quite understand that until I traveled. But I will say that some things are pretty simplistic, like the fact that novelty and challenge bring happiness.

Please take a minute and fifty-seven seconds out of your life before you continue reading and watch Jason Silva's "Happiness Lives in the New," from his *Shots of Awe* series, then you'll hear what I'm talking about.

Learn.

Explore.

Be stirred.

Here is hoping you book a flight after you read this book and that you're doing it while you're young—not waiting until you're grey downstairs. Get on a plane. Take advantage of the free alcohol and this one life you've been gifted.

PART I

"The only true wisdom is in knowing you know nothing."
Socrates

If you did something daring.

If you decided to move around the world for a year or twenty, seeing every flower, fish, and freak you desired…you might gain and lose things. Some expected—others, not so much.

Long-Term Travel Possible Gain List

1. THAT story. The one that's too crazy to be true. The one that blows minds, even your own.
2.
3.
4.
5.
6.
7.

Long-Term Travel Possible Loss List

1. Your naivety.
2.
3.
4.
5.
6.
7.

A Good Bad—That Story

CHAPTER 1

"Wanna go on the prison tour?" Deirdre asked in the same way someone might toss around an invite to a matinee.

Her hazel eyes blinked once and then slanted to match her smile, persuasion lasers burning "YES YOU DO" onto my forehead. She sat across from me on her bed, legs crisscrossed, hands cradling a *Lonely Planet*. Her fresh-out-of-the-shower hair was brushed back into a shiny curtain of onyx. She looked happy. It made me happy too.

"Mmmm..." I mused. "Tour..."

It was a response intentionally devoid of meaning. Lounged out, I returned the smile but not an answer. Instead, I went back to watching the 1980's classic *Purple Rain*. Prince pelvic-thrusted his way across our ancient, rabbit-eared TV in his crushed velvet and bejeweled shoulder pads, his skintight pants accentuating his mammal toe.

I was in heaven. The movie was a stroke of good luck that I couldn't have imagined if I'd tried. My foot bounced to the beat of "Let's Go Crazy." The drum kept rhythm not only with Prince's stage humping, but also with the distant thud of machine gun fire outside our window.

Supposedly there was some coup going on in the city we were in—La Paz, Bolivia. At least, that was the rumor on the street. We'd also heard that gunplay was pretty common for La Paz, and somehow that made us feel better. Gat shots = normal. If the locals were cool with it, so were we.

It was just a bit of random banging coupled with a more random eighties flick in the middle of twenty-first century Bolivia. No biggie. The outlandish was becoming standard during our South America escapade.

So, despite the reports, I was relaxed. Deirdre was her usual spunky self. The third leg of our traveling tripod, SeDessie, was tucked deep into her turn in the shower. I could hear the water splashing extra loud against the tub every now and then, probably caused by a squeeze of her long hair. The smell of coconut wafted through the crack below the door. It made me eager and I sank deeper into my pillow, imagining how good a hot shower was going to be.

For the past three days I'd been fantasizing about it. Soap. Hot water. Hot water. Hot water. Give me the hot water.

Now it was only minutes away, and I promised myself I'd kill both SeDessie and Deirdre if the hot water ran cold by the time I made it into bathroom. I'd go medieval on their asses. I wanted and needed that hot shower.

We'd had a rough week prior—intrepid traveling at its finest. I'd even suffered the first stages of frostbite, so that shower was worth its weight in gold. It meant the world to all of us. It meant a slight return to normalcy.

"Don't you want to go on the prison tour? You heard that chick say it's pretty cool," Deirdre pressed again.

"Huh?" I asked, ripped back into reality from my shower daydreams. "The prison tour? I dunno. I just really want to go see the pink dolphins."

"It's booked out. We can't," Deirdre reminded me.

I stared at Prince's high-heeled boots and thought *he's short as shit*, and *I can't argue Deirdre's point*. She was right. The flight to see the dolphins was booked out, but I desperately wanted to fly into the pocket of the Amazon that boasted those rare creatures—an area not far from where we were in La Paz. I was dying to go, even if it meant actually *dying* to go.

To get there, we would have had to board one of Bolivia's flying pig airplanes that reeked of gasoline and seated six or fourteen passengers, depending on how many Bolivians could cram into one seat—no seatbelts, smoking optional. The thought made me want to trifecta—poo, spew, and pee all at once, but I was still willing to aneurism my way through it if it meant seeing those regal albino animals.

Now, so close and yet so far away from them, I imagined missing out on a photo op with a pink porpoise—my new best friend—both of us wearing Amazon4Life headbands and doing synchronized swimming moves in the river. The heaviness of disappointment I felt made my bottom lip protrude.

"No, I want to see the dolphins," I pouted.

"So, you want to take death road there? That's our only option if we can't fly," said Deirdre.

"Well, no. I don't really want to take death road there," I said.

"Well then, since we're not making it to the Amazon, let's do this tour thing, hun. It will be great! I promise."

I huffed and readjusted my pillow.

"Look, I know the flight to the Amazon is booked out, but those dolphins are majestic."

"Yeah, but the tour is gonna be just as wonderful! Please? I mean, we might as well while we're here. Can you at least just call and ask about it?" Deirdre urged.

"Uuhhhhhggg…"

I sat up to face her, swinging my feet to the ground. The tile was slick under my rainbow-knitted socks. I slid them in figure eights while I sulked.

"Fine. I'll call, but I really want to figure out a way to get to the Amazon. Pink dolphins are Plan A. There has to be a way. I mean they're pink dolphins. They're fucking exceptional."

"Okay. Dolphins Plan A," Deirdre agreed, but her grin didn't.

XXX

As one of my best friends in New Zealand, where I'd been living for a few years, Deirdre was allowed to be a bit pushy. She put up with my shit on the regular.

"Stay in your lane, Simpson," was her mantra.

Boundaries sometimes don't occur to me, and it turns out that I can really annoy people, but D (as many call her) was good at reeling me in. Whether I was trying to move someone's indoor furniture outdoors or insisting the lead singer of a band wear my mullet wig on stage— "WEAR IT! W E A R I T D A M N Y O U!"—Deirdre was great at serving me gulps of logic to keep me out of trouble. The rest of her efforts were spent throwing us headfirst back into it.

A strong-willed Kiwi chick with an artsy side and entrepreneurial brain, D started her own graffiti art business at age twenty-three. She's a weapon of mass destruction. I met her at a party in Auckland, New Zealand, where I explained how I had almost impaled my labia climbing over her front gate, and we were practically inseparable ever since.

When I told her I was going to South America for three months, she bought a ticket too. She didn't ask if she could join me. Didn't need to. She simply met me in Argentina two days after I arrived. I trusted Deirdre's judgment, and if she was super keen to go on a prison tour, there had to be a good reason.

She tossed the travel bible toward me—a *Lonely Planet* guidebook. It landed equidistant between my hand and the ancient rotary telephone sitting on the nightstand, mockingly convenient.

"It has a number for the prison. I think you can make reservations for the tour or something," she said.

I didn't move.

"It's under San Pedro," she encouraged.

"But...my dolphin friends..." I groaned as the bathroom door swung open.

"Oh mah gawd! Gurrrrrl, that might just have been the best shower I've ever taken. I'm pretty sure it changed mah LIFE!" SeDessie drawled, gliding out of the bathroom wearing a fluffy towel as a turban. Steam trailed her moist footsteps. Fog pillows poured into our room.

"That good, eh?" I asked, leaning back on my elbows.

"It was awwwwwe-some. What ch'all doin?" she asked, plopping down on my bed and massaging a thick coat of cream that smelled of peppermint and Frangipani into her delicate skin. "Oh, holy shit no way! *Purple Rain*! Does this place have room service? I mean if they have *Purple Rain* they have to have a club sandwich. I feel like an Orange Crush. Yum!"

"Deirdre wants me to call about some prison tour thing, because we can't get a flight to the Amazon," I said, fingering the pages of the guidebook.

"Hell no, I'm not going to some Bolivian prison," SeDessie replied, moving onto towel-drying her chestnut mane.

She took her time squeezing, tousling, and occasionally smelling her clean hair. She grabbed a bottle of elixir, then considered.

"But...if it means I hang out alone while you two go off for the day, then yeah, I guess I'll go."

"What?" I asked, eyebrows hitting the ceiling. "Soooo, you're saying you want to check the prison out too?"

"Sure."

She transitioned from hair care to lip luxury, then to rummaging through a make-up bag that I knew held only topline beauty potions and lotions, keeping one eye on Prince the whole time. She smelled like a slice of angel food cake drizzled in fruit sauce.

To my right, Deirdre was doing a celebratory hand jive.

"So you're for sure in, SeDessie?" I asked again.

"Uh-huh," she muttered, making love to her products and the sight of Prince's ruffled shirt.

That was it. I was chest-bumped out of the dolphin trip. The vote stood two to one, and I owed SeDessie a solid anyway. I felt compelled to do whatever she wanted. She'd been a trouper throughout this trip, and I'd invited her along knowing damn well that it wasn't exactly up her alley.

She was champagne, spa treatments, swimming pools, and cabana boys, but I'd brought her to a world of bloated goats, warm Coca-Cola, dust facials, and unpredictable sleeping arrangements. So far she'd been amazing, but every day I half-expected a bitch slap across my cheekbone.

SeDessie is one of my "big-baller" American friends. At the time, she worked in hospital management for a major medical company in San Francisco and made more money in five minutes than I saw in four years.

I'd taken her out of Knob Hill and dropped her smack dab in the middle of alpaca sandwiches and altitude sickness. But, for part of her reward, Deirdre and I granted her two of her La Paz wishes:

1. A place to drop off her dirty laundry.
2. A nice hotel room instead of a hostel.

We'd found the laundry mat in the middle of town.

We'd found the archaic hotel tucked away on a steep cobblestone road that threatened to collapse our lungs during our climb to its ancient wooden doors.

At thirteen thousand feet above sea level, the city of La Paz was literally breathtaking. It was funky, ancient, weird, and cool. The thin air gave it that deoxygenated charm you can't put your finger on, because everything seems rather indescribable when you're about to pass out.

Our hotel room was a palace—outstanding by poor country standards. It had a TV, hot water shower of course, clean sheets, two beds, a floor, AND a ceiling that was fully enclosed. It even had some pretty nice décor; decorative tiles, intricate bedspreads, and a dresser for our things.

Our room, the hotel, and the city of La Paz were all princess status compared to where we'd come from.

Compared to our past three days, we were in gangsta paradise.

CHAPTER 2

When I decided to travel through South America, I saved money for about a year in order to afford three months of travel. I had three things I just had to do during those three months—three non-negotiable requests. The rest could be improvised, but I absolutely had to:

1. Dive the Galapagos Islands.
2. Go to the Bolivian Salt Plains.
3. See the albino dolphins of the Amazon.

I was even willing to forego lots of popular South American hits to complete those three things, mega-hits like Machu Picchu and Iguazu Falls. I knew I'd have to give up something, because for the first time in my life I was traveling with a group of friends. When you travel with friends, you learn when to stand by your agenda and when not to. Everyone has something they want to do and places they want to see. So, unless you want to be a first class asshole or split from the clan, you get flexible real quick-like. You adopt a hive mentality, because if you don't, it can all disintegrate into mad stress, tacky comments, and goat stubbornness. Lifelong friendships can breakdown in a matter of days.

I got my way with one thing on my list: the Salt Plains.

Deirdre and SeDessie agreed to take a Jeep tour for three days into an area of the world that resembled the moon.

The world's largest salt flat, Salar de Uyuni, is a crusty layer of hexagonal salt patterns in Bolivia that connect across nearly four thousand square miles. It's empty—a frosty white landscape broken only by rich blue sky and the occasional hill.

No trees. No life. No rocks. Nothing but freezing air and the random Jeep full of shivering tourists.

You drive on it for days, weaving salt lanes into the predictable and stark scenery, until you magically arrive at a cactus island. Beyond that, more prehistoric salt…blue sky…and then all of a sudden a lake full of disco-pink flamingos. It's a supernatural universe, one that you have to visit to fully grasp. And out there, things are very basic.

Our Jeep had no heater or stereo. The place that we stayed overnight, a building made out of nothing but salt, was lit only by candlelight and heated by nothing more than a pot-bellied cast iron stove. Its tummy radiated an auburn hue that we attempted to absorb into our bones before retiring to our bitterly cold rooms for restless sleep, but there was no beating the freeze. It froze our electronics. It turned wet hair into icicles. It made our innards chilly bins.

Body heat was our only bet. We huddled and convulsed in the cold.

We wore every stitch of clothing we had, including bathing suits over our underwear, which took an act of God to get off to use the bathroom. More than once in the middle of the night we discussed pissing ourselves instead of using the bathroom, because it would be easier and warmer. In the mornings, in order to get into the Jeep and continue our teeth-chattering expedition, the drivers had to blowtorch the vehicle's frozen doors open.

I went through the days dressed like a gay onion—layers of rainbow-crocheted garb, pink and blue cotton pull-overs, and colorful wool blankets wrapped around my body. Sometimes I would shove hand warmers into the front of my reindeer beanie to keep my forehead from pounding out an altitude induced staccato onto my frontal lobe.

And all along the Bolivians pretended to be immune to the frigidness, but they really weren't. They used moonshine jackets to stay warm. They wore two layers of cloth and swigged on lighter fluid, floating through the plains like Floridians on Daytona Beach.

Contrarily, sardined into the ten-passenger Jeep was the only place we tourists found a bit of warmth. Our Jeep was made up of three long passenger seats that we deemed our happy place. There were six of us foreigners on the trip.

Deirdre, SeDessie, and I usually claimed the back. A single Irish guy—very nice, kind of hippy, cool, and fun—took the middle. A friendly German couple with wicked senses of humor took the front. The male in that couple was named Enis. We were forced by rhyming laws to call him Penis. His wife played along.

Two Bolivians, a married couple, were our guides on the psychedelic salt trip. The man sat at the wheel and never spoke a word. His wife sat shotgun wearing a navy blue head wrap, maroon sweater, and turquoise skirt. The turquoise was the only bright reflection of the usually cheerful clothing sold in the country. She spoke maybe two or three words a day and only when engaged, and only in Spanish.

XXX

On the second day while driving in silence to the cactus island, the German guy got out his iPod. He started to plug it into his headphones when the Bolivian woman uncharacteristically broke the silence. Instinctively, or maybe running on an alcohol-induced urge to hear some hip-hop, she leaned toward the German dude from the passenger seat and with her cracked, mocha-colored hand, she extended a shiny cable toward him.

"E-pode?" she asked.

We all gasped simultaneously.

How that drunk magician produced such a modern device was a mystery. The truck didn't have a heater or stereo, but it had a bangin' speaker system with an auxiliary outlet. Good enough.

From the "E-pode" moment onward and with a simple thumb click, we went from bygone days to rollin' salty with Biggie's "Juicy" as our theme tune.

These are the strange things that happen abroad. You might find yourself somewhere with no running water, no electricity, and no sophisticated spot to relieve yourself, but one evening a native might mysteriously whip out a plasma screen TV and hook it up to some dude's gold tooth while he jogs in place to get reception. Minutes later, everyone will be enjoying *The Hangover* in the middle of a destination not available on maps.

So in our Jeep, newly entertained with modern music and lulled into relaxation with bit of body heat, we happily rolled across the Bolivian plains toward the famous cactus island. After about an hour it appeared out of nowhere in the distance, as if someone had turned the page on a gardening pop-up book. We parked on its spiky edges, got out, and climbed onto the oasis.

On that cactus island was the first I heard of the prison tour in La Paz. Deirdre had struck up a conversation with a bubbly backpacker, an American chick that had actually gone on the prison tour a few days before.

SeDessie missed the prison chat.

She'd returned to our Jeep to chew on coca leaves and drink hot tea in an attempt to ease her altitude head bomb. If she'd been there for the conversation, maybe together we would have asked the right questions. It's not that I'm stupid or careless, especially when traveling. I'm quite the contrary, but Bolivia was just weird. Getting to the Salt Plains, being out on them...it was Freak Town. I think my adrenal glands were sizzled. I was numb—mentally and physically.

So, without SeDessie's help and armed with only my popsicle brain against Deirdre's desire to do the prison tour, I had a fart's chance in a hurricane of noticing the shiny lure dangling in front of my dizzy face.

XXX

"You guys should totally go," the American chick with curly blonde hair told Deirdre.

She sat on a park-style bench in the middle of the cactus wonderland. Legs crossed at the ankles and a big smile, she was cute and friendly enough. It was like talking to a Care Bear. All I could think about was how she was an American and how few Americans I usually ran into while traveling. She was a unicorn. I wanted to pet her.

"We go to La Paz after this. I want to go on the tour! I've heard a lot about it," Deirdre said, lounged against a rock that sat between two giant, thousand-year-old cacti.

I didn't quite follow the conversation.

"Wait, so it's a prison tour that people go on? It's like…popular?" I asked, chilling out mid-path and scratching my stocking-capped head.

Equally-dazed tourists crisscrossed around me, and somewhere in my sea-level thoughts I told myself to move out of their way, but my stupid high-elevation brain kept me rooted. I was Frankenstein in a hoodie.

"I read a book about the prison and its tours," Deirdre explained. "The tours have been going on for a while. They're run by the prisoners."

"Uh-huh. Ask for Mike, the South African. He's cool," Curly added.

"So, it's in La Paz?" I asked, stretching my arms toward the sky.

The cold was cementing my blood.

"Yeah, it's that fortress in the middle of the city. Stone walls. Built like a castle," Curly confirmed, fluffing her fro with a gloved hand.

"Cool," I grunted, staring off into the white horizon.

Space cadet. Ground control to Major Tom.

Maybe my deoxygenated brain was the cause of my imagination picturing the prison tour as something Alcatraz-ish. Head set-esque. Sit on Al Capone's toilet-kinda-sorta doohickey.

Of course in reality, it was anything but. Although, to give credit where credit is due, it was actually organized. Well organized. Well-organized crime.

Two days later, the phone call I made from our hotel room was my first hint.

XXX

Back in the hotel room, I finally picked up the *Lonely Planet* Deirdre had tossed on my bed. Inside, I found a small paragraph describing the San Pedro prison tours in La Paz. They called it, "The world's most bizarre tourist attraction." I scanned to the phone number tagged at the end of the blurb.

"I guess this is it?" I asked, placing my fingernail under a row of numbers and holding the book up to Deirdre's face.

"Yeah. Guess so," she nodded.

I sighed and reached for the old phone. With my pointer finger I spun the rotary dial wheel, its clicking sounds triggering a memory of my grandma's house. I was just about to tell the girls about it when a man answered.

"Sí?" the cavernous voice crawled down the telephone wire, scratching on my eardrum.

It threw me off. I don't really know what I expected, but it definitely wasn't the Bolivian Dirty Harry who answered my call.

I cleared my throat, "Um…hola. ¿Trabajas para la prisión de San Pedro?"

Hello. Do you work for San Pedro prison?

Long pause.

"Sí," the man grumbled.

"Bueno. Quiero comprar billetes por el tour por favor," I stated, with as much correct pronunciation as possible—round vowel sounds—ah-eh-ee-oh-ew.

We'd like to buy prison tour tickets, please.

The line crackled. I heard raspy breathing that I imagined to be stinky. When the man's words finally came, they sounded like they were mashed against the mouthpiece.

"Sí, señorita. Necesito un número de tarjeta de crédito," he replied.

I crinkled my nose. *Credit card number? Is this guy for real?*

"I'm so fucking sure," I said in English, before slamming down the headset onto the cradle.

"Whhhaa happened?" Deirdre asked—saucer-eyed.

"Deirdre, Whiskey-Tango-Foxtrot? I'm pretty sure some prisoner just asked for my credit card number."

SeDessie ignored us, focused on her now clothed and newly clean self.

"Well, then we'll just have to go down there and see what's up?" said Deirdre.

"Yeah I 'spose," I agreed, sinking back into my pillow.

"Can I wear this on the tour?" SeDessie asked.

She twirled in front of us in the only outfit she'd not dropped off at the laundromat earlier. I couldn't help but cackle. My bling-bling friend was dressed as a bag lady who just happened to have shit-hot hair and perfect makeup.

She wore a naughty muumuu—a long, multi-colored polyethylene blend with a deep V in the front. It was retirement home with a bit of tit. Over that, she had on a thin, black cardigan. Around her waist, another cardigan, this one grey. On her feet, wool socks and flip-flops. It was the most fucked up outfit I'd ever seen one of my friends put on with the intention of going out in public.

"That's totally prison," I said.

"Should we go after your shower?" Deirdre asked me, jumping up and clapping her hands like a cheerleader. "Is that cool with you, SeDessie?"

"Fine with me," SeDessie drawled, spritzing her face with a tiny bottle of cucumber aloe mist.

I shrugged, "Sure, that's fine. Okay then. SHOWER-POWER TIME!" I yelled, giving in and joining Deirdre's enthusiasm.

We were going on a prison tour—yay.

In retrospect, I blame the hotel room. It relaxed us to the point of cerebral mush.

I stood and danced toward the bathroom holding gun fingers in the air. I fired four imaginary rounds into the ceiling, because I had no idea what I'd just signed up for. If I had known, maybe I'd have shot one through my temple.

At least my shower was hot.

CHAPTER 3

"Aquí, por favor," I alerted the taxi driver with a shoulder tap.

"San Pedro?" Deirdre asked, pointing to the rock wall on our left.

The driver nodded. I leaned forward and handed him a crumpled ten Boliviano from my jacket pocket.

"That was quick," said SeDessie, climbing out of the cab into the crisp air. Deirdre and I followed.

In the blue afternoon we stood as a threesome, happy to be shower-fresh and in a city. SeDessie straightened her muumuu and stared at the structure in front of us. To me, it looked exactly like what the curly-headed American chick had described to us back at the cactus island. It was an old fortress. Pockmarked stone walls. A worryingly vacant watchtower. No door that we could see.

La Paz's air smelled clean with a hint of animal fur. The temperature was, of course, so cold that you could cut glass with your nipples, but the sun had teeth—barracuda sharp. When it peaked, it was a cranked furnace battling against the bitter altitude. But even so, I came prepared. The cold and I are enemies.

I'd worn my black, puffer jacket and SeDessie wore a highly similar one over her homeless outfit. We were twinsies. Deirdre was in her signature green Adidas jacket. We were girls again—earrings, vanilla body spray, spearmint chicle, and good chitchat to accompany our walk around the prison wall—your usual Tuesday afternoon.

"I guess we just keep going until we find the front door, eh?" Deirdre asked.

"There has to be a way in. I'm pretty sure they don't just catapult convicted prisoners over the wall," I said.

I shaded the sun with my hand to investigate the height.

"They might," said SeDessie.

We giggled. It was all funsies and ha-ha's, even as we approached a dark-skinned man holding an AK-47 machine gun. He was young and dressed in dull army greens. We'd found the door and the gatekeeper.

"So...what kind of deal is this, D?" I asked, stalling about twenty feet from the guard so that we could formulate a plan.

"I dunno, but you should go tell him you think his gun is sexy," she replied.

"Maybe I'll tell him you wanna clean it with your tongue," I said, glancing over my shoulder at statue boy.

He was nothing but stern brow, unblinking black eyes, and big gun. It didn't look like my type of gig.

"You go talk to him," I told D.

"Shelby, you're the translator. Stick to your role," said SeDessie, flicking her hair and swaying her weight from her left to right foot.

Talking to SeDessie is like being rocked to sleep by a Georgia peach momma—a gentle glide, side to side. Swaying with her, I knew she had a point. Traveling in a group, we'd each assumed a certain character.

D played the part of marijuana locator. SeDessie was the toiletries master. I was the translator. And as more friends joined us in South America in the weeks to come, our troupe gained a trip planner, luggage carrier, and a sponsor—the most cashed-up of us all. The sponsor paid for a nice hotel room down the street from the hostel where the rest of us stayed. By the end of the night, we'd all be in the hotel room. Thank you, sponsor.

I kicked a pebble into the street.

"Translator shmlan-shmlater. Sucks, but fine. I'll do it. I guess you guys stay here while I figure out what's up with this tour thinga-ma-jig," I said, already turning and hopping over a pothole to approach the soldier.

I smiled bigger the closer I got to him. People usually like smiles.

He glared at me. Guess he didn't get the memo.

I stopped within a couple of feet from him. It was a planned buffer, a squishy barrier of personal space that left plenty of wiggle room for his weapon.

"¡Hola!" I grinned. "Con permiso señor, queremos ver el prisión. ¿Hay un tour, sí?"

Excuse me sir, we want to see the prison. There's a tour, yes?

He stared at me through icicle pupils.

I smiled bigger—cheeks burning from the stretch—and waited.

He said nothing, but what he did do was readjust his grip on his machine gun and turn away from me to prove just how much he was going to ignore every word out of my mouth. So, I tried again in true annoying-American-tourist form.

"Um, señor. Lo siento, pero mis amigas y yo queremos un tour…por favvvorrr señoorrr. POR FAVOR," I said, shuffling back into his line of vision.

Sorry, but we want a tour plllleeeaaassee. PLEASE.

His eyes narrowed.

Through taut lips he said, "No hay tour."

There is no tour.

And then back to soldier-corpse mode. I was invisible.

It was hardball time.

XXX

"He said no," I told the girls as I re-entered the circle.

"He's full of shit," said D. "Offer him money."

"I've got fives," said SeDessie.

Between the three of us, we came up with a small wad of greenbacks. I rolled the money into a tube and returned to attempt conversation with the unfriendly guard. This time I wore my biggest smile yet and left only a foot of buffer between us.

"¡Hola otra vez, señor!" I chirped.

Hello again, sir!

He scowled at me.

I leaned in with my shit-eatin' grin and poured the syrup on thick.

"Señor, hay un tour. Yo sé. Otra extranjera me ha dicho. ¿Está seguro no hay un tour?"

There's a tour. I know. Another foreigner told me. You sure there's not a tour?

To make sure he heard my question, I showed him the roll of Hamiltons that I was small-pimpin'. And just like that, the statue came to life.

"¡Sí! Sí, tour," said the new Wayne Brady.

I was a winner on *Let's Make a Prison Tour Deal*. He flashed a surprising full mouth of pearly whites.

"¡Excelente!" I said, having to refrain from patting him on the shoulder like a good puppy.

"¿Quiere un tour? Habla con ellos," he directed.

Want a tour? Talk with them.

He pointed with the butt of his AK-47 down a hallway behind him. Through the slender archway I could see a desk and two other guards dressed in the same uniform.

Further beyond the desk and guards I saw something eerily familiar. It was a scene that reminded me of the part on the *Pirates of the Caribbean* ride at Disneyland, where all of the old, scraggily pirates are hanging their arms through jail cell bars. They're attempting to coax a bony dog with a key ring in his mouth to creep just one inch closer, desperate for the mangy mutt to get within reach.

Down that dim hallway in the Bolivian prison, seven shifty characters draped themselves through the bars and yelled at me in English. They'd waited until the guard and I were done with our deal—obviously not their first rodeo.

"Tour right here. Get your tour. One-of-a-kind guide. Five years experience!" one hollered.

"Hey, hey, chicky! Need a tour guide? I'm the best. Come and get it. Safe and sound. Better than a safari!" another shouted.

I turned away, feeling less confident and a little queasy.

"Ummmmm…" I said to the guard.

He just smiled, nodded, and waited for me to proceed. Confused, I signaled the girls to come over.

"¡No! No. ¡Sola!" the guard insisted.

No! Alone!

"¿Porqué?"

Why, I asked, but the girls were already walking our way.

"Are we in?" Deirdre asked.

"Um, yes, but I need to talk to those guys first," I signaled toward the prisoners down the hallway. "I have to go alone. Guard's rules."

"Sounds good," said D. "We'll wait here."

"Have fun," said SeDessie, through arched eyebrows.

"Always," I muttered and walked my booty toward the hall of pirates.

XXX

Dankness clogged my nostrils. Inside the prison walls, I could feel its personality. It was a cranky, old bastard steeped in very questionable things.

I eased past two more guards lounging at the desk with their feet propped up on it. The soles of their chunky Doc Martens stared at me, but they didn't blink an eye. The convicts, though, were visually dining on my flesh.

"You know you want me, girly. Good price. I keep it real nice," a dude with dreadlocks down to his waist cooed softly.

He seemed like he was about to pass out—exhausted, done with his tour guide gig.

I veered to the right toward an old man with long, grey hair and round glasses. He looked like the love child of Gandalf the Grey and John Lennon. I thought, *He looks like a nice prisoner.* His face crumples were charming.

"Yeah, come on over here. I'm your man—one of the originals in this fine establishment. I'll cut a good price, take real good care of you," he spouted in an NBA sports highlight voice.

His accent was South African. I zeroed in on him. The other prisoners disassembled, peeling themselves off the bars and moping back to the jail yard. Their disappointment hung behind and mixed with an aftershave that smelled like Old Spice. It was cologne radiating from the hippie dude.

"Hi. How are you?" I asked him.

"I'm in prison for life. How are you?" he returned, pressing a gangly finger to the nosepiece of his sunglasses and sliding them up onto the bridge of his bulbous nose. The lenses were oil-slick purple and made my reflection look like a human wombat.

"I'm good. We'd like a tour, please."

"I'll give you ladies a nice tour for forty dollars a piece," he said, glancing left and right.

I almost gagged.

"Forty! That's highway robb…"

I stopped myself. I was talking to a prisoner. Of course it was robbery, or larceny, or breaking and entering, or smuggling, or worse.

"Ten apiece?" I asked.

I have the negotiating skills of a brain-damaged inchworm.

"Ten? You shittin' me? You think you're payin' for a new sweater? Thirty-five is as low as I can go."

I took a small step toward him and lowered my voice.

"Twenty is all we have," I lied.

He leaned back from the bars and rubbed his chin.

I fiddled with my jacket zipper, yanking it up and down so it sounded like a turntable remix. I looked around and sniffed, missing my friends. Years were passing. As messed up as this may sound, it was kind of exciting. I felt like I was living a movie scene.

"Okay, girly. Twenty apiece," he finally said.

And so it was done.

After that, the guards took our cameras and everything else that we had, except for our money and the clothes on our back. I watched Deirdre empty her pockets with a smile. SeDessie started to lay her camera on the desk then pulled it back at the last second. She popped open the little door that holds the memory card, removed the card, slid it into her cleavage, and then handed over the camera. Travelers don't part easily with their memories. Photos are babies. The rest can be sacrificed.

I pulled two finger puppets out of my left jacket pocket, a grey elephant and bright blue Cookie Monster made out of alpaca wool. I'd purchased them from a street vendor the day before. I laid them gently on the desk, promising I'd be back soon. They looked worried.

We stood together, empty of our possessions and ready for the next step. The guards nodded in satisfaction then turned away. We followed, plodding across cold concrete straight for the bars at the end of the corridor where the prison yard beyond was flooded in sunlight. Our hippie-dude tour guide waited patiently on the other side, a lit cigarette dangling between his cracked lips.

CLANK CLANK, clank clank clank.

A half-asleep guard slid the bars back in slow motion. With the same jolly attitudes of *The Three Amigos*, SeDessie, Deirdre, and I stepped inside.

CLANK CLANK, clank clank clank. SLAM!

The bars crashed shut, locking behind us. My muscles tensed. An angry pterodactyl flapped its wings against my tummy lining. And I know how utterly stupid it sounds, but for the first time that day my brain decided to crunch some numbers.

I thought, *what the fuck are we doing?*

CHAPTER 4

"We're going to have to split you up," Hippie Dude said.

"What? Why?!" I spat.

"It's better that way—safer," he said, glancing over his shoulder.

"I'll go on my own," Deirdre volunteered, when a slender young Bolivian boy walked up.

His skin was buttery brown. Clean clothes. Great smile. Sooooo not prison style. He was the kind who might cause conjugal visit fantasies.

"This is Angelo," said Hippie Dude, shaking a thumb at the young boy. "He's good. He'll take care of you."

"Are you sure?" I whined, scanning the prison bait—his model features stark against the prison setting.

Things were going from weird to weirder. It was all happening too fast. My palms felt moist. The guards had disappeared into the shadows beyond the bars, reclining in their chairs a million miles down the hall that we'd stupidly left. Pressure built behind my eye sockets and I clenched my jaw, trying to figure out what the hell to say.

"It's fine," D said, smiling.

She looked genuinely excited and chill.

"I'll stay with Shelby," SeDessie offered.

"Good idea," said D.

Deirdre leaned in and hugged me, then did the same to SeDessie. While my friends exchanged goodbyes, I looked around the yard. It was a part-grass/part-dirt rectangle with soccer goals on either end, but it was the rest of what surrounded us that totally blew my mind.

We were in a thrown-together, ghetto-LEGOLAND shantytown. Lines of drying laundry strung from crooked banisters to exposed rebar. Shop signs hung at tilted angles and prisoners chilled on stoops outside of doors that looked like apartment entries. Some paid attention to us, most didn't.

I mentally hunted through my "prison education" in search of comparisons.

Nothing.

This place was funky—the opposite of anything I'd seen on *CSI Miami* or *Shawshank Redemption*—but somehow civilized.

I turned back to Deirdre.

"I don't know, D. Are you sure this is okay? I mean are you SURE, SURE, SUUURRRREEEEE this is okay?" I asked.

I tried to eye-signal her so that she knew I was serious.

"Yup. Bye!" she squeaked through her perma-grin before disappearing around the corner with her new prison candy.

SeDessie, Hippie Dude, and I stood there. I looked over at SeDessie and her low-cut tropical robe. Her girls peeked out the top. I swallowed a porcupine.

"We need to get out of the yard. There was a fight yesterday, so stay close. Stick to the wall," Hippie Dude instructed, turning and scurrying toward a row of doors.

"Jesus," I muttered, falling into footstep behind him with SeDessie by my side.

And just like that we were off on our official prison tour.

XXX

We scampered like mice into the bowels of a maze made out of every scrap piece of building material you could ever imagine: tin, cardboard, plaster bits, compressed mud, concrete chunks, graffitied two-by-fours, waterlogged plywood, your mom's underwear.

It was Picasso's barrio—a shape-shifting neighborhood that appeared to have been created by a bunch of guys who got together, smoked crack, and built a fort out of the city's leftovers, which is basically what it was.

"Zip your jacket up to your chin," I whispered to SeDessie as we turned the corner of a leaning brick wall.

"Hell, I'd zip it over my forehead if I could," she whispered back.

With a unified zzzzzzziiiiiiiipppppp, we both locked our jackets shut, complete with matching zippers jiggling under our chins. I hoped we looked like a couple of charred marshmallows or possibly a pair of butch dykes. Either would do. I was ready to let a loogie swing from my chin and shart in my pants if it helped keep us un-raped.

Hippie Dude shouted out descriptions of the fun house as we wound through its misshapen arteries, but I wasn't listening. My eyes were busy downloading. It was such a spooky mixture of a hoarder's wet dream and a well maintained, but poor, neighborhood. Faded posters pinned to mudbrick walls. Rusted iron pathways lined with the bottoms of broken bottles—ghetto flare. Organized chaos. A junk mansion built on broken dreams.

We passed no people.

I didn't know where they were, but I had my sneaking suspicions that just because I couldn't see them didn't necessarily mean they couldn't see us. In my head, if I turned and really took the time to peep the scene, I figured it would look something like every werewolf movie ever made—yellow, slitty eyes blinking through the gaps in the walls.

Where is he taking us? I worried.

"This is our library. Over there is a restaurant. Here is a string of apartments that aren't so expensive. Up there are some of the nicer places to rent—two thousand a month," he noted with the professionalism of a Hollywood Hills expert talking through a PA system and pointing to Keanu Reeve's estate.

"You mean two thousand Bolivianos," I verified.

"Nope, two thousand American bucks, chicky," Hippie Dude replied, running a shaky hand through this long hair. "Hurry, we need to hurry."

He pushed us forward into a dark, constricted hallway lined with corrugated iron.

"I can't see anything!" I yelled back to him, my sweaty palms now waterfalls.

"Just climb. Climb up that ladder at the end!" he yelled.

I did as I was told. I felt my way around the end of the tunnel, begging my eyes to readjust in a hurry as my hand passed over a ladder. I put a hand and foot on it, bit my lip, and climbed, even though it didn't feel right. I knew I was climbing into something bad. Every cell in my body raked fingernails down my danger receptors. My legs were licorice whips. My follicles stood on end. Fight or flight kicked in so hard, I had about two minutes left before I freaked the fuck out.

But I still climbed. I scaled the shaky ladder robotically. I could hear SeDessie right behind me—her heavy breathing and flip-flops slapping on the wood. Her proximity did little to comfort me. When I reached the top, popping out into an open-air room half-shaded and half-sun flooded, I tried to think.

"Hey…" was all I got out before SeDessie surfaced.

Right behind her came the crown of the hippie's head, the ladder hole birthing out the South African prisoner into our private veranda. I considered kicking him in the teeth, grabbing SeDessie, and bailing hard. I had no idea where we were at this point, which meant I had no idea where we'd go, but it didn't matter. I was adrenaline soup. Electric nerves. Bat ears and wolf teeth. I was ready to remove testicles from body with one grip-and-rip if needed.

"SeDessie," I huffed into the collar of my puffer when Hippie Dude moved toward the balcony, "we need to—"

"Come on," he barked. "Hustle!"

SeDessie fell into step behind him. I followed, but the cogs in my brain were cranking.

No. Don't play along. Grab her and go. This is your chance.

I flexed my balled fingers in the pockets of my puffer as we walked. We were on the second floor of what could have been any shifty apartment complex—a long, beat-up balcony passing all closed doors, some with numbers, most without. The hippie's footsteps slowed in front of one of the numberless doors; movement and voices leaked through it.

"Wait for me," he directed.

The dragon's nest.

"W h a t   t h e   f u c k?" SeDessie mouthed to me when Hippie Dude turned and banged on the door.

This was our window of opportunity. I leaned into SeDessie, the smell of her coconut hair reminding me just how out of place we were, and put my lips right up to her ear.

"We need to leave," I whispered.

The door swung open.

CHAPTER 5

"HHHHHEEEYYYY, come on in!" a tall, hot, and obviously drunk Australian boy slurred. "Come on in, mates. You're late."

He stood aside as we entered the small but well-equipped apartment. It had a kitchen, dining area, bed, and bathroom. The ambiance was homely—the kind of place your second-grade teacher Aunt might live in. Lace curtains, framed family photos, pastel pink coffee cups in a cupboard, and a fluffy woven rug under our feet.

Bob Marley's "Could You Be Loved" bumped through an early nineties stereo system. My heartbeat slowed to match the rhythm.

And there weren't just a couple of people in this room, there were about fifteen, not prisoners, but tourists—average, every day, mainstream tourists—sitting around partying. They were drinking, smoking, shooting the shit, and in the middle of it all sitting at a circular sixties-style kitchenette was a black-haired man with a greasy ponytail.

The Don—an older South American man with leathery features and a brooding demeanor. He slumped in a plastic chair. He was big but not huge, the kind of bulk that probably didn't intimidate many until their clocks were already cleaned. Dragging hard on his cigarette he exhaled even harder, and then dropped the burning butt in an already overflowing ashtray.

Just past where he sat I spied Deirdre. She leaned on a wall with her prison beau next to her. They both clutched beers. She looked like she was on a date.

"Hey!" she yelled and motioned for us to join her.

It was cramped. Moving was tough. SeDessie and I took baby steps and our sweet time weaving toward her, but before we got there the Don took over.

"Okay. Now that we're all here, everybody pay attention. Listen up. Get comfortable."

I stopped and looked around. The only unoccupied space was the bed, so I reached behind me for SeDessie's hand and together we maneuvered toward it, sliding between the warm, happy bodies that partied and chatted like they were in the middle of a bar in Manhattan. At the bed, we plopped down on its corner.

"GET THE FUCK OFF MY BED!" the Don shouted.

His anger froze the room—needle off the record.

I looked behind me to see who was jumping, peeing, or letting their rank dog up onto this guy's bed, but there was no one.

"I said, GET THE FUCK OFF MY BED! I fuck my girlfriend on that bed. No one but me and her get on that bed, *comprende*?" he hissed.

He glared at me and SeDessie, got out a new cigarette, and lit it.

I could feel my heartbeat in my face as SeDessie and I moved to a vacant patch that had been kindly cleared by the wall.

"Fucking foreigners..." the Don mumbled.

He slicked his hair back and took a long drag without exhaling.

"Do you understand where you are and why you're here?" he asked.

Silence.

"Everybody. I'm asking everybody! FUCK!"

A soft murmur escaped from the crowd, but no one spoke up. The Don huffed and picked up a tumbler filled with copper liquid. He titled his head back and shot it, then flicked a lizard tongue over his thin lips.

"These tours started a long time ago. I'm not the one who started them. Thomas McFadden did. Has anyone read this?"

He pounded his pointer finger on the cover of a book that sat next to his ashtray. The book looked old, or maybe just well used. The corners curled and it had what appeared to be five lines of cocaine scraped into tally marks lying on top of it. The title read *Marching Powder*. He picked it up, keeping the coke in place on top. It was an optical illusion, a flawless photograph of nose candy looking snort-ready.

Deirdre looked over at us and gave a "yup" head jerk. That book was what she'd read a few years back and also the whole reason we were there inside a Bolivian prison.

"That book is why you're here. If you haven't read it you need to, and I don't know how the fuck you ended up here, but since I'm nice, I'll give you a quick and shitty little rundown of what it's all about."

He slid the book across the table. It stopped against a Crocodile Dundee buck knife.

"San Pedro ain't like no prison you know, man, especially you fuckin' Americans. This side of the prison is for foreigners—the drug dealers. I'm not gonna tell you my story, because I don't fuckin' feel like it. All you need to know is that you're in the nice side of San Pedro. The other side, that's where they keep the locals, the real killers. *Animales.* No guards, self-governed Mad Max shit."

He let us marinate in his words and lit another cigarette. He poured another drink and ran his hand down his ponytail…again.

"We have our own little society on this side. We can have our girlfriends stay the night…hey baby," he cooed, slapping the ass of a woman with jet-black hair who stood to his right.

"Wives live here. Children are born here. We have jobs. We have apartments. It's a family and business thing. We LIVE here. You can buy or rent, depending on how good you are at earning extra cash. Thomas was really fucking good at making extra cash. That's why you're on this goddamn tour."

I squeezed SeDessie's knee. She gawked back.

"Thomas McFadden was a British drug trafficker who got busted and thrown into our humble home here in San Pedro. In this prison, we cook the world's finest cocaine—right fucking HERE in the guts of this stone pig—and we sell it onward. As you may guess, this is one motherfucking corrupt joint."

We all laughed. I don't know if we were supposed to, but we did. Some travelers lit up their own smokes, took drinks, readjusted—it was story time at Mr. Trafficker's house.

XXX

"Thomas was smart. He just got out of San Pedro last month, the lucky bastard. Me, I got out last week."

I titled my head, trying to get my ears to work properly. I thought I'd heard him wrong.

"That's right. I GOT OUT last fucking week, but I stayed. I've CHOSEN to stay to make sure the tours are set and to make sure a couple of young Americans that just got busted for trafficking understand San Pedro business...fucking Americans," he grumbled.

Ciggie drag. The smoke fell out of his nose.

"I stay for Thomas's legacy, man. It was his idea to start the tours. The tours are how we bring the buyers to us and move the coke outta here. Plus, we get to tell our stories."

He stopped and stared down at the shiny knife and tattered book. A grey snake of smoke slithered onto his forehead.

"Let's get started. Everyone paid...except for you, amigo."

He slowly turned his head and aimed a predatory snarl at a skinny, blonde, blue-eyed, brand-new red sweater-wearing boy who sat pretzel-style on the floor.

The boy's jaw dropped.

"Um, yeah, sorry. My friend...she was supposed to come in here with me. It was her idea, but we got here and didn't have enough money. She said she's coming back with it. She has all our money. I can get it for you when I leave. I promise I'll come back and pay you," he rattled.

The Don gritted his teeth, face mangled into the kind of battle expression I imagined pirates to have used when they boarded enemy ships. He reached for the knife and with one fluid motion the mofo snagged it, raised it, and stabbed it four inches deep into his kitchen table with a sickening THUNK. The handle vibrated—a greasy palm print left behind by his nasty grip.

Dead silence.

We all stared at its erectness while the blonde boy shriveled into a sickly pile of fear. The Don laid into him.

"You're damn right you'll fucking pay, 'cause if you don't fucking pay, I'll fucking find you and MAKE you fucking pay me, cojudo! ¿Me entiendes? I don't collect like your landlord would, motherfucker!"

"Yyyyyyes. Yes, I'll pay you. I promise. I swear to God I'll pay you. I'll go right now if you need me to. Wha…wha…whatever you need," he stammered.

Tears pooled in the boy's blue eyes. It didn't match the cold beers, cheap cigarettes, and Rasta verses. So as though on cue, the entire room erupted into money propositions.

"I can pay for him," an Aussie offered.

"We've got extra cash," said a French man.

"I have twenty quid you can have. It's not a problem at all," a Brit hollered from the back of the crowd.

We were strangers bonded through instinctual protection of human life. Travelers are pretty good at helping each other, usually. In this case, if we didn't step in the possibility stood that this kid might get scalped by Psycho McCrazy. No one wanted his stab wounds on their conscience, hence the outpour of donations.

The Don looked around and smiled.

"Okayyyy…you have lots of friends, amigo. Lucky you. I was just fucking with you anyway…or maybe not. Maybe I was gonna slit ya. Nah..nah. You're cool. Don't worry 'bout it, man. Money later."

He hyena laughed through his smoke cloud, throwing his head back and sticking out a coated tongue.

I recoiled.

"Okay, let's do this shit! Each of you came in with a guide. Each of you leaves with one, and you come back here when you're finished, entienden? Good. Now get the fuck out of here."

He reached for his girlfriend's thigh and aggressively pawed at it. She giggled. Hovering by the front door, Hippie Dude signaled to me and then scampered outside.

I watched Deirdre and her guide leave the apartment before us. She never looked back. They were long gone by the time SeDessie and I filed out of the party zone along with the rest of the tour herd.

"This tour come with a brain scrub at the end?" SeDessie asked as we emptied onto the balcony.

Hippie Dude leaned on the railing outside, smoking a fresh ciggie—sunglasses on.

"Ready?" he asked through a pillow of white.

"Spose," I answered.

XXX

We moved from bizarre space to freaky room and every inconceivable possibility. All were matched with some whacked out story. I was neither relaxed nor scared. I was something else, something I hadn't felt before. I was caught somewhere between mental block and morbid fascination.

I listened like a good little student, taking in every boiled, candy word. It was campfire and flashlight under the chin stuff, the kinds of tales that mesmerize me.

Yes, mister scary drug dealer. Tell me more about the blow that got you into this silly mess and the time an undercover cop sprayed your Lambo with bullets in Miami.

"This is our law office. We keep track of our own files because we can't trust the pigs. They're always telling us we've been here five minutes when we've been here fifteen years. This is the only way we can stand trial fairly."

Hippie Dude nodded toward a row of filing cabinets.

"So, who represents you?" I inquired.

"Each of us represents ourselves. That's why it's so important that we each keep our files straight," he said, squinting at the row of cabinets.

We toured some more and stopped at a pay phone attached to the wall.

"This phone is tapped. That's why we do our business on cell phones. Cell phones are for the deals we don't want the pigs to hear," he said with the concentrated voice of a lawyer.

"But, on this phone," he ran his hand down the side of the old pay phone, touching it with the gliding sensuality usually reserved for curved hips and plump buttocks, "we say the things we want the pigs to hear. Ya know, both private and tapped conversations are important. Good behavior/bad behavior 101," he said.

"I took that class in college," I said. "My parents reckon I skipped all the days we covered good behavior."

He let out a short but sincere chuckle.

"I took that class too, but at Florida State," chimed in SeDessie. "I slept with the professor and got an A."

We all laughed that time and I watched as our guide's scraggily face collapsed into a million folds of enjoyment. It wasn't the first time in my travels that I was shocked I was able to share a good belly shake with someone I:

A. Was basically a stranger to.

B. Had nothing in common with.

C. Was kind of scared of.

D. Am pretty sure was a few sandwiches short of a picnic.

Traveling has taught me that it just doesn't matter. People are people. That's where it all starts and ends.

"You have a big dimple, eh," he said, raising a craggy finger to my cheek.

"Yeah," I bowed my head and felt a warm wave crash on my cheeks. "It gets me into and out of trouble."

"Dimples are good. I used to have one on my ass until this place dropped me fifty pounds I didn't need to lose."

We stopped laughing.

I stared at the old phone. It was probably the same one I had called from the hotel room. I'd had no idea it was this, though. I was clueless to the fact that I was calling a relic payphone in the middle of a civilized hellhole.

We moved on in silence.

He pointed out this and that—stopped in an open-air room that he said was supposed to become a club. He got out another smoke, but this time offered to share.

"Smoke?" he asked, fanning the open pack in our faces.

"I'm good." SeDessie waved it off.

"Sure," I said, reaching out. "When in San Pedro, right?"

I sat on wooden crate, crossed my legs, took his offered light, and inhaled sharply. The hit was strong—a local blend.

"What are you in for, if you don't mind me asking?" I said through a slow exhale.

"Unpaid parking tickets," he replied, straight-faced.

Hippie Dude seemed so quirky, harmless, and nice—genuinely nice.

I took another drag and reminded myself not to get too comfortable. We weren't hanging out with Winnie the Pooh and friends.

"You have an apartment like the one we were in earlier? You know, the one where all the other tourists were hanging out?" SeDessie asked.

"No. That's expensive, man. Here in San Pedro, we're encouraged to keep our day jobs, if you know what I mean. Gotta make money to have an apartment like that, be really good at keeping up the game. He keeps up the game better than me. His contacts are closer."

I wondered how far away his contacts were. They were probably back in South Africa. I started to ask him about it but decided against it. Drugs were a better topic.

"So, you guys are in here for selling drugs, but once you're locked up you're encouraged to cook and sell more drugs?" I asked.

"That's the gist of it," he smiled.

He flicked his ciggie off the balcony without putting it out or looking down to see if a passerby would take it to the head. I crushed mine under my shoe and slid the mangled butt to the wall, too scared to try the same maneuver.

"Let's go. Now you're gonna meet the man that plays the game the best," he said, turning to walk off without having to tell us to follow.

CHAPTER 6

"Estás nerviosa?" an older man asked me from his nice armchair.

Are you nervous?

When we'd entered his apartment, he folded the newspaper he'd been reading. It rested neatly on his lap, but the niceties did nothing to calm my nerves. My leg tapped out of control, slamming up and down like a rubber ball against a hand paddle. I pressed a shaky hand on my knee to make it stop.

I was nervous, because Hippie Dude had taken us into this new apartment and just left us there this time. He slid out just in time to avoid the door slamming shut on his skinny ass. A slender man with a rat face bolted it shut behind him.

This apartment was different than the last. It was VIP—massive. Nice couches, a TV, a nicer stereo than I had back home, side tables, art, and basically all the convenience and detail an average home would contain.

Inside were six large men. They milled about, talking in hushed voices. The older man I was speaking to was the only one sitting. He'd motioned for us to take a seat on the couch across from him, so we had.

From his big armchair he stared at me and awaited an answer—*was I nervous?* He had his hands crossed in his lap. Slight smile. His chair was the kind a man in charge sits in. Black leather. Fancy.

"Sí. Estoy nerviosa," I answered.

Yes. I'm nervous.

I made eye contact while I delivered my emotion in clear, concise, and truthful words. I hoped my tone was dipped in confidence. I wanted him to understand how I felt, because I thought he might respect my forthright attitude. Maybe he'd leave us alone.

And the truth is, I was beyond nervous.

I was freaked the fuck out and feeling dumber than I ever had in my entire life. It's one thing to realize you're in a bad situation, but it's a complete other to drag that knowledge out for over two hours on a "bad decision tour".

The roller coaster of emotions I'd felt since entering San Pedro became overwhelming in this man's apartment. Locked in a room with his wolf pack, I felt San Pedro's jaws snap shut around my neck.

I swallowed a lump of tears.

"Tranquila," said the older man tenderly. He cracked a soothing smile.

Be calm.

"Nada va a pasar a usted mientras está aquí."

Nothing is going to happen to you while you are here.

His eyes stayed glued to mine while he used the *usted* address instead of *tú*, and my gut relaxed. It's formal usage of Spanish. It's respectful.

I had no idea why we were locked in this room, but I decided maybe it was going to be okay. The guy who seemed to be the boss said it was going to be okay and he said it in front of the entire gang. I figured, just like in the animal kingdom, when the Alpha spoke, it's bond.

I leaned back into the sofa.

"What are you guys talking about?" SeDessie asked.

"Oh, sorry. We're just getting acquainted," I told her, gently patting her knee and shooting her a weak smile, totally denying my former anxiety.

Usually the key to tight situations is remaining calm. I once watched a documentary on a man who went deep under cover with the FBI to take down a highly ranked motorcycle gang. He'd never intended to enter the world of criminals—breathing their air, sharing their vocabulary, and partaking in their nasty habits—but he did. He'd been asked to do so by the good guys, his boss, our government.

In the few hours I watched him on TV, I could tell he was one of those guys you could easily be friends with. He was just cool. Friendly. The show explained that, when it boiled down, what made him so attractive to every human, criminal, or saint was that he was calming and listened. He looked people in the eye, made them feel like they mattered.

Those attributes saved his life numerous times, even while staring down the double barrel of a sawed off shotgun held by a jacked-up murderer. He said he couldn't count on two hands and two feet the number of times his steady composure kept rooms from erupting in gunfire and kept hammers from splitting skulls.

I filed the memory of that man away in my mental cabinet marked DIRELY IMPORTANT LIFE TIPS, and, since then, serene demeanor had gotten me out of plenty snug situations.

XXX

I was trying my hardest to play it cool.

"Traducir para mí," the older man spoke again, this time waving a hand in the air like the Godfather.

Translate for me.

A gangly fellow stepped forward from the hovering group of men, his hands stuffed in his pockets, a button-down shirt tucked into clean jeans.

"I will translate for him," he said, pointing to the Alpha dog.

The older man in the big armchair started speaking in rapid Spanish while the gangly man translated in good English. SeDessie and I sat back and enjoyed the show, our mouths catching flies, listening to each exciting syllable.

"They call me Jorge. I'm the president of this prison—the voice of the population. I'm here because I got taken down by the United States government in the biggest drug bust ever made here.

"I was drug running on a very large scale. I was one of the top cocaine distributors in the world, and when I finally got busted, I was in a gutted 737 jet trying to leave the middle of the jungle. The plane was filled top to bottom with cocaine. It was a big takedown. I was shot three times."

Jorge, the president—the Alpha—quit speaking.

The gangly man stopped translating, slumped his shoulders, and looked at Jorge. A nod of approval followed, then the gangly man turned and reconvened with the wolf pack.

"¿Quieres comprar tarjeta San Pedro? Te mantendrá seguro durante el viaje," Jorge asked me.

Want to buy a Saint Christopher card? It will keep you safe while traveling.

I turned to SeDessie.

"Want to buy a San Pedro card from this guy? He says it will keep us safe."

"Like a San Pedro gift card?" she asked.

We simultaneously started cracking up, rolling around on the couch a bit.

Jorge stared at us, unblinking.

We faded the laughs into chuckles, and finally into a couple of uncomfortable coughs. I recomposed myself, rubbed my eyes, and sat up straight.

"Lo siento. Nos reímos cuando estamos nerviosos. Sí, queremos comprarlas," I said.

Sorry. We laugh when we're nervous. Yes, we want to buy them.

He grinned and all was forgiven.

And that's how SeDessie and I wound up owning a couple of "good luck travel cards" —from a man who got busted for the biggest cocaine take down in FBI's history. The cards are actually pretty cool. They feature a sparkling Saint Peter on the front. Ever since I bought it, I keep mine tucked safely inside my passport. It's truly my travel totem.

After buying it from the drug lord, I flipped it over and over in my palm, testing its vibe. Jorge watched me.

"¿Quieres mi autografo?" he asked if we wanted his autograph, like he was Brad fucking Pitt.

"Sí, claro. ¿Tiene una pluma?" I asked.

Yes, of course. Do you have a pen?

He produced an expensive, heavy looking, CEO-type of pen from the pocket of his khaki slacks. He was all business, and I could tell this was the part in his show that he loved best. Clout, baby—it's world-renowned.

He signed the back of my Saint Peter card, his hand swirling black ink into what has become my travel charm—a card that is still my own personal American Express—I never leave home without it.

SeDessie suggested we pass our cards onward to some of the wolf pack to get their signatures too.

"I mean, you don't just ask for Clyde's autograph and skip Bonnie like she's a lump of belly button fuzz," she said, doing her trademark sway—left, right, left, right—all southern smile and prison muumuu. "I mean, that would just be rude, and I'm a lot of things, but I'm not rude unless I have to be."

"Well, I think you're right," I said, and together we worked the room. I got three guys to sign mine before Hippie Dude finally came back.

"All good?" he asked, sidling up to me and squishing his wrinkled hands into his pockets.

He gave the room a once over and head jerked an "hola" to the boys. Without his sunglasses he looked naked and wrong.

"Got some signatures. I have no idea what they were telling me while they signed it, but they signed it," SeDessie said, flashing her card in my face.

It shimmered a lenticular print of Saint Peter holding two keys and looking toward a plum colored sky that, when twisted to the correct angle, had beams of lights coming from it. A halo formed around the Saint's head.

I examined mine to make sure I had the same card. I did, and before I pocketed it, I noticed two words that one of the men had written. The first word I couldn't make out, but the second said FREEDOM.

"Yeah, it's all good," I told Hippie Dude.

"Then let's party," he said, producing his sunglasses from his jean pocket.

"Party?" SeDessie asked.

But our new hippie-prisoner friend was already doing secret handshakes with the wolf pack and halfway out the door—sunglasses back on.

XXX

The party was back at the Don's quaint apartment, the same place we'd started our perverted carnival ride. Once again, it was overflowing with tourists, party smells and sounds—but this time, a small pyramid of cocaine was piled on the Don's kitchen table.

After everything we'd seen and learned, I don't know why this shocked the hell out of me, but it did. After hearing about the culture of corruption that the prison was soaked in, I didn't get how everyone was so willing to party between the warped walls of this twisted fun house. How'd they feel safe? There's a time and place to kick back and have a good time, but I'm pretty sure it's not at 3:00 p.m. in a Bolivian prison.

"Hey, welcome back," a British boy yelled into my face, slugging me on the shoulder as I passed by.

I ignored him and followed SeDessie deeper into the swaying crowd. The music was louder this time around. The party train was gaining speed.

"Yo!" a familiar voice shot across the room, and I caught a visual of Deirdre as she pushed her way toward SeDessie and me.

Her smile stretched around her head as she dove for both of us, wrapping warm arms around our necks.

"So happy to see you girls!"

"Same! Oh my God. I was worried we wouldn't see you again," I said into her shoulder.

I held her for longer than the usual pal-hug time limit. She returned the feeling of relief with a back pat and deep sigh. The potency of the embrace communicated that we knew we'd made a crooked decision to enter the world of San Pedro. Splitting up was sketchy—we'd do better in the future.

"Hey…is that Jack Black?" I asked.

I nodded toward a boy across the room that looked exactly like the famous comedian, Jack Black. Round face. Dark hair. *School of Rock* smirk.

"Holy shit! That totally looks like him," said SeDessie, eyeballing the boy hard.

"Nah, it's not him. Well…uh…damn! It might be," said Deirdre.

"I've gotta find out," I said, lunging toward him.

I broke through the two girls and landed right at his feet.

"Hey!" I said a little too loudly in his face.

"Hey. What's up?" he asked in a British accent. High voice—not Jack Black.

"I bet a lot of people tell you that you look like Jack Black," I said sheepishly.

"All the time."

"Well the resemblance is uncanny. The accent makes it funnier."

"Yeah, it's a blessing and a curse. Lots of photos, the occasional autograph and piss-take."

I laughed and stared, then realized I was staring.

"Ah hey, can you sign my card?" I asked, fishing Saint Peter out of my pocket.

"Sure."

I found a pen on the kitchen counter and the British tourist signed my San Pedro card—*Jack Black.*

The tour could be finished as far as I was concerned. I'd stuck the landing.

"Okay…who wants to taste Bolivia's finest? Time to do some real blow. Some good blow. Some rrrrreeeaaaaaallll good blow!" the Don cackled at his own joke and his guttural laugh carried over the racket of the room.

He held out cupped hands to the crowd and a rainbow waterfall of money flowed into them. The party got rowdier. Pavlov's coke bell had rung and the slobber started. I shot a glance behind me to Deirdre. She shot a look to SeDessie, and SeDessie nudged me.

We shuffled through the partiers, opting out of the cocaine festival, but we were the only ones. Hippie Dude was propped up on the wall next to the front door, ciggie in mouth, with a watchful eye scanning the crowd.

When we got to him I leaned in and said in my most courteous voice, "Thanks for the offer, but we actually have to get going. We have some laundry to pick up."

I couldn't believe laundry was the excuse I'd come up with. I felt like Baby in *Dirty Dancing*—"I carried a watermelon."

"Laundry?" our guide asked through pinched features.

"We have to go," I repeated, without the lame laundry addition.

"Okay," he shrugged.

Maybe this wasn't normal. Maybe people only went in San Pedro to snort jumbo lines of cocaine and talk endless shit for three days, but call us crazy, it just didn't seem prudent.

Still, offending prisoners wasn't on our to-do list either, so we thanked everyone with genuine gratitude for being fabulous tour hosts.

"We have to go, but thank you so much for the tour," I yelled to the Don.

"Yes. Thank you, guys. We really appreciate it," Deirdre said.

"Thank ya so much, gentlemen," SeDessie added.

We exited like we were tea party guests, bowing and waving gracious goodbyes.

The Don gave a heavy wink.

"Suit yourselves. You know where to find me if you change your mind," he growled.

We reached the door just as the Don leaned into his collection of rum bottles, ciggies and cash, grabbed his knife, and hovered above the small pyramid of ivory powder.

"Fuckin' Americans," he grumbled.

He licked his cracked lips and cut the pile into perfect snowy columns.

CHAPTER 7

Back at the metal bars that had let us into San Pedro, I felt like I'd hiked Mount Everest.

"You ladies be safe. Hope you had a good time," Hippie Dude said, weakly saluting us and lighting another cigarette.

"Thank you. Thanks for keeping us safe in there. We had a great time," I lied and told the truth at the same time.

We watched the metal bars get pulled back in slow motion by one of the guards, then we stepped over the threshold in unison. We greeted the guards like old friends. They shook our hands and asked how it was, like we'd just ridden *Space Mountain*.

We got our cameras back, and my finger puppets. We externally reassembled into the people we'd come in as, but internally we were different.

We waved goodbyes as we walked away from the fortress and its very odd guts. The sun seemed brighter than when we had started. Maybe it was higher in the sky, or maybe it just pretended to be so we'd feel better. Either way, it was a token that I greeted with arms of praise thrust into the air.

"Oh, thank you God! I know we don't talk much, but for real—thank you."

I dropped to my knees and kissed the ground for the first, but not last, time in my life. I actually let my lips touch the pavement.

Before, whenever I saw people kiss the ground in movies or on TV shows, I always thought two things: *yeah right* and *gross*. But after exiting

San Pedro alive and without incident, kissing the ground was my natural instinct. That was how happy I was to see the free world. Kissing the ground wasn't gross—it was the right thing to do.

I pushed myself back up onto my knees and turned to my girls.

"So, now what?" I asked.

"Anything outside of those walls is good with me," SeDessie said, shaking a thumb at the fortress. "We can pick up my laundry. I'm pretty sure this outfit is done."

"That was crazy, eh?" Deirdre said, sliding her hands into the pockets of her Adidas jacket. "I actually liked my tour guide. I got his phone number. He said I can come back"

From her left pocket she produced a small, triangular piece of paper. *Angelo (591)454-8898. Smiley face.*

"Wha-wha-wait. We go into a prison that cooks cocaine, and you leave with digits?" I asked.

"I know I look nothin' like your momma, but I'm one hundred percent positive you will NOT be callin' that number. NO ONE is coming back here," said SeDessie, wagging a finger in the breeze.

I stood up and stretched my legs.

"I guess that's par for the course. Let's go to the room and regroup, maybe *Breakfast Club* will be on TV."

XXX

SeDessie, Deirdre, and I still talk about San Pedro. It's a bizarre story and people don't really get it. Neither do we. The message of San Pedro morphs for me, but more than anything, I think it was a lesson on deception and knowledge and deception of knowledge.

Traveling can be a test of patience.

Now I wait, because I've met flowers that smell like rotting corpses and ugly ducklings that become swans.

PART II

"The only source of knowledge is experience."
Albert Einstein

Long-term Travel Possible Gain List

1. THAT story. The one that's too crazy to be true. The one that blows minds, even your own.
2. International work experience.
3.
4.
5.
6.
7.

Long-Term Travel Possible Loss List

1. Your naivety.
2. Confusion about what you really want to do with your work life.
3.
4.
5.
6.
7.

Twork It

CHAPTER 8

We're all coin operated—every person on every chunk of dirt on this planet. So, of course you'll need money to live overseas. If you don't have it, don't stress—earn it.

You can make and save enough money at home to get you to your dream destination overseas. It doesn't take much to get going. Find out how much it's going to take to get you there and get started. Be disciplined with your savings, and then go. Once you're overseas, you can start the whole process over again. Find work, live, and save. Travel to another new country when you're ready. It's a tasty recipe when cooked right.

Sound difficult? Yes, it can be. Sound impossible? It's never impossible. Just like anything else in life, finding work depends on you. I found work in Melbourne in just a couple of weeks, when I'd been told that people had been searching in vain for six months. The only difference between me and the other backpackers was that I was relentless on the job hunt. I competed like I was in my comfort zone.

You can do the same, no matter what corner of the planet you're calling home, because there are always ways to make money, or at least afford room and board without trading in your sanity, morals, ethics, or kidneys.

I've seen travelers do all kinds of jobs—boat cook, photographer, bank teller, nanny. I've even seen a traveler trade room and board for a bit of grass-roots PR while she was passing through. Her job was to hang out in the bar area near the beach and nonchalantly make her way from table to table, asking if anyone had been out on the fishing trip or catamaran ride—both great fun and worth the money.

With computers making us more mobile than ever, the possibilities are truly endless. But, if you're not a techy—don't fret. There's work for you too. You just have to adapt and play the game. Don't be scared to wheel and deal. There are always jobs—both over and under the table.

When I worked overseas, I obtained work visas and found legitimate positions, but I've known people who got jobs without the papers. I don't recommend depending on this method, but I'm just sayin'—you will survive.

The point is that you don't have to have a job or your life lined up before arriving somewhere. Just go with the right paperwork to get yourself started, and then trust the universe. It'll come through if you put in the grit.

The following stories are a few of my most potent job experiences overseas—the best lessons, brain burners, and laugh inducers.

CHAPTER 9

Surrounded by the baby blue skies and electric green trees of Napier, New Zealand, I was in fruit picking utopia. The apples, though, were causing me hell. I had no idea orchard life could be so complicated.

I didn't need to be picking fruit for a living—I chose to. My decision came about because I was visiting Auckland for two months, before heading on to Southeast Asia to teach English, and I accidently had too much time on my hands.

The days were getting long and lonely while most of my friends went to work and I poked about town. Also, I was spending more cash out of my savings than planned. Mostly though, I understood that idle time for me is devil's play. That's why I started sniffing around for something to fill the minutes of my days during my extended New Zealand layover.

Then one day, my answer came. On the news there was a report about odd weather patterns causing the New Zealand apple crop to unexpectedly ripen early—way too early. There were thousands of juicy apples hanging from healthy trees months before harvesting schedule. They begged to be picked, but there was no one to do it. Unfortunately, the influx of seasonal fruit pickers hadn't yet arrived.

The New Zealand apple industry panicked as dollar signs dropped from limbs before their eyes. To fix the problem, farmers pleaded for anyone and everyone who was willing to head to the bottom of the North Island and help save their precious crop. They were so desperate that the government stepped in to issue short-term work visas to travelers who wanted a little extra cash.

I thought it sounded cool. My boyfriend at the time, Steven, could go with me, because he was cashed up and available after completing a building contract.

So that was that, and a few days after I saw the news report we were cruising our way south to hit the orchards. But when we got to Napier, things weren't so cool. Turned out farming is brutal.

We were supposed to get up at the butt crack of dawn and pick hundreds of apples to fill a crate that could fit fifteen people in it—all for about fifty dollars a pop. Picking apples was backbreaking work that I could barely handle, and I wasn't a stranger to hard physical work. I just didn't know *farming hard work*. For those who don't know, it's a totally different ballgame than your average hard labor.

Farming is no joke.

We were constantly on the move, walking here, bending there, and climbing ladders everywhere like crazed firefighters. We wore giant baskets attached to thick harnesses that wrapped around our necks. By early afternoon, they were torture devices. We twisted achy spines, we lifted exhausted arms and craned frozen necks, and we CLIMBED—up and down, all around, sweating, holding, pulling, stretching, pouring, and carrying.

The farm owners were more concerned with the bruising of the fruit than our bodies. My muscles screamed. My brain was apple jelly. Boredom, pain, and realization of minimum payment for maximum effort piled up on my conscience until finally, Steven and I started playing by different rules.

XXX

Steven and I started waking up at seven a.m. instead of five. We would drag ass into the "picking area" and supply ridiculous medical excuses as to why the dawn hours had slipped away from us.

"My tonsils are pregnant."

"I think I might have zpchqrbermist."

"My finger fell off last night in the shower. I just got it re-attached."

The sunburnt orchard manager would stare at us dubiously.

"Uh-huh. Good one, mate. Try not to get any blood on the apples," he'd say, giving us a once over that was full of warning, before taking bowlegged steps into the next row of trees, but he never asked us to leave.

The orchard was that desperate. Every morning that we were late, he'd still hand us our brutality baskets and sadistic ladders and point with a callused finger to the next area that needed rid of Royal Galas. No questions. All work no play.

We weren't the only ones dying in the apple picking war, though. Workers were dropping like flies. Some even transferred over to the sorting area where we had heard rumors of people having mini-meltdowns from staring at a conveyor belt of rattling apples for eight hours a day, six or seven days a week.

But no one got fired. We were needed. My boyfriend and I were special though, we were needed and hated. I think the orchard manager wanted to run us over with his tractor, reverse, and repeat. We were most likely the worst version of help he'd seen in a while...if not ever.

On top of slacking, we stood out like throbbing thumbs in a field of healthy fingers. Even our tent screamed *interlopers*. It was the Hilton of tents compared to the others in the orchard, equipped with three bedrooms, a queen sized blow-up mattress, and side tables we'd bought at a thrift store. We thought having a cool tent would enhance our stay, and it did, so much that seven a.m. became seven thirty-ish.

The farmer growled.

We groaned, but still pressed on.

As the days passed, I became obsessed with the shapes and colors of the apples, pocketing prized ones that had rosy cheeks, creamy bottoms, firm everything, and perfect symmetry.

"This one. Oh my God, look at this one! This is the best apple in the universe!" I'd announce to Steven, picking the apple with respect and holding it at arm's length for ultimate viewing.

Oh the beauties I found in that orchard. They were too good for the crates, and slowly our tent started filling with perfect apples. Little piles of apples in the side table drawers. Big stacks of apples in my bag. Single apples in Steven's shoes.

At night, I'd dream of apples, plump pink and vanilla ones, spinning in fruity kaleidoscopes. Apples, apples, apples. Apples here, apples there. Apples everywhere. My brain was mushy apple sauce, and slowly I started wigging out. I wondered what we were doing in that orchard. I was losing my apple fucking mind.

I mean, it was clear from the get-go that we weren't going to make any money. Some workers did, but they had to snap every tendon and slip every disc to do it. I wasn't interested in doing that, and my man wasn't either. He was into fuckin' around…

XXX

Turned out, Steven wasn't there for the money or to pass the time— no, no, no, noooooooooo. He was, without my knowledge, there to be the Director of De-Pantsing.

He quickly went from attentive apple picker to very seriously, and with extreme dedication, finding any opportunity to yank my shorts down to my ankles. Whether I was mid or top-ladder, it didn't matter— both were equal opportunity. He would wait until my basket was full to the rim with chubby apples and I was absolutely helpless, then he'd pounce.

On the ladder and loaded down, I couldn't pull my pants up without returning to the ground. When you're at the top of a tree with a basket full of fruit balanced around your neck, you can't just take your gear off unless you want to fall fifteen feet to a C4 spinal injury. Everything about the situation was too intricate, heavy, and cumbersome to fix quickly, and this is coming from a decently coordinated and athletic person. I couldn't bend over. I couldn't disconnect from the basket, and there was no way I could rapidly descend carrying fifty apples, a metal contraption, and wearing my shorts as ankle cuffs. And, there was something else about the de-pantsing that added insult to injury.

It was my summer of going commando, and since I wasn't in the mood for underwear that season, my boyfriend thought his little joke was the best ever.

There I'd be, bare-assed and mid-way up the ladder, when my boyfriend would yell out, "Naked apple picker! Nothing but butt on row eighteen! Ass orchard!"

He'd yell at whoever would listen, even if it was just the birds and leaves.

Half-naked and on top of the ladder, I was forced to climb down slowly, trying to protect my coochie from splinters and my butt from mosquitos, with a waterfall of cuss words spilling out of my mouth and a curtain of apples tumbling out of my basket.

He adored it.

I had plans to stab him in the trachea with a dull pencil during dinner.

Fortunately, we were far enough from the other pickers that I'm pretty sure no one got too many glimpses of my flat butt or hot pocket. I'll never know for sure, but I do know that after about my fifth de-pantsing, I was done.

I took off my basket and with clenched teeth and laser beam eyes said to him, "Fuck you. Can I please have some fun? Take me to the local waterpark."

I needed fun. He'd had his, so he understood.

As I shot down the Master-Blaster thrill slide at Splash Planet and joyfully absorbed every minute of the summer heat, chlorine water, and apple-free splash zone, I swore off farm work.

At sunset, we returned to the orchard and talked to the manager about bouncing on the apple life. He was thrilled. I guess it was a mutual loathing.

Picking apples opened my eyes to what life could really be like with few options. There are jobs that will mangle your body, pay you little, and deaden your brain. If you don't have one of those jobs, be thankful. If you have options, be happy.

If you don't have options, fight to make some for yourself, because no one else will.

CHAPTER 10

In Melbourne, Australia, holding a three-month work visa and standing alongside thousands of British people holding highly superior one-year work visas, no one wanted to deal with me. I was too short-term, even for the short-term employers.

Plus, there were tons of travelers to compete with. If I saw an advertisement for waitressing, by the time I responded it would be gone.

Cash jobs vaporized before my eyes, snatched up by Brazilians, Italians, and people from nearly every country around the globe. Everyone was competing to make enough money to fund their drinking, backpacking, and surfing circuit. It was dog eat dog.

I tried to rely on my education, but since I wasn't a hotshot at anything, no office was going to hire me for such a short stint of time. And since all the casual positions were in such high demand, I quickly realized that I was going to have to settle for the bottom of the totem pole.

After about a week of "NOs" in Melbourne, I became an early bird while my peers slept off their hangovers. I'd rise with the sun to search and apply for sandwich-making positions, waitressing gigs, or anything that had to do with food and drink, because I'd done some of those jobs in college.

I'd march around town to show up for group interviews, and when I'd get there with my face painted to girly perfection and my dress pressed to a level of professionalism way beyond ham and cheese on rye, my optimism would melt as soon as I saw that I wasn't the only one desperate to get paid.

Day after day there would be never-ending lines with hundreds of fresh-faced twenty-somethings fighting to get employed. The queues wound around buildings and there were "interview stations" set up where employers could hit you in groups instead of one-on-one.

At the time, I was perplexed by the mass amounts of young folks trying to get work, but I would later understand that Australia (Oz) is a super popular destination for travelers. A ton of Europeans and others can get working holiday visas for Oz, and it's the kind of country that has mad visiting and living appeal, so the math makes sense.

The surf, the cities, the bush, the animals—the everything you would expect out of Oz just happens to be true, so it's no wonder that casual work during summer months is bursting at the seams with eager beavers ready to fill any vacant, paying slot.

Melbourne knew it had its pick of the litter for casual workers, and so did basically every other town or city along the eastern and southern seaboard. I just didn't know that.

At one particular cattle call, after hours of waiting and shifting my weight from one sore, high-heeled foot to the other, I finally got my chance to shine.

XXX

The interview was for a restaurant that distributed gourmet sandwiches to other businesses at lunchtime. The restaurant seemed awfully popular, so my hope was that they were hiring by the hoards.

"Hi! How's it going?" a young man sitting behind a table asked me.

He wore a black t-shirt with swirly logo on the pocket. Dark-skinned and fit, he had nice smile and blue eyes that glowed sandwich lust.

"I'm good, thank you," I replied, demurely sitting down across from him.

"So, do you have any sandwich making experience?" he asked.

"Well, no. But I've worked in many restaurants, and I love sandwiches. They're my favorite food. They'd be my death row meal," I answered.

"Hmmm," he hummed, looking down at my resume and blindly scanning it for redemption.

I had to make a save.

"But, although I've never been a sandwich chef, I've helped make lots of other foods. I've been responsible for designing desserts and salads, and other items that come separate from the main dish," I said, oozing the type of enthusiasm that would make anyone think I wanted to get married in an IHOP—because I love making whip cream smiley faces THAT MUCH.

I wriggled in my chair. The guy was so damn cute. He made me want the job even more for all the wrong reasons. He pressed his pencil to his puffy lips.

"So, you've been around food, and you've helped plate desserts and salads, but you've never made sandwiches."

I wanted to be his tube of ChapStick. I paused, mesmerized by his mouth and considering the question while re-crossing my legs slowly.

Those lips. Where was I?

"Sandwiches! Um...no. I haven't made sandwiches before, but I've been making them at home my whole life. It can't be that different," I offered.

That was it.

I'd hit the kill switch.

Hottie went sour. His mouth shriveled. His brow furrowed. His back stiffened, and I got slapped in the face with an imaginary slice of bologna.

In that cold moment, I learned two very important life lessons:

1. Don't ever compare what someone does professionally to what you dabble in, and

2. Perfect the art of bullshitting.

I didn't get that sandwich-making job, and I would have rocked that sandwich-making job. I would have spun pickles on my fingers, tossed summer greens with my Jedi mind tricks, and toasted bread with the heat of my passion for sandwich artistry.

I really do love sandwiches, and when I make one I take my time to make sure every bite gets its fair share of spread, veggies, cheese, meat, and whatever other great sandwich yum-yums I've chosen to be part of my food sculpture.

I am a legit sandwich maker fo-real, but no, at that point in my life I had never gotten paid to grab a hoagie and go to town on it for someone else.

The problem was that hottie-boy didn't care about my able-ness, he cared about my experience. He forgot that ambition is a worthy opponent of experience, and desperation can make mothers lift trucks off babies. My desperation would have given him the hardest working roast-beef-on-wheat-roll worker he'd ever seen. I needed a job. I would have worked hard for him and the restaurant, but he was done with me.

Wah-wah. It was one more work opportunity down the garbage disposal for me. Up his.

As I dragged my feet down the street toward my hostel I made the decision that, from there on out during my job search in Melbourne, I would say what people needed to hear. Not because I'm a liar—lying is something I loathe and try to avoid at all costs. Plus, for me the truth is the only thing that keeps me sane. I like to hear it, no matter how raw, and I like to speak it, no matter how difficult. But my new plan wasn't about naughty lying, or at least I didn't see it that way, it was about healthy lying. Faking it until I made it.

XXX

That night I scoured the want ads for anything close to suitable. Buried in the back, I found a café position that called for:

1. Coffee making skills (check) and
2. Sandwich artistry (fucking check-check).

The next morning, after a phone call and some resume tweaking, I headed in for an interview where I was better mentally prepared than I had been for any interview I'd ever had in my twenty-three years of living.

The café was located in an uppity part of Melbourne. I'd ridden the city train to get there, and instead of zoning out to the sway of the rails, I spent the minutes running over the interview conversation in my head. I covered every possibility, every curveball, and even mentally practiced my smile follow-through and unbreakable eye contact—I was the most interesting barista and sandwich maker in the world.

"Hello, nice to meet you," a lovely woman greeted me as I walked into the cafe.

She looked friendly, motherly. For the first time in Melbourne I felt comforted. Even though my gut did a tiny twitch as I shook her hand, knowing that I was getting ready to fib the shit out of the interview, I felt like maybe this women would understand my predicament. Mothers get necessity, and necessity is the mother of invention, so I figured she'd probably reason my innovative tale forgivable.

"Please sit," she said, extending a hand toward one of the shiny café tables.

I slid a chair out and sat down, making sure to stay on the edge of my seat as if to physically express my eagerness.

"Are you American?" she asked, settling in across from me.

"I am. I've always wanted to come to Australia, and now I'm here. I can't believe it. I love it, but I just really need to afford my time here."

I dropped my eyes. I felt like crying for some reason. I had to get this job. My year overseas depended on income yesterday.

"Oh, yes." She softened her tone and glanced at my resume. "It can be very competitive for casual work, but I'm sure you'll be fine soon. Let's see, it says you've worked in Blimpie's Sub shop? Tell me about that."

I dove into my Blimpie's job description—the fake job description. It was a glorious tall tale of pepperoni on white bread with green pepper. I gave details about my adeptness at upselling people to large combos. I swore by my pastrami and swiss.

The truth was, I ate at Blimpie's a few times my senior year of college, but during my one-shot interview moment I owned that motherfucking sandwich chain. I invented it. I was the genius who thought of putting bacon, lettuce, and tomato together with meat and cheese.

Once my tongue warmed up from all the steamy bullshit, I spread my wings and flew on the wind of lies.

I told the lovely lady of my time as a barista at a café called Froth, an imaginary coffee shop where I was master of all things caffeine. I used vocabulary from Starbucks. I folded my hands into weird origami shapes to perform an invisible latte making session, describing not only my expertise on the matter, but also my passion for coffee.

I hated coffee. I'd purchased maybe two cups of coffee during my two-ish decades on the planet, and I hadn't finished either. Coffee made my tummy feel like I needed to poo my pants or vomit on my shirt, or maybe both. The strong caffeine simply disagreed with me.

It didn't matter, though. I was the actor of the decade—*I'd like to thank my mom, the Academy, my agent, and that hot dude at the sandwich shop for snubbing me. Dreams can come true if they're built on grit and fibs.*

When I finished my coffee legends, I leaned back in my chair, ready to reap my harvest.

"Wow. Interesting," said the lady. "You're perfect! When can you start?"

"I can start now. I'm ready when you are!" I replied, leaning in to hug her.

BLAM! Mission accomplished.

I became weepy, I was so happy. Yes—I'd lied. But yes—I could do this job. I was going to do better than well. Because this woman had given me a chance, I was going to work my fingers to the bone for her.

XXX

She told me to start in the morning and I did. I showed up fifteen minutes early for my 5:30 a.m. shift. She wasn't there, but I was introduced to the manager—a tall, gorgeous, cocoa-colored, Brazilian woman with the most amazing boobs I'd ever seen. She didn't have them out, but she didn't have them in either.

She wore a tight, black, V-neck t-shirt that allowed her girls to plump their way into perfect half-domes. They were like vortexes, those boobs. All the workers and customers had to worship them, not because she asked us to, but because the boobs demanded it. They were powerful mind readers and true works of art that belonged in the Louvre. Her face should have detoured me from her boobs, but it didn't.

She was South American beautiful—unfair beautiful. It still didn't stop me from being hypnotized by her perfect boobs. She'd come up to me and start talking, and I'd start staring at her boobs. I was that creepy, fifty-year-old guy who threatened to play pocket pool every time she asked if I could refill the cup stack.

Thank God she didn't seem to mind my creepiness, and later she would be so cool with me that she'd explain to me why her boobs were exactly circular, perky, and flawless. It wasn't because they were fake. They just looked fake, because of her trick—she'd never taken off her bra since she'd developed breasts. She wore it all hours of the day, even through the night, so that they'd never move. No jogging. No jumping. Boob protection first—everything else second. Long live elasticity.

That woman turned out to be hyper-unique, and her jaw-dropping life story is one I plan on writing about, but when we first met on that oddly cool summer morning in Melbourne, she and her boobs were all business.

She showed me around the tiny café without friendliness or foulness—just work focus. She and her boobs pointed out knives, towels, aprons, refrigerators, the stockroom, cash register, the juice bar, sandwich bar, and, of course, the coffee machine.

The high performance espresso machine was really fancy-shmancy, boasting copper piping, chrome housing, and other sleek and very mechanical looking buttons, dials, and drains that made me retreat in terror. It was the size of a church organ and wildly intimidating.

To avoid the mean machine, I'd take care of every other aspect of a customer's order except the coffee part. If they wanted a tuna fish sandwich and cappuccino, I would rush to the sandwich bar. If they wanted a bagel and flat white, I was already at the toaster with my cream cheese.

"I'll grab that muffin for you, Jen."

"I'll press that juice for you, Stacey," I'd announce, sprinting in the opposite direction of the belching steam monster that threatened to end my paycheck.

I did though, keep one eye on that damn coffee machine at all times, because I knew sooner or later we'd throw down. While I made sandwiches and juices, I'd glance behind me to see what buttons were pushed, what handles were twisted, and what cups were used. My mental list of steps to espresso success was growing.

Finally, it happened. On that first day of work at about ten a.m., a speedy co-worker beat me to dibs on a ham sandwich. I was left with two lattes. *Two wha-what*? *Sheeeeeee-it.*

I wasn't getting out of this one.

XXX

I tiptoed my way toward the espresso, biting my cheek until I could taste metal in my mouth. I quietly confronted it, stepping up to the silver, drip tray and eyeing the gadgets, gizmos, thinga-a-ma-bobs, and whose-it-whats-its.

This was the moment of reckoning. I took a deep breath and wrapped my shweaty palmshz around the handle-thingy. I knew I needed to fill it with coffee grounds. That step I'd witnessed the other girls taking as the first one to coffee magic.

I held the handle up to the bean cylinder and clicked the big button below it a few times, thrilled to hear the beans get pulverized into a super fine grind. It spilled out into my handle.

Aces.

Next, I moved on to pressing the coffee filled handle-thingy up into another thingy-area to do whatever it was supposed to do at that point.

I'd watched them do that too. Later I would learn that this was called "tamping". I guess the tamp, which means packing the grounds down tight, ensures equal water contact with the grounds, which will in turn make a more uniform cup of coffee.

To be honest, whatever it did, I didn't care. I just wanted to make sure I got the step right to keep my bullshitting on a professional level.

From there, I remembered that I needed to attach the handle-thingy to the bottom of the overhanging shelf on the machine. I knew water would come out of the overhanging shelf, run through my handle-thingy, and dump an espresso shot into my awaiting cup.

I attached the handle without incident, set up my shiny cup and saucer underneath it, and pressed the ON button on the machine. The metal dragon gurgled to life and I could see the beginning stages of black heaven oozing from the nozzle.

I'd done it. I was making coffee!

I loved myself, and I would have done a little celebration pelvic thrust with an *uh-uh* sound for added enthusiasm, but I wasn't golden just yet—there was one more step that had yet to be completed.

I had to steam the milk.

I grabbed a silver pitcher that I'd watched the other girls fill. I whistled while I poured milk into it and carried it over to a slender arm sticking out of the machine. I figured it was the steamer, and I figured right. I was crushing Coffee Making 101.

I reached up and turned the dial above it to the left. The arm roared to life, spitting indistinguishable vapor out of its eye. I held my pitcher up to the screaming appendage and started frothing/foaming/steaming my milk. But the thing was, I wasn't frothing/foaming/steaming my milk, I was killing/slaughtering/truly fucking my milk.

I stood there smiling, totally oblivious to my mistake while the nozzle emulated a dying cat. I gently turned it and pulsed it up and down, like I'd seen the other girls do. It screeched and moaned like a moody goat, or like ten zillion screaming babies competing against a billion howling dogs. It burped burnt milk bubbles onto my apron, and at one point it started farting.

I smelled campfire, but still smiling, I frothed that freakin' milk anyway for about a minute. I would later learn that milk should only be steamed for about ten to forty seconds.

I don't know why anyone didn't stop me—probably because the owner had told everyone there that I was the Pablo Escobar of lattes, born on a coffee plantation in Columbia and raised wearing a bean grill over my front teeth, snorting lines of espresso while I threatened to beat bitches with my robust flavor.

While I killed the milk, all the other employees turned their heads in slow motion to gawk at me.

I whistled, working my fake coffee expertise into a singed pile of dung. Then, I stopped. It was the confusion on their faces and the sickly stench coming from my pitcher that made me quit, and my manager and her perfect boobs confronting me.

Brazilian-perfect-fun-bags asked me in a controlled but super pissed hush, "What the hell are you doing? *Parvo*."

She yanked the pitcher out of my hands and I was pleased to see it go. I dropped my head and stared at her nips while I waited for my red slip, but then she switched gears.

"Here—watch," she offered, taking mercy on me.

"Thank you," I whispered, memorizing the movement of her adept hands.

A week later, with her espresso lessons and my work ethic, I ended up being a badass coffee maker and one of the owner's favorite employees. I worked there for the duration of my work visa in Australia, and I was invited to come back in the future.

My lies got me in the door of that job, but my effort and skill kept me there. I made good friends and have great memories. And without that experience, I wouldn't have learned how certain arenas in the game of life work.

I haven't since told any whoppers like I did during that interview, but I would again if I had to. As long as I could perform the job well and knew that I was being blackballed from getting that job because of a ridiculous reason, I wouldn't feel bad about stepping slightly outside the facts. If I knew that unless I bent the truth I had no shot in hell of becoming employed, I'd level the playing field every time.

Life isn't fair—not for me, not for you, the next guy, or the chick after. As long as you're not hurting anyone…play ball. You just have to be able to back your bullshit.

CHAPTER 11

A good way to earn money overseas is by teaching.

If you were born in an English speaking country you are extremely fortunate for many reasons. One reason is that English is the third most widely spoken language in the world. English is also currently the dominant business language in the world, meaning that many people in non-English speaking countries want to learn English. Therefore, teaching English is an excellent gateway to exploring the planet.

I decided that teaching English was something that I wanted to do for a bit, so I braved up and jumped into the pool of Teaching English as a Foreign Language, aka TEFL.

I got my TEFL credentials in Thailand. I went there because a British friend that I'd met in New Zealand had signed up for a two-month course on Koh Samui—a badass, gorgeous island off the southeastern tail of Thailand. I had no idea about Koh Samui or the entire country of Thailand, but I knew I needed TEFL credentials, and I trusted this British dude. He was quite the researcher.

"So this TEFL training center is good? Do they still have room in the class?" I asked down the telephone line, squinting at the pathetic website he'd suggested for information on the TEFL training school.

It looked like Helen Keller had designed the graphics and Patrick Star from *Spongebob SquarePants* had written the content.

"This website is bunk. You sure this place is legit?" I pressed.

Stuart cleared his throat.

"Yes, it's good...enough. I've done a lot of research, and it seems they're all a bit dodgy, but we need the certificate to teach. Schools want the certification. We have to have it to teach in most countries."

"Okay. I trust you," I said.

"It'll be great. We'll get our teaching certificates and then go wherever we want. You're going to love Koh Samui, it's amazing. I promise," he said.

I clicked on the money tab of the website and investigated the cost of getting TEFL certification. The numbers were so-so—not super expensive but not hella cheap.

Overall, I figured the time spent in Thailand was worth the price tag. It would be a good jump-off point to working anywhere in Southeast Asia.

"Okay, I'm in. So, you said you wanted to go in about eight months from now, but do you think you could push it out to ten months?" I asked, typing in my bank's website to confirm how much I needed to save in order to make this whole venture happen. "There's a June session. I just need a bit more time to save some cash."

"I guess I could wait a couple of months. That would let me put back a few extra quid myself. My boss would like it too," he said.

"Great! Then we'll plan for June."

"Excellent!"

And that was that.

Eight months later I was headed to Thailand to train for my new teaching career.

When I landed on Koh Samui, I was surprised. It was anyone's island—an odd mixture of day spas, manicured golf courses, gold-chained German sunbathers, poor street food vendors, ladyboy knife fights, modest villages, and backpacker squalor. All this was nestled among serene jungle and giant golden Buddhas. It was hands down the most amazing place I could have chosen to get my TEFL certificate.

My life there was the perfect balance of education, relaxation, and celebration. I studied and went to school all morning, floated in crystal clear ocean water for lunch, and got crooked on Chang Beer to the thud of the Bee Gee's at some random jungle hut by night.

I rented a nice apartment with my British friend. It was a few blocks from our school on a great little street with a peculiar French Quarter feel.

I long-term rented a scooter, even though we were warned of scooters being the number one cause of death on the island.

Driving on Koh Samui was just sketchy. An American boy that graduated from our school the year before had gotten drunk, ridden his scooter too fast along a backstretch of the island, and lost control on a sand patch. The accident took off his leg, but it didn't detour me from owning my own moto while there.

I drove my moto fast, cruising windy roads by sun and moonlight, and hoping with every overhanging palm tree that it wasn't in the mood to spit from its fronds one of its many loaded coconuts onto my helmetless head. That's the way the Thais rode—fast and helmetless—so that's how I rode.

Most foreigners who found their way onto Koh Samui for a few months or years switched to the Thai way of doing things, which meant most of us accepted life-threatening hazards as a part of daily routine. Riding a scooter at high speeds without a helmet and perhaps a few beers in your system was fine and normal. Riding with four people on your tiny scooter was normal. Once I saw a Thai family of six riding on a scooter—SIX people on one scooter!

Although we'd memorized the warning tales of cars passing on curves, falling coconuts that cracked skulls like eggshells, and that often not-so-random stray animal that chooses precisely the most dangerous moment to make their way out of the jungle in front of scooters, we still rode without much care.

I fit right in with the rest of the crazies on that island—both Thai and foreign. The dangerous aspects of our lives were something not to be dwelled on, because the beauty of it all was more potent.

XXX

Everyone's life out there was unpredictable yet magical, and as gently as the island could kiss you, it could also violently bite you. You just hoped for the best and tried to make good sober decisions to make up for the bad boozy ones—all the while embracing the amazingness that is Thailand.

Teaching English there was eye opening. The schools were so basic. I wanted to be sad for the kids, but once inside I realized there was no need.

Without doors, air conditioning, supplies, and sometimes even tables and chairs, the children still smiled and laughed, approaching their education with the zest that all youngsters should possess for new things. They loved learning and they cherished it, looked forward to it.

The respect we were given as teachers was moving. In my experience teaching in Thailand, I was awed by the reverence offered to those who help others to expand their minds with knowledge. As teachers, we were bowed to when we entered the classroom. I never had a child act up or had an adult roll their eyes at our lessons. They were happy and polite, eager and humble. I was equally delighted, respectful, excited, and modest.

The whole time I was in the TEFL certificate program, I loved waking up in the morning and going to the school to teach. It was so much fun and equally as gratifying. We'd sing the names of colors, repeat sentences about days of the week, and pla y heaps of games.

My favorite game was hangman, but instead of hangman, I would draw a picture of a stick man hanging from his parachute, floating over the ocean. Below him, a prehistoric-sized shark breached the water— jaws open, eyes squinted. With every letter they missed, I'd erase a string on the parachute and give the stickman a more worried facial expression.

Sometimes I think they got letters wrong on purpose, because when all the lines on the parachute were erased, they'd roll on the floor with laughter and screams while I took my time stretching out the death of the stick man. I drew him falling inch by inch. I'd add sound effects. I'd use my red marker when he finally entered the teeth of the shark, drawing red geysers that squirted into the clouds—the shark smiling, his belly swollen with dinner. The kids couldn't get enough. We all loved it. Great laughs.

After each amazing day at school, I'd slide right into even better nights. I cruised under the stars to the aroma of jasmine incense, walked jungle paths dotted with miniature Buddhas holding giant offerings, or got ripped drunk with a rainbow of humans from all around the world. I danced a lot in Thailand.

Somehow I graduated my TEFL schooling without bodily harm and with a lot of student teaching under my belt. I did well. I earned top grades and I very badly wanted to stay on Koh Samui and teach. I'd fallen in love with it.

I had local and foreign friends. I knew every back road that led to shacks filled with bright colors, spicy food, cold beer, and amazing candlelight conversation in hammocks.

I had my favorite Buddha, my preferred beach, ultimate Thai massage spot, and the local pub quiz on lockdown.

I was so into the scene of Koh Samui that I even knew the usual money trail of a local six-year-old who earned a living for her family by challenging drunk Westerners to a game of Connect Four. This girl was a Connect Four missile. She had every possible combination of moves memorized and was unbeatable and cocky about it. I hated her and loved her at the same time.

I knew her hustling spots more than the ones of other children, and there were a lot of kids working the streets. I saw them every night, but like most morally intact travelers who've been educated on the reality behind the situation, I didn't buy their goods.

Not if they begged.

Not if they nearly cried, which they did sometimes.

I offered them food or a hug, but not money. The food they usually declined. The hug they sometimes took.

This kind of discipline was heart shattering and crazy difficult, but I understood that I couldn't buy what they were selling unless I wanted to contribute to their exploitation. The less money they made the less likely their family was to continue sending them out into the streets alone with a bag full of neon sunglasses and hand-painted shot glasses.

Four years old, maybe three. It didn't matter.

A lot of children were sent by their family out into the night to earn a living.

As a teacher, we were told to watch for these kids in our classrooms. They were easy to spot, because they'd be puffy-eyed and fading in and out of consciousness, slipping off of their chairs into exhaustion comas in the middle of a lesson on how to sing in English about a dog named BINGO. They were present and absent at the same time, because they'd stayed out working the streets until 4:00 a.m.

I learned that being poor, truly poor, could lead to acts of survival that I don't understand.

XXX

It was common among impoverished Thai families to use all members of the family to bring home a buck or ten, whether the person was sixty years old or six.

In some families, kids were the top breadwinners, because they're cute, and we all know that in the grand scheme of the world cute and pretty win. It's why puppies get commercials for donations to PETA and not snakes. Imagine if the animal rescue commercials set to Sara McLachlan's single-tear melody zoomed in on a Cobra's missing eye, a Rattler's bent fang, or a Python's busted fork tongue—the purse strings would be double knotted.

If you're fuzzy, sweet, mini or cuddly, innocent and adorable, you have a better shot in life than the wrinkly, oversized, annoying, dodgy, and fugly. It's pretty easy to get a drunk Welchman to buy a plastic rose that lights up in hot pink LED lights as it plays Beyonce's "Crazy In Love" if you're three-feet-tall with watery eyes and a pouty bottom lip that mouths, "Please. I'm hungry."

Most people want to help kids. It's the adults that we turn our backs on. Thais know this, and their laws don't prevent them from working their children. They're desperate to feed them and keep them alive, so you'd see these kids working the streets, rolling deep with their kiddie-gang and out WAY past a decent bedtime. They haunted all of the most inappropriate places, but that's the set up over there. That's the set up in many countries that don't have well-enforced human rights. Plus, is it wrong to let a child work to survive if it's the only way they might do so?

The situation is complicated and layered. Survival has different definitions in different locations. Judging is impossible, unless you walk a mile in their shoes.

Life is dirty—dirtier in some locations more than others. The cleaning crew might not show up for years, if ever, so what do you do to get by for now? You do lots of things that fortunate American minds may not understand.

And even I was bent on the subject. With my understanding of the situation, that giving money to these kids probably fueled the fire, my firm stance was flexed to the point of shattering. With intact morals and a confused bleeding heart, I couldn't help but track down the Connect Four girl at least once a week and empty the cash from my pockets into hers.

I liked her. She was different. She was ambitious. At six years old she was too smart for her little britches—savvy well beyond her years.

I'd spy her weaving her way through a bar looking pissed off and bored, and I couldn't resist. I'd watch her slam down her worn out board game in front of some drunk twenty-three-year-old Irish chick and get to work.

"You play. Five baht," she'd scowl, shooting a stink eye at the wasted partier.

"Ahhhh, yooouuu shhhure are cute. Yoooou wahn-me-tuh play ya game, love? Hereyago then," the woman would slur back, pushing a wad of crumpled bills across the table toward the unimpressed child.

Connect Four girl would pocket the money and proceed to kick some Connect Four ass. Three moves tops, and the game was over. She wouldn't stop at one drunk chick. No...she'd take her, her friends, and every sucker in the bar, including the more sober patrons, until feelings eventually got hurt.

And they always did.

Getting taken by a kid feels weird, so at some point smiles turned upside down, and that's when the child gangster would exit the bar, pockets fat with fresh Baht and ready to hit the next victim-filled cantina with her Connect Four tucked safely under one arm.

She was uh-maze-ing at the game. As far as I'd seen she was unbeatable. That's why I trailed her like a starving tiger—I was intrigued.

I was so freaked out by this girl that I was willing to pay big bucks to defeat her. My stalking turned into a weird relationship and she got to know me, waiting for me. We'd eye each other from a distance down the dirt road—the scene reminiscent of an old Western showdown, whistles echoing softly in the background. Mano a mano.

When I would finally sit down to play her, I'd concentrate like I was taking the Graduate Record Examination. I slumped deep in focus over the suspended grid while she popped her gum and rolled her eyes.

Sometimes we'd chat.

Usually not.

Her English was pretty damn good, and she was really gifted at trash talk well beyond her years.

"You suck, lady," she'd say.

"You do," I'd retaliate with as much juvenility as possible.

"You never gonna win. You simple."

"Your face is."

We'd become archenemies and loyal business partners, me supporting the lining of her wallet and her annoying the shit out of my brain. I was determined to get a "W "in my column, but my determination was no match for her expertise. That six-year-old was smarter than me at Connect Four and probably at a lot of other things. Night after night, frustrated expletive after slammed fist on the table, she demolished me. I never even came close to winning. Sometimes she had me in four moves.

The mornings after a good beating, I wouldn't see her in class either. I wanted to, since the Connect Four take down wasn't going so swell, my backup plan was to show her up at naming "things on a farm". I needed my street cred back, but she was a phantom. I'd ask the other teachers if they knew of the Connect Four savant, but none ever did. I don't know why she wasn't in school, and it bothered me.

Sometimes I'd ask her about it while we played, but she never answered. She refused to say much about herself. The only things she ever offered was, "You boring me," or, "You too easy for me."

Now, I imagine she's taken over the island. I fantasize about her running a Connect Four ring, mastering algorithms with optimizations that include alpha-beta pruning. She's sporting black Ray Bans, a BMW, diamond incisors, and a castle made of gold and red discs. From her throne, she shouts down to the plebeians about horizontally, vertically, or diagonally ruling their worlds.

Their choice. Their move. She's in charge, a born business shark—the black mamba of *Milton Bradley*.

That little girl taught me just as much as my teaching—hopefully—taught some children. I think about her a lot and my time in Thailand. The random life experience I got there, along with living in a tropical paradise, made Thailand one of my favorite places in the world. It's a spellbinding location.

I loved it so much; I decided that I had to do whatever I could to stay there after I finished my TEFL certification. Unfortunately, though, most of the permanent teaching jobs on the island of Koh Samui were taken. My chances of continuing teaching there were small to nonexistent.

So, with sadness and reluctance, I did my homework. I found out that at the time, the best TEFL teaching options in SE Asia were in Japan, South Korea, and Taiwan.

Japan was expensive. I needed some cash behind me just to get started there, and I was nervous about earthquakes and tsunamis, so I crossed it off my list.

South Korea just didn't appeal to me, and today I still can't tell you why Taiwan did, but it did.

I went online, found the names of some school agents in Taiwan. They were the middlemen for bridging teachers to schools. I made some phone calls, and a week after finishing my certification I was on a flight out of Bangkok to Taipei, Taiwan.

CHAPTER 12

The school agent I'd contacted met me at the airport. He offered me a place to stay for four nights and promised me three interviews with good schools.

He was a good host. He explained the gig to me—the average pay for American teachers, the way most contracts worked, and some details about Taiwanese culture. He gave me confidence that things would turn out well.

The man referred to himself as an ABC—American Born Chinese. He spoke perfect American English and had a hot, Taiwanese model for a girlfriend who doubled as his business partner. They drove me around in a flashy, sports car, looking polished and gangster. I figured to drive that kind of car, get that kind of girl, and be on the ball like this dude was, I should have no worries. I was correct in my assumption. He worked hard for me, introducing me to people in schools and translating during different interviews. He even helped me negotiate contracts.

As a threesome, Mr. ABC, his arm candy, and I cruised Taipei in search of my perfect teaching job. I wore my best teaching clothes and tried my hardest to get excited about the schools that I entered, but Taipei was no Thailand. Obviously it was no tropical paradise island like Koh Samui, but in the grand scheme of things, it couldn't even hold a torch to Bangkok, and Bangkok can be a real slum.

Taipei just seemed off. It was modern and big. It even had shiny bits, but somehow it felt slightly distorted.

First, there was the pollution. The city was acid rain in your eyes, soot on your gums, and AA battery juice down your throat. It was the first place I'd ever been where I could actually see a cloud of carbon monoxide sitting on the ground at the bus stop and taste the invisible chemicals drip into my esophagus as I inhaled each stingy breath. Taipei might have had a polished outer layer, but when you scratched the surface its rotten insides spilled out. It was littered with stressed humans, soulless big businesses, unimaginative architecture, and it just gave me the heebie-jeebies from the get go.

The population of Taipei was comprised of walking dichotomies. Sharply dressed men spit phlegm globs everywhere. Little, hunched over grandmas in knitted sweaters preferred shoulder barging their way down the sidewalk instead of moving aside or muttering a soft, "Excuse me." Occasionally, if someone made eye contact they'd crack a faint smile, but always in a way that made me feel like their friendliness was based on a plan to eat my beating heart for dinner.

Harsh? Yes, but Taiwan is the first country that I didn't like, and it turned out my first impression was right. By the time I left my job and the country, I would have fantastic reasons to hate the shit out of it. But in those first days, I buried my gut instinct and gave it a chance.

Even though something felt off about it, things were friendly enough at the starting line to make me stay. The first few days were great, when Mr. ABC and his bangin' girlfriend escorted me to various job opportunities with smiles and laughs, but on the fourth day the fun slid down the gutter hole.

Mr. ABC and his model girlfriend broke up.

It turned into a Chinese version of Jerry Springer. Staying in the guest room of their downtown apartment, I listened to her yell in Mandarin while he bitched in Wu. They used me as a go-between to relay stories of cheating, stealing, regret, and chopstick-to-the-throat threats, so I made a snap decision on a teaching contract just so I could get the hell out of their space.

XXX

I chose a school located northeast of Taipei that offered both a salary and accommodation, something that is isn't uncommon with teaching positions. I agreed to teach English for a year at a grade school called Harvard. It was located in a major port city not far from Taipei, Keelung.

The gig seemed sweet. I had a cool classroom that was modern, fairly big, came with its own bathroom, and bursting with construction paper kites, toy trucks, and cotton dolls. The school made sure I had access to any books, props, or plastic playthings that I needed to help the kids learn English.

My students ranged from age four to seven. That was a weird and major gap in school age, but luckily I was assigned an assistant who we'll call Ms. Happy. She was super nice, translated everything I needed, and used bleach on her face to whiten her skin so she always looked like she was wearing a happy yoghurt mask.

She was amazing, kind, extremely helpful, and a walking Chinese caricature. She replaced her R's for L's. She was into all things pink and school-girlish, even though she was pressing forty. I loved her. Ms. Happy was a lifesaver—a really entertaining and spacey one. She seemed to kind of float her way through life, thrilled and bouncy-flouncy about everything from recess to toilet cleaning. I gelled with her immediately.

On the first morning of work, I was organizing a bookshelf before the start of class when I noticed something odd taped to the wall beside the bathroom door.

"Ms. Happy, can you come here a second?" I asked, setting down the books that I held. "Um, what…what is this?" I questioned, pointing to the picture taped to the wall.

"Oh. Dats for bathroom. It show kids how to go. Ha!" Ms. Happy chirped.

I squinted and tilted my head in disbelief at the photo. Yes, it was a "how-to" laminated menu showing boys and girls the proper way to use the bathroom, but it was a "how-to" using ACTUAL pictures of kids using the bathroom. It didn't show any nude body parts, but it showed girls sitting on toilets wearing grunt faces and boys with their backs to the camera, arcs of pee shooting out into the distance in front of them.

"NO. NO. NO. NO. Noooooo. We can't have these," I said, ripping the freakazoid bathroom guide off the wall and crushing it between my hands.

"But how they rurn to go pee and po-po?" Ms. Happy asked, demonstrating a proper squat right there in the middle of the playtime mat that was shaped like a kitty cat.

I halfway expected her to stand up, use her foot to kick some imaginary dirt over her imaginary mess, and lick the back of hand before running it over her pageboy hairdo.

"Their parents can show them how to use the bathroom," I said, shaking my head and tossing the guide in the trash. "They should know by now anyway."

Then the day started.

I welcomed kids, parents, and babysitters. It was always a parade of crazed faces—rushing, yelling, kissing, and hugging.

Most of the parents only knew how to say "hello" and "okay" or "bye-bye" in English, but most of the kids alternatively spoke English surprisingly well. With their black hair, beautiful Asian features, and delicate skin ranging from stark white to light coffee with cream, my gorgeous Taiwanese students introduced themselves to me one-by-one.

"Edward."

"Paris."

"Candy."

"Roger."

"Bridget."

Are these kids all midget strippers and movie stars, I wondered as they filed past me and into their miniature seats.

In Taiwan, not only are many people obsessed with learning English, but they're also dedicated to melting into the entirety of Western culture. They want to be like Mike, so the best way to do that is to call yourself Mike, get some Jordans, pick up a basketball, and learn to talk trash in the paint. They like names they hear on American movies, hence the random Pepper Potts and Steve Stiflers.

When I would get a new student, sometimes I was asked to give them an American name. I never wanted this job and I would explain to the parents that it wasn't my place, but if they insisted, I'd create a list of names for them to consider. I provided definitions for the names, historical referencing, and popularity statistics. I'd also throw a ridiculous name into the running, because I thought it was absurd an adult would want me to tag a name to their child—one that may stick. For instance, for one little girl I offered up April, Hazel, Lisa, Paige, and Sugarplum. They took Hazel. Good for them.

I thought the American naming thing was weird, but weird things would always happen while teaching in Keelung. Sometimes women wearing costumes would appear out of thin air in my classroom and start dancing around. I later realized that this was their version of music class, which was pretty cool for the kids. It wasn't that the music class was odd—what made it freaky was that I never knew when it would happen, and Ms. Happy always seemed equally surprised. The women just erratically popped in, all bells and ruffles and crazy songs.

One day a goat walked into my classroom while I was teaching the names of vegetables. He just waddled in, paused by the chalkboard, and stared at us like he was there to pick someone up.

Ms. Happy didn't flinch.

The kids kept reciting, "Carrot, broccoli, peas, asparagus."

So I kept going too, and the goat watched us for a minute before he turned around and left, his bell jingling softly as he meandered out. I guess he had the wrong classroom.

XXX

As time stretched on things went from peculiar, to very-less-than-normal, to just straight up freaky.

One afternoon recess, my kids were all excited about getting to play in the ball pit. The ball pit was the same kind of ball pit they have at McDonalds—rope walls, a ledge that ran the parameter of a square crater full of balls. Usually it was fun and average, but on this day it was neither of those things. When my students jumped in, I heard a loud splash and saw a giant wave of water come spilling over the edges of the enclosure. The students popped up from the shifting plastic mountain soaked, crying, and sputtering. Ms. Happy laughed, but I was disgusted.

"What's going on? Why is there water in here?" I asked, pulling drenched and sniveling children from the pit.

"They wash balls," said Ms. Happy, making a scrubbing motion with her hands.

"They could drown and we'd never know! We can't see them under the balls. Not to mention that putting a hose in a ball pen isn't washing the balls, it's feces soup. This is a floating fecal rainbow," I complained.

"No! Rinse balls okay. Kids play. Fun!" Ms. Happy laughed, totally unconcerned.

I scrubbed the kids down one-by-one Karen Silkwood style and forbade them from reentry. After Ms. Happy took the sopping students back to the room, I took some time to inspect the scene.

There were strange things bobbing in the water alongside the balls—hair ties, Band-Aids, sandwich crust from 1962, insect carcasses, pens, socks. It was a Hepatitis A party with a dysentery hangover, and I'm the opposite of a germaphobe.

It was revolting.

After that incident, I swore off the ball pit for good and promised myself a typhoid shot for dinner. It was the beginning of the end for Taiwan and me.

Each day that crept by after the ball pit disease festival, the principal of the school would lay a new set of rules on me. When she did, she acted like they'd always been in place and that I was smoking crack for believing differently.

"When you start crass at seven on Monday…" she'd say, flashing a slippery grin.

"You mean eight. I start class at eight," I'd smile back, figuring she'd made an honest mistake.

"Yes, seven, when you start crass Monday at seven. Crass arways start at seven. So, when crass start at seven…"

"At eight."

"Yes, at seven when the students get here, you teach corors okay."

"Coor ores?"

"Corors!"

"Colors. Ha! Okay," I'd giggle, forgetting that I was being ambushed.

"Yes, corors! Okay! Bye!" she'd say, disguising her presto-chango time flip trick with the charm of Mister Roger's.

Then she rushed off leaving me with nothing but a shrinking Hello Kitty on the back of her t-shirt and a new schedule I'd never agreed to.

The woman was good. So, I did as I was told and swallowed all the ill changes being made without complaint. I figured it was my duty to do so.

But then the principal changed my use of the office computer for personal emails from free range to a limit of one hour a week, to no use at all—no exceptions.

Then the classroom got overwhelming. The children were limited to only fifty minutes of recess a week—A WEEK. Remember, these are children under the age of seven, they were allowed to play for one hour a week.

Then I started paying attention. I figured out that the kids were in school all the time. They left long after I did—nearly permanent fixtures in a dodgy hotel disguised as a school. It was like the administration and the parents wanted the kids to live there, and I guess the idea was to get me to live there too, spending every available second teaching them about the farmer and the dell, hotdogs, baseball, and Britney Spears.

XXX

It was as though the main goal of all the parents was for their children to be more than fluent in English. They wanted their kids to be confused for a Texan or New Yorker. American English, particularly, was a blue diamond—a currency that promised a better life in a city that gets snow, has diners with checkerboard floors, milkshakes on the menu, and where in general the poor are fatter than the rich. To achieve this Nike, Oscar Meyer, white picket fenced dream, they took their English seriously from birth.

I, on the other hand, thought four-year-olds should be busy trying not to pee themselves, deciding whether or not to eat a roly poly they found on the windowsill, and/or running in circles and shouting made-up words like, "zeezle" and "shmlat shmlat".

I disagreed with the "work, work, work," thing so strongly that I finally started voicing my opinion, and I never fought back so hard as the day a thumbprint sent my classroom into hysterics.

I'd showed up about ten minutes before class, as I always did, but on this day the door to my classroom was crammed with the bugging eyes of parents elbowing a pathway to me. They bared their teeth. Some cried. Others were shaking and clawing at their shirts.

Zh-Ch-Sh-R sounds were hurled at me from every angle. Ms. Happy was doing her best to calm everyone down, and I just stood there in the middle of it with full moon eyes, wondering what the hell I'd done so wrong.

"They want to talk to you about the thumbprint," Ms. Happy said to me, cramming the door shut on the worried faces and carrying a wrinkled piece of paper over to me.

She held it out. All I saw were Chinese characters with a headshot of a child wearing that same slack-jawed facial expression that all the Taiwanese children seemed to wear when they took a photograph. Next to the child's photo was a black and white fingerprint.

"What is this?" I asked, scanning the document for anything that made sense.

Impatient knocks on the closed door rattled our silence and I glanced at it to make sure it wasn't threatening to bust open. It bulged with the weight of the unnerved families.

"It the Dr. machine prediction," said Ms. Not-So-Happy.

"The what?" I asked, confused.

"The Dr. machine. It terr you what your kid can rern, rike if your kid can rern Engrish really good or not."

"What? What Dr. machine and…wait," a memory flooded in. "Does this have anything to do with the kids being pulled out of class last week?"

"Yes! The thumbprint. They take the thumbprint! They put thumbprint through Dr. machine with all the lights. It print out paper about student Engrish skirrs," Ms. Happy shrieked, bashing the paper in my hands with her jittery forefinger.

It was like the bits of rationale that kept her nerves together were ungluing. She glanced over her shoulder toward the door. Her chest pumped hard and her breath was shallow. I felt for her.

"It's okay. Don't worry. I'll take care of this," I said, patting her shivering shoulder. "Come with me."

With a supportive hand, I led her toward the door.

XXX

"Okay, once I open this door just smile, stay calm, and please translate to everyone that I will see them one-on-one, but not until next week. Please tell them that I first need to talk to the principal about the test results before we can move forward properly. Make sure they understand that all of their children are very smart and learning English at a rapid rate, and tell them that I suspect problems with the testing. Tell them I think the results are incorrect. Everything will be fine, their children are doing great. You can do this. Thanks, Ms. Happy," I said.

"Thank you," she mechanically responded.

And together we calmed the rabid herd. The message worked, thank God. Everyone settled down, lowering their children's test results from the sky where they were being waved like an educational surrender flag.

I set up times to meet with each of them the following week, and after that I marched straight over to the principal's office to get the scoop.

I swung the door open harder than intended and froze in my tracks just inside small room. Inside the principal's office was my nemesis—not the lady running the school but the thing from Star Wars predicting my students' futures.

It was a shiny R2D2 type robot covered in lights, buttons, and futuristic non-sense. The thing lit up every so often making the principal turn her head to inspect the bleeps and buzzes coming from its innards. Caught somewhere between a memory of the State Fair's signature reading machine and the daleks on *Dr. Who*, I wasn't sure what to think. I took measured steps toward it, half expecting it to contact Sky Net if I got any closer.

The principal stared at me.

I took a seat across from her without asking.

"What is this?" I asked, flapping fingers of disgust in the direction of the supposedly telepathic droid.

"Oh, hi there, Miss America. You having probrems with crass?" the principal asked.

The Miss America title was dipped in sarcastic sauce.

I straightened in my seat.

"Yes. There are problems, but I don't believe I caused them," I answered. "I had a lot of parents come in this morning. They were really nervous about some test results concerning a thumbprint, this machine, and predictions on whether or not their child will ever be good at English."

"Yes, the test will terr them evelything," she said, offering a plastic grin.

She moved her attention away from me to a pile of papers on her desk. She started scribbling. It pissed me off. No more Miss Nicey-Nicey-Stars and Stripeys—it was time to get a bit Rowdy Roddy Piper.

"This test is based on a thumb print, right?" I asked, sitting forward in my chair.

"Uh-huh," she muttered, her face buried in her writing.

"A thumb print?" I repeated, leaning all the way over until I could place my thumb on top of the paper she wrote on.

She stopped and slowly looked up at me. Her face flushed a deep maroon and she replaced her smile with pursed lips.

"Yes, a thumb print," she fumed.

"That makes no sense," I said, shooting anger arrows out of my pupils.

She shot the glare right back and for a minute I thought she might whip a light saber out from under her desk and—with her cyborg—try to make sure I never taught English again. But instead, she simply rotated away from me and shouted something in Mandarin toward the door to my classroom. Ms. Happy came rushing in, and they exchanged machine-gun-fire conversation while I sat there wishing that I spoke more languages fluently.

"She says the test is important and you must follow it to exprain to parents how you'll teach their chirdren," said Ms. Happy, her words shaking as she angled them toward the floor instead of my face.

"Please tell her I don't believe a thumbprint can predict anything but a possible crime scene suspect. Tell her that letting parents believe their kids won't be good at English due to the prediction of a robot is the same as telling them their kid won't be good at English because a healthy looking cat took a poop in the shape of an F on their birth certificate."

Ms. Happy froze, her Clorox bleached cheeks changing from white milk to strawberry.

I stood up to continue my elevator speech.

"Tell her that if you convince these parents that 'Toby' is going to fail English, then they might turn around and convince 'Toby' that he's going to fail English, and then guess what—then 'Toby' fails English! He'll make sure of that. Whatever you believe is what will be. And please tell her the ball pit is a shit pit, just like this robot thumbprint scam."

I finished my spiel with a hip jutted out—my right hand placed firmly on it. My left hand did some ghetto finger wave that reeked of American girl attitude.

The office atmosphere went chilly for a nerve-racking handful of seconds and Ms. Happy looked like she was trying to keep her uterus from falling out.

"I don't know what you…how you… I can't say what you…" Ms. Happy fumbled her almost inaudible words.

Her eyes bounced between the mute principal and me.

"I can't say that to her," she finished. "Disrespectful…"

I started to get angrier, but then I stopped. I thought about where I was. I took a deep breath, and I accepted that I wouldn't win this battle—not because I was wrong, but because it was a cultural war. The argument was too complicated to end with a winner and loser.

"Have it your way then," I sighed, my former appetite for bionic destruction exiting the room before my body could.

I stood and dragged myself out of the office. I got why Ms. Happy couldn't argue with the principal. In Taiwan and other Asian countries, losing face or getting upset and fighting rank is frowned upon, not a little, but a lot. Ms. Happy couldn't go against her ingrained culture, or at least, she didn't want to. I didn't want to put her in the middle of my shit-shooting match.

Change at the school was going to be near impossible, knowing I could never disagree strongly with anyone above me. So, with a promise to myself that I would learn Mandarin, I resigned my seek and destroy thumbprint-reading machine mission and asked Ms. Happy to please tell the Principal that I said, "Sorry." I would talk to the parents later and take care of the situation.

I did just that.

XXX

The next week, other teachers kept their heads down and eyes averted from me when I passed them in the hall. They must have heard about my rant with the principal. It was like I was a pile of disgrace that burned their retinas. I'd been banished without receiving the official paperwork.

In the classroom things went back to abnormal, until one afternoon when a superstitious straw broke my back.

A parent asked me to privately tutor his child, so I invited the man and his son to meet me after class for a demo of my teaching style. With serious concentration, they both gawked as I scrawled big letters of schoolyard rhymes on the chalkboard, *the fat cat sat on a mat*. But the more I wrote, the more the dad's mouth pulled back into a grimace of, "Ewww yuck, oh God no!"

Halfway through my sample lesson, the man's prior excitement for his son's private English lesson was nowhere to be seen. It vanished without a trace into the stale classroom air.

"That was an example of a typical lesson…but…um…are you okay? You don't look too happy," I finally commented.

The man didn't blink. His son fiddled with a coloring book.

"Something wrong, sir?" I repeated.

"You are left handed," he said through gritted teeth and narrowed eyes.

He stood, took his sons hand, and together they backed toward the door like I was radiating AIDS from my armpits.

"Um, yes. Yes, I'm left handed. Is that a problem?" I asked, following his retreat.

"It's bad," was all he got out before yanking his son out the door and out of my demon's den.

It was times like that I wished I owned an "Elephant Man" costume and had giant incisors so that I could properly feed peoples' insecurities. Had I known he was so superstitious I would have excused myself, ducked into the bathroom to change, and came out looking like a monster. I gladly would have chased him and his son into the parking lot, lips pulled back over my tooth-daggers, hissing, and slobbering tomato juice yelling, "Vait! Vait! I vant to teach your keed!"

I would have dragged my evil left hand in a gravel train beside me, dropping skin nuggets along the way before raising it in offering to his kid, "Giblets, child?"

That was my first cultural lesson on Taiwanese superstitions, which are tied to Chinese superstitions, because Taiwan got its start from Chinese and Dutch dependents. These superstitions are very, very important to their daily life and flow deeply through the existence of most Taiwanese people.

Without these magical, wispy ideas to hover above their highly systematic way of being, I'm not so sure they could get by. They FOR REAL invest in lucky and unlucky, like they're tangible twins that live down the street, eating eggs for breakfast and riding bikes to work—two, real people with red blood cells and greasy livers who might just show up on your doorstep and change the course of your life, so you better show some goddamn respect.

From the benign to the bizarre, ghosts are serious business, zodiac signs reign supreme, and numbers breathe oxygen the same as any mammal. They're able to bring fortune or despair.

And let's not forget the ultra-sexy and super lucky mole, and the hair that hangs from it. Those bad boys not only occupy lips and chins, the hairs doubling as stirrers for soup, but they can also bring rain from dry clouds for your thirsty garden. They're that lucky. You really can't go wrong with a lucky mole—just check the mole chart to make sure it's in a lucky position. If the chart says it's not in a lucky position, get rid of it, because unlucky moles are not cool in Taiwan. But, what sucks more than an unlucky mole in Taiwan…your left hand. That thing will jack your world up hardcore.

Throughout history lefties have always been shafted. We get crammed into desks built for those who write with their right hand. Our hands are encouraged to curl around scissors meant for opposite angles. Our tender forearms get indented with the metal coils of spiral notebooks, and working a manual can opener becomes an uncoordinated stage show of twisty-awkwardness that goes against every natural inclination in our bodies. I actually trained myself to open cans with my right hand, because it gave me the heebie-jeebies so badly.

Right is correct.

Left is captain of the failboat.

In Taiwan, lefties are gross oddities with crossed eyes and corn nib teeth.

The word "left" holds negative connotation in many languages. The meaning can range from sinister to weak, evil to unlucky, and it even floats its slimy way into backstabbing and a metaphorical punishment from the Gods.

In French, "left" is a synonym for "clumsy".

The word *canhoto* in Portuguese is what you call a left-handed person, also how you call out the devil.

The Welsh use the word *chwith* to say "left", or to also say "strange" or "wrong".

The Swedes connect left, or *vänster*, to *vänsterprassel*—adultery and cheating.

In English, left can describe a direction or mean to abandon/neglect something or someone.

And for those who speak Mandarin, well, the character used to identify "left" is related to improper, unorthodox, or immoral behavior.

Lovely isn't it.

So, I guess this dude thought that if I taught his son English, I'd also be teaching him how to smoke dope, find hookers, steal milk money, and smack his bitch up.

"Okay, Toby, now what do you tell someone after they hand you an ice cream? *Thank you.* That's right! And what you do tell a woman with two black eyes? Nothing you haven't already told her twice. Zing! Oh snap, Toby. That's some shit right there. Fist bump."

XXX

I never saw that man or his son again. I guess he truly decided that he didn't want me tainting the pure world of his child with my icky left hand. So, I decided I didn't want Taiwan to taint my fascination and exuberance for life, new cultures, and teaching. I made plans to leave the country in the middle of the night—no shame in my game.

I was escaping undercover, because I'd heard nauseating rumors of schools withholding pay. I'd even heard of schools calling in work visa numbers to the police, claiming that the teacher was residing in the country illegally without authorized paperwork. This, to the school administrators, was fair play if teachers tried to quit in the middle of their contract.

In severe cases, I'd heard that teachers had even been arrested at the airport or fined thousands of dollars on their way out of the country, if they were told no and tried to leave anyway.

My school was scamming my visa. They used a cheaper loophole of listing me, not as a teacher, but instead as a student, and I had no doubt they'd use it against me if I told them I wanted to quit. Until this day, I still believe they would have had me arrested at the airport if I'd let them know I was leaving before the end of my contract.

I can still remember the noise my heart made in my ears as I packed up that random Tuesday evening. It was storm waves crashing on cliffs.

My apartment was located in the building above the school and I feared someone might hear or see me, so I had to make my escape efficient. I made sure my belongings were bundled into a get-away package that could exit my apartment door, out to the street, and then into a waiting taxi in less than twenty seconds.

When it was go time, my blood gushed through my veins at stroke rate as I loaded the last of my things into the rear of the cab and muttered a breathless, "Taipei," to the old driver.

I didn't say a word the whole ride there.

It only took about thirty-five minutes to get to the capital city, because it was late night on a mid-weekday. No action on the freeway—exactly what I needed. I mean, if a late-model Terminator dressed as a cop is sprinting down the hallway of a mental hospital toward you, silver blob parts morphing into giant hooks, you want the elevator door to close quickly. I needed my elevator door marked ESCAPE FROM TAIWAN to close quickly. I wanted the taxi driver to speed. I prayed for all green lights. I had to get the fuck out of there as fast as possible.

Lucky for me, things went smoothly. Wearing my sunglasses at night like Corey Hart, I crept into the international airport with erect arm hair and spastic nerves.

"I'm fl-fl-fly-flying to Auckland, N-N-New Zealand," I stammered, handing over my passport to the Air New Zealand desk worker.

My hands fluttered like a ninety-eight-year-old passing the saltshaker across the dinner table.

"Actually, there's a problem Ms. Simpson. There's warrant out for your arrest," was what I expected to hear.

Instead, the airline worker smiled and handed me back a boarding pass, luggage tag, and other flying paraphernalia. I was free to pass through security, which I did without any problems, but I was still nervous.

The superstitious culture had bled toxic platelets into my rationality. I was sure that my decision to bail out on my contract rather than talk to them like a sane adult would result in a bad karma volcano that would erupt mid-flight. Maybe we'd lose a wing, or maybe all the pilots would suffer a simultaneous heart attack. Who knew?

I somehow felt guilty, like a bad person, but I forced myself to take deep breaths and really think about the reality of the situation. Slowly, my worry muscles slackened.

I reminded myself that when I agreed to work for the school, the principal had promised the moon and delivered a pebble in a used napkin. She paid me less than agreed, wanted longer hours than contracted (for no extra pay or benefits), and barred me from all school activities that every other teacher engaged in.

I was an outsider—a filthy, begrudged, avoided bottom dweller that was needed but barely tolerated. I was used and abused, and later I would learn this was quite normal for English teachers in Taiwan.

I actually met a New Zealand man who shared an almost mirror image story to mine.

He also left Taipei in the middle of the night, wet-browed and clutching his passport as he ran through airport corridors, praying New Zealand soil would be his to walk on again.

As deplorable as I found my time in Keelung, I actually rank Taiwan high on my list of life lessons. Taiwan held a mirror to my belief system and its connection to my upbringing. Without it, I wouldn't have known how strongly I feel about being raised an American woman and how flooded in Western culture my personality is.

With all of the amazingness that is Chinese culture and the wisdom of thousand-year-old human tradition, there are, of course, things about it that I love. There are aspects I am moved by—like linking teachers and education to deep knowledge, leadership, and setting a moral example. Other traditions and belief systems in Taiwan simply didn't work for me though, simply because Chinese culture is so different from American culture, not bad, but just different.

In Taiwan, I got the chance to really examine my patterns and how I feel about them. Now, I appreciate who I am a lot more. Taiwan taught me that there are certain things about me I want to change and others that I will bear hug until the day I die. I feel lucky that I even got the chance to stare at my process. A lot of people never do.

From teaching to government project management, event coordinating to drink pouring, I've had a lot of different jobs overseas. There were many awesome and very professional ones that I haven't mentioned, but those were more mundane.

I wanted to deliver the oddities in hopes that my message is clear: that that you can make money anywhere if you try. You can survive and you will survive—anywhere— if you put your mind to it.

I've made great money and barely enough at times. Some jobs serviced me more than others. Some were amazing and some were horrible, but all had amazing and horrible moments. Surprisingly, one of my most interesting jobs was in a country closely connected to my own.

CHAPTER 13

"I'm appalled. Truly, I have never felt more disgusted in my career, and I assure you this will never happen again. I have insisted that everyone write an apology letter. I'll post them in the morning. Again…I am sincerely sorry, madam. Could I have your details, please?"

His embarrassment pulsated through the phone. With my feet propped up on my desk, I didn't share his stress. I understood it, though. I would have been chewing my fingernails too. The incident was pretty bad, but what he didn't know was that it took a lot to offend me to the point of tattling. I'm no snitch. Plus, I'd been around little shits before.

So what if his brat students royally pissed me off? I wasn't going to alert the media or tell anyone that could affect his job or ego. Even if I did feel the need to spread my rage, I didn't have enough clout to put a dent in his morning pastry.

What had passed was a dead incident, but I had no intention of letting him in on that. He'd been desperately trying to get ahold of me all day, so I stalled. Before calling him back, I sat through two voicemails and a handwritten message from one of my colleagues detailing his attempts to reach me and apologize on behalf of his classroom.

I didn't stall to be cruel.

I stalled because it was the non-boring move, and his students had been pretty mean. I'd let him take some responsibility for the shenanigans. It was only fair.

When I finally did call him back, he was a dribble of embarrassment and explanations. I listened intently to his regrets and responded with a little sprinkle of salt in the wound.

"Yes, I think written apologies would be nice. Thank you for taking that step. I do, though, hope there won't be a repeat for your next visitor. It would be a shame to create a reputation for your classroom...or school for that matter. Bad reps can be hard to shake," I said, twirling the phone cord around my pointer finger.

"Yes, yes I agree. Thank you for understanding. You're very kind to take this so well. Now, those details please? I'm eager to set this right."

I gave him my home address and hung up the phone. My job was getting better by the minute, and it was a far cry from the agonizing days it had taken to get employed at the joint.

When I arrived in London, England, I'd struggled to get employed for longer than usual. Usually I'm set within a month of arriving somewhere, but for reasons unknown, the London job world moved at a viscous pace.

I had a work visa through my husband at the time. I sweat and toiled eight hours a day, locating and applying for the jobs I wanted.

I took it seriously. I snarled. I clawed at the competition and was dialed in on my needs. I had a pretty specific job in mind, because although the jobs I took overseas didn't always have FOREVER written on their labels, they all were aligned with the big picture I had figured out.

I'd been trying things out around the globe long enough to know that I liked project management. I liked unveiling contracts, greasing the wheels of change, being the bridge of communication, and getting word highways flowing.

I'd decided corporations blew. I had worked for some big companies, and within their walls I felt like a crumb dropped in the corner that would either go unnoticed forever or maybe get munched by a rat. I didn't want to work for the Man—I wanted to work for people who were awake to every aspect of their company, responsible for doing good and moving forward with intention.

In London, I eventually pinpointed that position—a council job in my burro. After contacting the council, it took even longer to interview, then interview again.

Two months peeled off of the calendar.

Finally, after many weeks, a binding signature, and firm handshake, I became the Education Manager for a lottery-funded project aimed at helping children make better-informed life decisions. That meant I was in charge of getting into schools to discuss drug and sex education with junior high and high school students.

Turned out, this was a well-needed position, because in twenty-first century London parents and teachers weren't in the mood to talk to kids about boners or heroine. I guess at some point in the past, parents/teachers were okay talking about drugs and sex with their kids/students, but that feeling was long gone—dropped cold in the high-waisted jean streets of 1991.

XXX

In the early years of the two thousands, sex in London seemed to be something that most kids figured out through trial and error. Acid was something eaten late at night, not defined or discussed during a two o'clock p.m. classroom lecture.

When I went to the job interview, a panel of English people told me that the drug and sex education project had been created to fill a serious void. Through crooked teeth, Queen's English, and sentences that sounded way too polite to be interview questions, they explained the dire situation.

"The teachers feel they've lost authority if they have to finish their Trigonometry class by producing a banana and running a condom down it," said a woman wearing a grey suit and wire-rimmed glasses.

"The same coy sentiment related to sex and drug education in the schools bleeds into the home. Mom and Dad not only feel like little Aaron and Claire don't want to hear about the birds and the bees, but they also believe that they don't want to hear about it from them. Drug abuse is on the same level—Mom and Dad are simply too embarrassed to cover these topics," said a plump man with a bulbous, cherry-colored nose.

"That makes sense," I lied.

They went on to explain that the result was a bunch of horny and experimental teens going through life without knowing jack shit about birth control, magic mushrooms, herpes, or marijuana.

To London, it was recipe for disaster. To me, it was a heaven-sent job that miraculously equipped me with two *Men In Black* briefcases full of goodies.

The goodies in the briefcases were great for successfully completing the job and even better for hours of laughs at home. They were a gift from the directors of the program, because the directors believed that, in order for me to do the job right, the kids needed to get a good look at the stuff they were supposed to stay away from. I mean, if they couldn't identify it, how did they know if snorting it or having sex with it was going to help/harm them?

To give the kids a good look at the sex and drug paraphernalia that could screw up or protect their futures, my directors found a company— a REAL DEAL HOLYFIED company located in a giant factory—that dedicated their time to doing nothing but replicating every drug in the world to the exact size, shape, and feel of the McCoy, and every sexual health product available to mankind.

The fake—yet very realistic-looking—drugs went into one of my *Men In Black* briefcases marked DRUGS. That was my briefcase full of ways to teach kids about things that would make them really talkative, lose the ability to create short-term memories, paranoid, see things, or overdose in a dirty bathroom stall.

The fake and very realistic-looking sex paraphernalia went into the briefcase marked SEX. It contained things like pocket vaginas, dildos, condoms, dental dams, birth control, lube, and other sex whatchamacallits. That was my briefcase full of ways to teach horny teens how to get what they wanted, and what they didn't want out of bumpin' nasties.

Those briefcases went with me on the subway system—aka the Tube—double-decker buses, and across cobble stone streets all around the city of London. I was the safe sex pimp and plastic drug lord of the century.

What had two thumbs, a hog leg rolled with the finest oregano, and a diaphragm meant for an elephant? This chick.

XXX

My responsibility, which I was paid well for, was to contact the heads of schools and request a meeting, then go and teach the kids my knowledge.

To contact the schools, I was given an old wooden desk in a kinda-shabby room in an ancient building that looked like something out of *Oliver Twist*. With my computer and phone as my weapons, I was destined to keep boners clean and brains sober. I called and wrote schools to book appointments. I worked hard. I loved the challenge and I was damn determined to get into those schools.

My determination paid off. I actually did so well that I got into three times the amount of institutions that they had set as my goal, so with my new, full schedule, I attended meetings with educational professionals. At those meetings, I would convince Head Masters and district leaders that they needed me to educate their sexually stupid and drug prone students about what can happen if you get high and naked.

Within minutes of starting my presentation, they usually agreed to my services through sweaty upper lips and nervous nods.

It was true. They didn't want to talk about illegal, bare-assed young people stuff, not even with me. They would basically shoo me out of their offices, purple with embarrassment but pleased with the booked appointment they'd made for me to return and fill the educational gap. They knew that canyon was desperately vacant.

"Yes, yes that's fine. No need to carry on with the details. See you next week, then," the Headmaster would sputter as he hurried me out the front gate.

So, then my schedule was full with actual school visits. I'd done it. I'd booked sex and drug educational appointments for a slew of schools in my barrio. But even with my success, my American mind was constantly worried whether I was doing enough—even when I was backed by applause for the high numbers I was reaching.

Then one day I woke up and smelled the bangers and mash. I realized my numbers weren't really that important.

I recognized that my colleagues were awesome and dedicated to their cause, but not stressfully dedicated to it. They weren't freaked out, acting threatened by loss of job or scared of being raked across the coals if things weren't cranked to warp speed all the time. They just worked at a nice, medium pace. They were actually the opposite of stressed—super chill and reclined.

Within a couple of months I had a paradigm shift, a proper British turnabout. I learned that the job, the building, and the offices within it were simply a front. They were props in a game called, "Go somewhere for eight hours. Pretend to do something and we'll pretend that we care what you're doing. If the sun comes out, you should go to the park or pub instead."

It took me a minute to get used to taking cigarette breaks inside my boss's office with him and a co-worker. We met in there to play a daily crossword puzzle that I never knew the answers to.

I sat on the old windowsill in his office, smoked, and could even lean out to my death if I felt like it—a safety hazard of the old days.

I found it charming. Outside the sky was always grey, and it draped lazily over rows of crooked rooftops. It was the landscape of the chimney sweep dances in my Disney, childhood memories.

My boss was a ripe man—rotund and firetruck red in the face. He had the kind of voice that bubbled out of his mouth. His vowels and consonants mud wrestled until they spilled from between his puffy lips in a heap of English spittle. I liked listening to him, though. His lilt was poetic. He recited our crossword clues between puffs on his cigarette, saying things like, "Homophone for, 'We hear twins shave'—four letters."

"Whaaaa?" I'd ask, dragging hard on my Lucky Strike and relaxing into the open office window.

"Did you say something about twins talking on a gay telephone and shaving each other?" I would ask innocently. "I'm locking in the Thompson Twins. It's not four letters, but I'm locking it in anyway."

"Don't be daft. It's pare," he'd reply, unsmiling and without breaking stare from the newspaper quiz.

Then he'd move on while completely ignoring me. Someone in the room always knew the real answer behind my dumb-dumb answer. I think the British are pretty smart. I'm decently book and street smart, not that I'm the brightest bulb on the Christmas tree or a fair representation of grey matter built for crossword intellect, but I'm just not British book, street, and overall-knowledge smart.

My boss asked me many times a day not to be daft, and he meant it. I wondered what daft meant and was also too lazy to look it up. I figured it meant annoying and slightly witty. I didn't want to quit being annoying and slightly witty, so I kept giving ridiculous answers to his impossible crossword puzzle and he continued to ask me not to be daft. I figured I was nailing it.

In between being called daft, my smoke breaks, phone calls, letter writings, and other bric-a-brac jobs, I took my two briefcases to schools where hyper teenagers squirmed in their chairs ready to rip my throat out with their sharp, sugar-coated teeth.

Turned out, London wasn't only afraid to say *meth-vagina* but it was also afraid to say *discipline.*

There were even signs on school buses that encouraged kids to call the police if they felt they were being mistreated by mum and dad. The result was a *Lord of the Flies* feel at most of the schools I visited. Mind you, not all of them were like that. Some were downright lovely and the kids were outstanding, but too many were feral.

One time, I was talking to a class full of scaries when a trashcan that contained a small pile of burning garbage rolled down the hallway outside the classroom. No students blinked and no faculty members—or any one at all—came rushing after the barrel. It just rolled by like it had a hall pass to use the bathroom.

At that point, I was so used to the strangeness of what I was doing that I barely nodded at the rolling inferno and went back to talking about genital warts like we were diagramming sentences.

It was all very wacky, but there were two particularly wacky moments at that job that really defined my role as sex and drug guru.

CHAPTER 14

The first was when I went to a wonderful little junior high full of smiling faces and pleated uniforms to talk about sex. I was in charge of educating the fifth form classes.

When I first heard I'd be teaching fifth form students about sex, I freaked out. As open-minded and at ease as I am with many odd things, I was not—nor would I ever be—cool with explaining to a fifth grader what an orgasm is.

But it turned out, fifth grade wasn't the same thing as fifth form. Fifth form meant about sixteen years old, and I was fine with talking to young teens about sex. I believe that talking about things at an appropriate age, when exposure is certain, is a good thing. Knowledge is power. Ignorance is the true enemy—not slang terms, human nature, or anal beads.

From the outside, the school appeared better than most. It cradled the traditional London charm one might want and expect from a building within English borders—brownstone arches and a jovial aura that the Mad Hatter would be proud of.

Inside, it smelled of appropriate secondary education whiffs—used books, strawberry perfume, bubblegum, and stale vegetables. Chatty, plain-faced kids crawled the halls in ant swarms, laughing and occasionally shoving or teasing. I shuffled between them with my briefcase in hand, heading for the main office.

"Hi, I'm here for the sex education program," I said, leaning my weight against a check-in desk.

"Oh yes, wonderful. Please just sign in here and I'll walk you to Ms. Dunford's room," said a pudgy woman with a hill of silver hair and a hot-pink smile.

"Oh, lovely. I really like your school, it seems very welcoming," I returned.

I smiled. I like smiles. I'm like Buddy the Elf, "Smiling's my favorite." She smiled back.

After our round of smile tennis, she escorted me down the antique halls and out into a new annex. In the new wing, her boxy shoes echoed against the freshly painted walls. We slowed near the last door.

"Here we are, Miss," she said, reaching out plump fingers to pull the door open.

"Thank you. Oh, this is awesome! This is really nice," I said, scanning the room.

I absorbed everything—overflowing bookshelves, a few beanbags piled haphazardly in a corner, clean desks, and healthy plants hanging in front of windows.

"This is great. Really great," I reiterated.

I walked to the front of the room.

"Do you have everything you need, Miss?" the woman asked, hands folded primly together at her waist.

"Yes, I'm great. I'll just wait here until my victims arrive," I joked.

I set my *MIB* briefcases on a large table that I assumed had been set up specifically for my naughty teachings.

"Lovely. Good luck! Please don't forget to check out before you leave," she announced before turning and waddling away.

"Thanks!"

I grabbed a handful of condoms from a pocket in my briefcase and started lining them up at the front of the table. The classroom door swung open.

"Good afternoon, Miss. Hi. Ello." The students greeted me, as they filed in one-by-one.

"Hi everyone. Please take a seat wherever," I said, pointing to the empty desks.

They were a stream of plaid pants and evergreen sweaters, bouncy and energized. I was nervous as usual, but I also knew the nerves would dissipate as soon as I got started.

"Hello, thanks for doing this," a woman in her mid-thirties waved from the back of the room as the last student found a seat.

"Oh, hi!" I returned.

"I'll be back in about forty. Enjoy. Thanks again," she said, without waiting for further conversation.

She turned and disappeared down the hallway. Her "thank you" rang in my ears. *So polite,* I thought.

I presumed that she was their regular teacher, because she didn't stick around. The teachers didn't hang out for my show, which could have had something to do with the loss of credibility that I was told they were all frightened of. Most likely it had everything to do with personal discomfort.

I was okay with the teachers splitting. I liked the kids being mine for an hour. I think they felt better without their teacher hovering—less inhibited. I stared at their shiny, surprisingly attentive faces. Go time.

XXX

"Okay everybody. It looks like we're ready. You're fifth form, right?" I asked, glancing around at the grinning faces.

"Yes, Miss," said a ghost-faced girl with a ski slope nose.

She stared with steering wheel eyes at the condoms.

"Great. Today we're going to talk about sex. How's that sound?" I asked.

Not a word.

"Okayyyyy…well you'll get talkative soon enough. Let's start with the basics. Who knows what this is?" I asked holding up a condom.

The crowd stirred.

"It's a condom, Miss," said a stocky boy tilted back in his chair.

Giggles. Whispers.

From the condom icebreaker onward, the students responded with a steady flow of questions, sniggers, disgusted nose-crinkles, cavernous mouths of astonishment, and crimson-flushed cheeks that would have matched the Queen's tapestry, but they were also models of classroom etiquette—performing like scientists when needed and jesters when allowed. To me, it was exactly the balance I wanted and believe is needed when teaching anything.

I had fun. They had fun. We all learned.

Pun intended—we nailed sex education that day.

I thanked them profusely before their teacher came to collect them. With happy faces, they filed out as smoothly as they'd filed in.

I was packing up my goodies when I noticed a spindly, redheaded kid with a face full of orange freckles milling about by the door. He let everyone pass him, sinking into the shadows until he almost disappeared. I stared and he shrank into himself more. When the room was empty except for us two, I finally broached a question.

"You want to talk?" I asked.

He stared at his shoes.

"Um...yes, Miss. I have a question."

"Don't be embarrassed. I know it's cliché, but it's true there is no such thing as a stupid question, especially when it comes to sex ed. If you don't find out the answer to what you don't know you might make a fool out of yourself naked. Would you rather do that or throw one or two sentences at a woman you don't care about and will never see again?" I asked, smiling and trying my hardest to seem both hip and approachable, cool and sensitive.

He un-suctioned himself from the wall and took baby steps toward me.

"It's okay. Really," I reassured him, pulling up a chair, sitting, and motioning for him to do the same.

"Oh. Th-thank you," he stuttered.

He fumbled with a tiny chair that squealed in defiance as he dragged its metal legs across the tile.

"Ask me anything you want. I've heard it all. No one could ever outdo some of the things I've heard or some of the things I've done. Trust me."

I leaned back in my chair.

I wasn't lying to the kid. I'd heard enough stories to rot Larry Flynt's ears and I'd definitely had my share of sexual mishaps. He must have sensed my honesty, because he leaned back a bit in his chair too, mimicking my relaxed pose. He bit his lip.

"Miss…are condoms supposed to hurt?"

"No," I quickly replied. "No, they're not supposed to hurt, but there are many reasons why they would hurt. For one, you may have an allergy."

"No. It's not an allergy, Miss."

"Well, you wouldn't be sure until you go to a Doctor. Are you developing any rashes or…"

"It's NOT an allergy."

He inhaled a giant gulp of air and puffed it out toward the ceiling, sinking into his chair.

"It's not a bloody allergy," he reiterated.

I rethought my tactic.

"You're right. Sorry. It's better if you explain the problem to me," I said, leaning toward him wearing my listening ears.

He squirmed and sat up a little straighter.

"Okay…well like I said, I'm not allergic to condoms. I don't get a rash or anything like that. It's just that they hurt when I put them on."

"Hmmm. Okay. Well…you might be trying the wrong size. There are varying sizes of condoms available. Possibly the ones that you're buying are too small."

He waved me off.

"I thought about that and I've tried the biggest condoms available—extra-large, lots of different brands."

I thought, *Surely this four foot nothin', soft-around-the-edges schoolboy isn't hung like an elephant.* But, as a woman who talks a lot with her girlfriends about all kinds of things, I can solemnly swear that you never can tell.

"And the large condoms still hurt?" I asked through sterile features.

"Yes, Miss. Actually all the sizes hurt. The weird thing is that all the sizes are also fine when I first put them on. They don't hurt at first."

"Uh-huh," I answered, brow furrowed.

"They're comfortable. Some fit better than others, but all the sizes feel just fine until I stretch them over my balls. That's when it hurts."

And that's when I used the Force, my ninja skills, a prayer to God, and all my karma to stop myself from busting into hysterics in front of this poor kid.

My cheeks burned.

My throat hurt.

Tears brewed in my ducts.

"Uh-huh," I coughed. "I know the problem. You don't need to pull the condom over your testicles. Unrolling the condom to the base of your penis is fine. Your testicles are lone soldiers, able to fight the good battle without armor," I said through a difficult straight face.

"Really?" he asked.

"I swear."

"Okay. I'll try that. Thank you. Really…thank you, Miss. I was starting to worry," he said, grabbing his bag and exiting the room with perfect posture.

Over and out. Easy as that.

XXX

I'm sure his testes would have written me a thank you letter if they could, and no doubt somewhere in this kid's dating line-up there's a chick who should thank me that she doesn't have to watch her boyfriend grimace and scream anymore while he creates a scene similar to a surgeon trying to stuff a piece of KFC original recipe into a finger frock.

And my year went on like that, vagina lessons here, Ecstasy stories there, and then one day my job finally peaked out—THAT DAY happened—the grey afternoon in London when I sat at my desk with my feet propped up and my ears listening to the worried teacher on the other end of the line. He promised me a stack of apology letters. I wanted that stack of apology letters, a fat one. I deserved that fat stack.

I knew that the teacher would deliver on his promise, because he sounded so rattled. He had every reason to be. I'd visited his class earlier that day to teach sex education, and his students had behaved terribly.

Embarrassment makes people react strongly. I had no doubt that he was sprinting to the nearest post office and nicely folding each apology note into a bag that he sealed with the sickly stickiness of his shame. He'd been made a fool, and he didn't seem like the kind of guy who would take that lightly. The Professor Snape type, he would make his class pay. And I...I would reap the benefits.

So, after our short conversation I hung up the phone feeling pretty smug. After work, I basically skipped to the bus stop—extra sass in my step. I took the two-five-one bus home with my fingers tapping to the beat of scheming. When I got to my front door, my package of apology letters was waiting. BOOM—pelvic thrust—hands accenting crotch area.

"Babe! Babe! Come here!" I yelled at my husband before I'd even opened the front door full tilt.

"Well, hello to you too," he sneered, poking his head out from the kitchen.

"I have the most magnificent thing to show you," I said, jutting the package in his face. "Come sit down."

I ran to the living room couch and flopped down in a huff. He followed me to the couch without question. Together we curled up, carefully opening the package.

"Exciting," he said, slurping on a popsicle.

"It's my gift from a bunch of shits," I said.

"Even more exciting! Is this from the class that went crazy on you a few days back and you walked out on?" he asked, eyebrows raised and a sneaky smile stretching across his lips.

"Uh-huh. Remember how I told you the class was actually super well-behaved and almost scared of their teacher? And when the teacher left they all went ape shit. They freaked out and went totally nuts. Anyway, the teacher found out that I walked out and he made his students write me apology letters. He said he's ultra-sorry and embarrassed."

"Sweet," Gareth said, leaning back into the blue polyester cushions.

That day in that classroom—yes—I had lost control of the class.

It didn't start like that, though. The students were fine at first.

When the teacher had first introduced me to his students, they'd sat with straight backs, laced fingers, and mouths clenched shut like photos out of a military school pamphlet.

But after the teacher left us to it and my sex paraphernalia came out, the kids were more like Gremlins at Dorry's Tavern—smoking three ciggies at a time, playing the synthesizer with their tongues, swinging from chandeliers, flashing, and doing lines off strippers' tits in the middle of a poker game.

Even though I was talking about basic things in scientific terms, all hell broke loose. Safe sex education was a pixie stick of pineapple flavored spaz dust that over stimulated the area of their brains interested in boobs and balls.

As my control of the classroom unraveled, I tried my hardest to reel order back in, but it was useless.

The students had gone berzerk. It was like they'd been kept in a sophisticated, refined, and tactful tearoom their whole lives, unable to mention the urge to get naked and freaky.

They spazzed. They foamed at the mouth. They randomly started shouting things like "nuts", "dong", and "jack off". I tried everything to reassert command, but they were long gone down a sexually paved path of mayhem.

My reign was over.

And so I'd warned them quietly at first that I would leave, and then I threatened them loudly over their "beef curtain" chants that I was about to bail. Then, I bounced.

The last thing I heard as the door to the classroom slammed shut behind me was one of them saying, "She's really leaving! We're in the shits now."

They must have known their teacher was going to go nuclear on them. He seemed like the type of guy who ran a very extreme kind of scary, tight ship. He would have probably preferred to lop off a leg rather than hear that I chose to leave his classroom due to horny commotion.

Back at home on the couch, sitting next to my husband with my stack of apology letters from the naughty kids, I smiled at the memory.

The anger I felt at the time of the incident was worth the delayed amusement. I pulled the neatly folded pile of about twenty-five letters out of the oversized manila envelope and lowered them onto my lap like precious gems.

"Here we go. Let's see who's crying now," I said.

XXX

The letters—oh the apology letters. I wish I still had them. I lost them in the divorce years later and it breaks my heart. They were worth more than the settlement. Those letters ranged from kind, to awesome, to WTF.

Some were pretty nice like, "Sorry for being so rude, Miss. Sex is cool. I wasn't."

One was to the point, "I liked your willy. Sorry it didn't seem like it."

Another said, "Sorry I laughed at the banana wearing the condom. I thought it was funny, but I was being immature. Bananas are the closest fruit to a penis."

And my favorite, "Dear Miss Sex. I'm sorry for laughing at your dick."

I just couldn't believe I was actually getting apology letters from fourteen- and fifteen-year-olds who wanted to say sorry about my diaphragm, regrets about my dental dam, and please come back with my lube.

My husband and I laughed until we cried, and then we tucked the special letters away for a rainy day or a plateauing dinner party.

Thank God for that job and all the others. Without them, I'd have a lot less laugh wrinkles, but I'd also have a lot less experience. Working all of those different jobs overseas made me who I am today and led me to becoming a writer. Through those positions, I gained courage and wisdom about work life. I learned to function successfully in highly diverse environments and became super resourceful, resilient, unembarrassed to ask questions, and well-versed in a wide variety of topics.

Sometimes I wonder what the future would look like if high school graduates took time to explore life for a year or two before signing up for college. What if they went out on their own to earn their way through life by tasting a buffet of jobs? What if we were forced to really think about what we want out of a career before pursuing one based on a shitty advisory talk or solely on an annual salary?

Maybe some would figure out that they don't need a degree but instead technical training, saving thousands of dollars and staying out of debt. Maybe during their time out in the world they might have a run in with a stranger that seals their fate, booting them off the fence of indecision. They decide that becoming a neurosurgeon is his or her fate, no matter how challenging. The needed desire, determination, and tolerance of the job are naturally instilled.

If young people REALLY knew what they wanted out of a career and had a deeper understanding of the work world, by experiencing before studying it, then higher education might become a treasured and fully-utilized springboard to a dream rather than an apathetic motion for survival.

What if a wanderer veered off the beaten path and discovered his or her passion hidden in the rough—staying with it forever and changing the world in the process.

What if…

PART III

"Quit your job. Buy a ticket. Get a tan. Fall in love."
Island Company

Long-term Travel Possible Gain List

1. THAT story. The one that's too crazy to be true. The one that blows minds, even your own.
2. International work experience.
3. An island life.
4.
5.
6.
7.

Long-Term Travel Possible Loss List

1. Your naivety.
2. Confusion about what you really want to do with your work life.
3. Weight.
4.
5.
6.
7.

Nest on the Chest

CHAPTER 15

Ever heard of someone wanting to run away to a desert island? After finally escaping the concrete jungle, they'd swim and fish their life away. The design of their island days would be very different from the city ones. Island days would be structured solely around pleasure and relaxation—a hedonist's playground.

One healthy tan.

Three hammock naps.

Endless mimosa baths.

Evening would be quality lover time—a cuddle in the sand—constellation spotting followed by wild sex. At bedtime, sleep would come fast and easy, the kind of stress-free shuteye reserved only for places void of urban din and internet connection.

Growing up, I didn't think this was possible without either a billion dollars or becoming a penniless beach bum. I was wrong, which is pretty normal for me. It wouldn't be the eight hundred and seventy-fifth time.

I lived the island life without having to change anything about myself, except the amount of clothes that I usually wore. Same goes for you, if you're down with it.

XXX

Fiji was on my travelling bucket list. Everything about the place, including the name, fascinated me. My imagination told me it was the exotic, rainbow-colored, swaying palm tree, clown fish utopia that exists only in movies.

In my head, Fiji had too much tropical pizazz for reality. That's why I had to go, I had to make sure it existed.

Tucked into a happy snooze on an Air Pacific flight from New Zealand to the islands, I woke up to the clank of the landing gear lowering out of the belly of the plane. It startled me less than the view out of my miniature window. Outside and below was another world—a green-blue fantasy.

Even from miles off of the ground it didn't fail to amaze. It was the portrait that my imagination had painted so many years ago, and this was abnormal, because usually my imagination takes liberties that the planet can't afford. But Fiji, it was beyond imagination.

Our approach was smooth and our landing smoother. When the doors to the jet opened, the heat hit my face like a blow dryer—a tropical blowout that smelled of coconut oil, mountain flowers, and salt. I was sweating already. The dense air reminded me of what a fellow writer refers to as "conception weather". It was a Pacific steam box, and I couldn't get enough. I absolutely love and live for tropical weather—the hotter the better—the more humid, the happier. This was the tropical flavor I'd been craving and I wanted to rip my shirt off mid-tarmac, but I didn't. Naked time could wait until I wouldn't be arrested for it.

"Bula!" a giant man wrapped in a neon orange and red hibiscus flowered skirt greeted us on the tarmac.

He played a ukulele. Three men swayed beside him.

"Hi!" I waved back and stared.

Upon closer inspection, I realized that all three of the men wore skirts. Granted, they weren't like spandex skirts. Each was a rectangle of cloth wrapped around the hip and hanging down to just below the knees. The thing that got me about the man skirts was that they looked really good—I dare say sexy. I'd learn later that the skirts were called sulus, and a sulu is traditionally worn by men and women in Fiji. They're even regarded as Fiji's national dress. The longer I was there, the sexier I found them. Nothing like a tan man wrapped in a nice, flowered skirt.

"I like your outfit," I said to ukulele dude, grinning and waving again.

"Vinaka—thank you," he replied—all white teeth and thick cheeks.

I moved past the welcome crew, following the herd down a corridor marked *Baggage Claim*. Lucky me, my suitcase was one of the first three off the carousel, something that always makes me feel like I won a slot machine pull.

I grabbed it and glided toward customs to the soft tune of Fijian harmonization. I was gagging to get out of the airport and into the moist day.

XXX

Growing up, my family had been to Barbados and some other Caribbean destinations, so I was used to basic airports. Island airports aren't your Denver International types. They don't always have walls or paved runways, and sometimes only a stick jammed in the ground with a Mellow Yellow t-shirt tied to it by some random dude missing all but one tooth are the only indications that your plane has arrived at its correct endpoint.

In Fiji's case, Nadi International is a real building, it's just not a real-nice building. I examined the antiquated posters and dusty customs booths—they were from another era. The customs worker seemed to have warped in from the same timeframe. She looked weary but healthy. A sheen radiated off of her perfectly formed helmet fro and dark skin.

"Hi," I said, handing over my passport.

She barely moved her lips—a half-asleep attempt at a smile.

"I have a non-customs question. Once I leave the airport, where can I buy a ticket for the yellow boat?" I asked.

"You buy the yellow boat tickets at the airport exit just beyond the gates. You'll see," she replied, stamping my page with a weak-wristed THUNK. She slid it back to me.

"Think I can still catch a boat today?"

"They leave when they leave," she said, flashing an orthodontist's wet dream grin. Her full, ebony lips offset their whiteness.

"Okay? Thanks again," I said, pocketing my passport and moving along.

That conversation was my first introduction to "island time". I really don't think it should be called "island time" though, because time has nothing to do with it. The way Fijians keep track of what's going on at a certain space in the day is by mood and readiness. Everything just takes as long as it takes.

A schedule is more like a soft guideline in Fiji. They throw the numbers in for us stressed-out, Western multitaskers, but they really have no relevance. You try to stick to them and you'll end up pissed off and crazy. Seven may mean eight, maybe even ten. Maybe never—no one knows. Just accept that something might happen at some point or not, then drink some kava and find a tree to lean against. That's Fiji time.

Fiji time was as chill as their customs check, which had the biggest lack of security welcome into a country that I had ever experienced. I felt like I could have worn a marijuana jacket with a hat made out of dynamite sticks and carried in a bag full of teenagers with price tags stuck to their foreheads, and they still would have greeted me with a warm hello, sweet smelling lei, and tried to teach me thirty ways to tie a sulu.

"Super chill in Fiji," I mumbled to myself as I made my way out of Duty Free and around to a strip of stores at the mouth of the airport.

Up ahead I spied an old sign that read "YELLOW BOAT" in simple block letters, nothing fancy. I made a beeline for it.

"One ticket please," I requested, stepping up to the counter and a woman with poofy hair and dark chocolate skin.

She was lounged behind a makeshift desk, looking half-business ready and half-drugged. She looped letters across a piece of paper that wasn't quite notebook paper and not quite printer paper. It was something I was sure came out of the sixties, and I watched in awe as her giant hands and baby powder-white nail beds dwarfed the Bic pen.

"Where to?" she asked without looking up.

"Um…the Mamanucas, I guess."

I'd done a bit of research before arriving in Fiji, and when I say research I mean that I asked one person if they knew of a place to go in Fiji. They mentioned an island group called the Mamanucas and I just said, "Okay." There are over three hundred islands in Fiji and I wasn't about to do thorough investigation of them all.

The Fijian woman continued scribbling on her paper.

"You want to go to the Mamanucas? Which island?" she asked.

"I'm not sure. You pick," I answered, reaching into my purse for my wallet.

She stopped writing and shot me a look of bemusement.

"Well, if I were picking for you I wouldn't pick the Mamanucas. I'd pick the Yasawas, sweetheart."

"What are those?"

"They are the best island group in Fiji. My sister lives in a village on Waya. Not a lot of travelers go there, so it's beautiful. It's real Fiji, if that's what you want."

That was exactly what I wanted. I considered jumping at her proposition, but my quick decisions have gotten me in trouble before, so I slowed my roll.

"Well, can I get the yellow boat from an island in the Mamanucas to Waya in the Yasawas?"

"Yes, of course. Is that what you want?"

"Yes, please. You know of a good backpacker hangout in the Mamanucas?" I slid my debit card toward her and she extended a massive hand.

I have this thing for hands. I like them a lot—the way they look, the way they move. I invest a lot in the way a guy uses his hands, not only on my body, but also shuffling cards, using tools, or driving a car. It's my litmus test.

This woman had fantastic hands, and later as one of my hobbies on the island I would spend hours staring at the MASSIVE hands and feet of various Fijians. Fiji is the land of colossal appendages. It's quite impressive. I once saw a Fijian man's foot take up the entire width of a ladder rung.

This woman's hands weren't quite as giant, but they were still big. I watched them grab my card and tap it gently on the desk.

"Beachcomber Resort is a very popular backpacker destination in the Mamanucas. It will be about thirty dollars USD to get there. I'll run your card and you'll be set. I can even make your reservation at the resort if you want."

I did want, and two minutes later I was inside a taxi on my way to the yellow boat dock. I was thrilled about leaving the mainland and heading for island paradise.

I had my ticket to Beachcomber Resort, a place the taxi driver described as "MTV Island", and a reservation in Beachcomber's bunkhouse for five nights, thanks to the nice man-hand lady. It was only twenty dollars a night to stay there at that point in time. I couldn't believe my tropical fantasy was not only coming true, but also costing basement bargain prices. This was a total steal.

It was time to get island funky.

CHAPTER 16

Rolling over the South Pacific waves, I was absorbing the atmosphere of a place I never thought I'd actually be able to visit. I was soooo happy and proud of myself. I'd made it to a renowned destination with only three thousand dollars to my name.

In the middle of the open ocean, the air was clean and cool. The groan of the yellow boat's diesel engine was the loudest sound. I stared at the water. I was just starting to wonder how long it took to get to Beachcomber Resort when a spot of land miraculously appeared on the horizon.

We crept toward it. The boat gears turned from a loud moan into a low growl as we slowed down. We completely stopped about two hundred yards offshore and a little water taxi chugged out to meet us.

"Come on! This is it!" a shrill voice screeched from the upper deck.

I shaded my eyes to get a good look at the group of people coming down the stairs of the yellow boat, a young Fijian boy in a hibiscus-splattered shirt helping them along. They were obviously retired. They looked almost ready to die, maybe in their early eighties, and they seemed exhausted but stoked. I was stoked for them—their grandiose vacation was finally happening. They were laughing, talking, and helping each other along as much as they could, but of course it was a slow and precarious process.

Some balanced on canes against the motion of the ocean while others grasped bony fingers around the handrail, stepping ever so carefully down each stair, one at a time. It was all sunbonnets, polyester slacks, and Terminator shades. They'd probably waited most of their lifespan to see this place, and now they were only minutes away from enjoying the white sugar sand between their wrinkled toes. It was nice to witness, but it was much nicer to be in different shoes—ones without Orthowedges.

I shook my head at the memory of questioning myself before leaving the United States and waved the Jurassic Park crew past. You couldn't power scrub the smile off my face. Traveling young is next level shit.

The retirees departed and the yellow boat's motors roared back to life. We chugged through deep ocean for about thirty minutes more to reach the next island—my stop—Beachcomber Resort. My water chariot and strong cocktail awaited.

XXX

Beachcomber is tiny. You can walk around it in about ten minutes, but it's packed full of good times.

Young people, loud music, and alcohol—lots of alcohol. Towering palm trees in broken shell sand. Teal and cobalt-colored sea that licks the shoreline in splashes of vanilla froth.

I was staying in the resort's bunkhouse, because it was cheapest. The bunkhouse was an open-air pavilion and there was a waist-high partition that created a barrier between where we slept and what was considered "outside". That was the substitute for actual walls. Inside the bunkhouse were forty-three bunk beds, a vaulted ceiling, concrete floor, and a couple of gigantic wooden posts that held the structure together.

It was quite a site—thatched-roof set off by wagon-wheel-sized fans that spun in quiet unison above. The varnished, Mahogany poles accented the polished floors. It was nicely made—the kind of a place a carpenter would roll around in, giggling, drooling, and scribbling down mental details of its craftsmanship, which perfectly walked the line between exotic and homey.

And don't forget the heaps and tons of bunk beds. They created a bed maze through the shared living space, each mattress lined with a thin but comfy bedspread decorated with butterflies.

Because I believe in my prior life I was raised by wolves, this place was right up my alley. I could sleep outside for the rest of my life and die a very happy woman. And this place was pretty damn close to sleeping outside, which was perfect because of the weather.

For most of the year, the temperature in Fiji is three shades of hot without much rain or wind. In the months I spent there, it rained zero times, got windy on no occasion, and was overcast only a handful of days. Open-air sleeping is made for Fiji.

After settling into my accommodation, I was ready to start my first day of island life. I started by sniffing around the premises, having a peek here and a probe there. The island was not what I expected, and although the topography was kind of what I thought it would be, it was all manicured. I wanted rugged.

The resort itself was definitely MTV style. The foci were partying, sulu tying classes, cramming occasional food down your trap from an all-day buffet, and hooking up with other backpackers.

Although I'm opposed to none of those things, what I wanted and what I envisioned was untouched beaches, loin cloths, raw tropical paradise, and no Kanye West, Snickers, or Nike running shoes.

Because it lacked the serene atmosphere that I craved, I grabbed the Fiji *Lonely Planet* that was wedged into the overflowing bookcase of share books in the dormitory. I tucked it under my arm and strolled out to the beach to kick-start my tan and get my read on at the same time.

It was an overcast day, and although I knew better, I decided to not put sunscreen on. I figured I'd only stay out for about an hour and read until I determined my next island stop—no big thang. A bit of unblocked sun on my pale skin would be good. I'd just settled onto my towel when a girl broke my concentration.

"Just get here?" a pleasant female voice asked from behind me.

I turned to see a friendly face smiling at me from a supine position—a girl about my age, American accent.

"I did. Fresh off the boat. This place is kind of small, huh," I said, fluffing my towel and re-settling onto the pebbled beach.

"Yeah, it is small. I walked around it yesterday. It looks the same all the way around. The food is awesome and the alcohol works. I learned how to tie my sulu like a diaper," she said, pointing to the pink cloth wrapped around her hips and knotted at the side.

"Really? I haven't done any walking yet, or swimming, or anything. I literally threw my bag down about ten minutes ago, put my bikini on, and headed out here to work on my skin cancer. Where ya from?" I asked.

"Oregon. I'm on my way back to the US actually, well…after I hit China. I'm going to Beijing and then around that area for a bit. I want to see the Great Wall."

She nonchalantly brushed her short black hair back from her face. Her features were plain with no makeup, no frills, just creamy skin. She was granola. Oregon crunchified. I liked her already.

"I like Oregon. Haven't been to China, but I've heard good things. I'm here for about three months. I'm trying to figure out where to go next," I said, waving the chubby *Lonely Planet* in the air.

"Wow. Three months! You'll have plenty of time to get a tan. This is the only place I'm going in Fiji. I wanted to get some good beach time in before I head to China. Are you staying in the dorms or do you have a bure?"

"Oh, you mean the private rooms?" I nodded down the beach to my left.

There was a string of little beach houses lined up together on the edge of the island. They each had a patio, flowers and shrubs edging the walkways, and palm trees shading their doorstep. It looked too rich for my blood.

I was unfamiliar with any Fijian speak yet, but I figured "bure" meant better than dorm. Either that or she was staying in something similar to a donkey. I figured the former was correct.

"The bures are pretty nice. They're like a little house. I'm in number four. Hey, I wonder if you'll have trouble falling asleep in the dorm with all the drunkies piling in at night," she said, tugging at her sulu.

"I didn't think about that," I frowned.

"But you know what they say. If you can't beat 'em, join 'em. Wanna grab a drink or something?"

She flexed her eyebrows, making them jump up and down.

"Sure," I replied, standing up and brushing off a patch of crushed shells that had adhered to my calves.

We walked together to the bar and bought four drinks—no need to start small. All hosted miniature, Pepto Bismol-colored umbrellas.

"Sex on the beach," Oregon winked at me and held up one of her double fists to cheers me.

"Sex on the beach," I recapped, bumping my plastic cup to hers.

XXX

With our nasty Kool-Aid concoctions in hand, we commenced a crazy, tropical throw down. We laid out some more and bullshitted about a million random topics. We took shots and floated in the bathwater warm ocean, with water so clear it looked like vodka. We watched different ocean creatures plunge, dart, and hover around our bobbing bodies like we were swimming in an aquarium.

I bought a sulu and wore it around my waist for a few minutes before tying it into a halter top dress, and then an adult diaper. Oregon did the same.

After more shots, we proudly stumbled around the diminutive island, slurring our sentences and dressed like anorexic sumo wrestlers. We laughed at chairs, talked to spindly-legged birds that roamed freely on the island, and marveled at the flora—leaves that unrolled like dragon tongues and hyper-colored flowers.

We watched about four minutes of Fijian dancing and about three hours of random make-out sessions between backpackers. It seemed like a biplane had crop-dusted the island with Viagra. The orgy was accentuated by really cheesy American hip-hop. Nelly's "Hot in Herre" was a favorite of the DJ, a song he played on loop while people swayed and dry humped in between sloppy kisses and public gropings.

Oregon and I got rowdy. We did the robot. I tried to do the kick worm down the shoreline. We were having a wicked time until I looked down and noticed that I was pink. My olive-skin is used to a summertime bronze glow, but that doesn't mean I'm immune to a rotisserie baking.

At that point in my life I'd had at least four bad sunburns, and if I knew one thing it was that if you look red in two o'clock sun, then by six o'clock you're cooked. Throw in the finger test, where you push a fingertip into your skin to see if it leaves a white mark when you remove it, and you should know exactly where you stand.

Swaying back and forth in front of the bamboo stage and attempting to focus crossed eyes on my tummy, I pressed a forefinger down on my lobster shell. When I lifted it away, it left a mark the color of a marshmallow.

"Um, I think I need to go find some aloe vera," I shouted over the throbbing speakers.

"What?" Oregon yelled back, grinning like I'd just told a good joke that she kind of didn't get but still found amusing for no reason at all.

"I SAID I NEED TO GO LAY DOWN!" I shouted back, cupping my drink-free hand around my mouth.

"Oh. Okay. You sure you don't want to go to my bure? It's super nice. Radisson shit," she said, scrunching her lips into a fishy face and rattling her noggin side to side.

Her black shades sat askew on her nose. She reminded me of Bernie from *Weekend at Bernie's*.

"Thanks for the offer, but nah. I'm out," I kind of said to her, but more to myself, as I dragged ass off the makeshift dance floor toward my sleeping quarters.

XXX

Inside the bunkhouse the air was cooler and blowing in a soft stream through the maze. It was quiet—all of the action was back on the dance floor. It didn't really matter anyway, because I had enough booze in my system to help me peacefully snooze through a chainsaw making love to a jackhammer.

I stumbled from bed to bed, looking for the number forty-one. The numbers were painted on plates attached to the side of each bunk and my vodka pupils strained to focus. Eventually, I made it to my bed and started the process of peeling my swimsuit off my body.

In the soft light of the bunkhouse I got the first good look at my skin, and it was badong—bad and wrong. This was no ordinary sunburn. This was professional idiot shit. I looked like someone popped me in the microwave for thirty minutes, covered me in Crisco, and finally slid me under broil coils for a solid searing—an extra crispy finish.

I whimpered while locating my aloe. In the bathroom, I gasped and winced through slathering it over my raw body. By the end of it, I was dead. All I wanted to do was drink water, swallow Advil, and sleep it off. I told myself...

Go to bunk.

Lay down on back.

Pass the fuck out.

Don't move until morning.

That was my plan. It worked until a three a.m. surprise woke me up.

XXX

"What? What is it?" I heard myself ask, my eyes Super Glued shut.

It was late. I could smell sunscreen, hear snores, and feel no movement. I wanted to look around, but my lids weren't ready to open yet— boulder heavy due to my day's extracurricular activities. I felt like I'd been eaten by Godzilla, regurgitated, then flattened and torched by a flame tank.

Up until that moment, I'd been completely and happily passed out to the world, lying dead on my bottom bunk bed. I was sleeping on my back; it was the only position I could hold, considering my sunburn. Thank goodness for the alcohol.

Shortly after putting my head to pillow, I slipped into a coma—my hands cemented to my sides, doing my best impression of a cadaver.

Something was waking me up though, I just had no clue what the hell that something was or what was going on.

"What's it? WHAT?! Mmmmuuhh," I moaned.

A "feeling" had magically stirred me from the dead. This "feeling" was a quiet one, an almost nonexistent nudge, but it was there. My brain fired sluggish signals to the rest of my body, until I finally realized that the "feeling" was coming from my chest. It wasn't a heavy feeling. It was just enough pressure to feel wrong.

Groggy and confused, I grunted until my left eye opened. Trapped in a world between awareness and dreamscape, I could make out lots of black blobs. The blobs were backpackers. They were spread out across the dark dormitory, sleeping soundly. Moonlight splotched the floor and I guessed it was three, maybe four a.m.

Then I peeled my other eyeball out from underneath its lids. That's when I saw it. On my chest, busy and non-concerned, stood a bird about two feet tall. It was a good looking bird as far as birds go—long spindly legs, a shiny white chest offset by midnight feathers, and an orange beak that held three tiny sticks.

I froze and stared. The fowl brazenly returned my glare, but not for long—it was all business. It turned and went right back to work. It strutted in a miniature circle and shifted its hollow weight from left bird foot to right, kneading my boobs like a cat.

It seemed obsessed with figuring out where to lay down the bundle of sticks it held in its mouth, which made sense, because who would want to carry around a bunch of sticks in their mouth all night. As it rotated its feathery and very rude back away from me, I noticed that in between my breasts was a small pile of beach debris—twigs, something that looked like a cigarette pack wrapper, and what I think was a piece of Styrofoam. The ambitious bird bent and dropped the remaining sticks from its beak onto my chest, right on top of the dirty Styrofoam. Then it fiddled with them, scooting them here then there.

That's when it occurred to me that a fucking bird was making a fucking nest on my chest.

"What the shit!" I yelled, swinging my arm in slow motion across my torso at the bird's head.

"Sssquuawk!" it retaliated, using my right tit as a diving board and springing off my nipple onto the bed next to me.

It was on a full-blown fowl rampage.

Its wings flapped across noses. Feathers floated onto sleep masks, stuck to lips, and tickled necks. Its toes scraped its initials into cheeks.

Sleepers jerked into sitting positions, insolently awakened by Larry Bird as he hopped across faces and torsos like he owned them.

"What the fuck?" a girl who was still wearing her bikini top sat up and yelled as the bird did a gainer off her stomach.

"Arggh!" a muscular boy screamed.

He swatted a prissy hand at the bird as it bounced off his forehead.

I sat back onto my seared skin and watched the show, wondering what the bird's problem was. I mean, when building a house, it's all about location, location, location, and this bird chosen a rough neighborhood.

I lowered my head back onto my pillow and watched the bird do one last karate kick off someone's face before escaping over the partition. It disappeared into a fluorescent green bush. As it went, it raised one wing in salute. I'm pretty sure it gave me the middle finger, or I guess more correctly, flipped me the bird.

I closed my eyes and mumbled.

"I need the real Fiji."

CHAPTER 17

The next morning I woke up with swollen everything. Sore liver. Self-loathing. Sufferin' succotash.

I'd bought a house on Struggle Street.

"Sorry. Excuse me. So sorry," I mumbled and stumbled my way through the bunkhouse out into the sunny day.

The heat of the sun was agonizing.

"Ouch! Owwww," I whimpered with each tiptoe.

The beach was dotted with bikini clad twenty-somethings who seemed just as worse for wear as I was, minus the hot sauce tan. I weaved through them. Most of the chicks had gone from island video hoes to sand trolls. They wore black shades, spoke in drones, and lounged sloth style on their bloated bellies. Drool pooled on their sun soaked chins. They refueled with banana slices and papaya juice.

I stepped on peoples' towels and crunched their plastic cups under my bunions with little less than a muttered, "Shoot." I didn't care. When on a mission, there's no time for niceties.

Through my pain I did notice that Fiji looked, smelled, and felt exactly the same as it had the day before. It was an imprint of yesterday, and I got my first hint that island weather would probably act similar to a nesting doll—one day opening up the same as the day before, except maybe a tad bit shorter based on how long I wanted to stay in bed.

I zombie shuffled up to the bure marked number four.

BOOM. BOOM.

I hammered my fist twice on the wooden door.

"Hello?" a husky voice came from behind it.

"Hey…um…hey it's me. The American chick you partied with yesterday," I said into the wood, leaning my warm forehead against the cool and smooth surface.

It smelled like damp forest.

I couldn't remember her name. I squeezed my eyes shut, trying to imagine a nametag floating in my memory. *Julia….Amy….Cate….ughhhh.*

No hope. I was kidding myself. I have a disease that blocks blood from feeding the cells in my brain that enable name memorization. It's a sad truth and horrible problem that's cost me many embarrassing moments and offended the masses. It's really bad, like sometimes I don't even remember family member's names. That's why I'm the nicknaming master—for whatever reason, I can remember Cake Badger, Juan Juanson, or the Informer way better than Matt, John Johnson, or Stacey.

Oregon. I remembered that.

"Oregon! Please take mercy on me," I pleaded into the number plate.

I heard the slide lock move. The door swung open.

"Oh hey, what's up?" she asked.

Air-conditioning hit me in the face like angel breath and I slumped my shoulders against the reprieve.

"Oh my God. YYYYYeeeeesssss. Oh, that's good. That's so good," I moaned.

I took a deep breath and exhaled slowly.

"I'm sorry Oregon, but can I please hang out here with you for a bit? I baked my bread. I cooked my chicken. I'm fucked," I said, waving a limp hand over my body.

"You look like a baboon's butthole," she replied.

"I know. I probably taste like one too."

"Weird. Come on in," she said, signaling for me to follow.

I was in. Mission accomplished.

And it was bliss. Her room versus the bunkhouse was like a steak at Wolfgang Puck's versus a corn dog at the state fair. I felt warm tears of relief sprout in the corners of my still sunglass-shaded eyes.

The bed looked comfy. The walls had all kinds of art, but it was the AC unit that held my attention, because it worked phenomenally. Without asking, I sprawled like a parachute jumper onto her bed.

"Sorry, I have to lie down. I think I would have been facing some hospital-level burns if I'd stayed out any longer yesterday."

"You're probably right. You look pretty hospital-ish," Oregon said.

"Thanks for letting me collapse here. I honestly didn't know what else to do."

"All good."

I was already on my way out, fading into dream land with my shades still on my face. Being hurt or sick overseas can be rough, but if you have a person like Oregon with a good heart and an awesome air conditioner, you can get through it. When overseas on your own, don't be shy and ignore someone's hospitality—it changes new experiences from great to amazing.

"You going?" Oregon asked.

"For sure. Beachcomber ate me alive," I said.

XXX

Two days after Oregon welcomed me into her private bure/princess palace on Beachcomber, my skin shifted from a shade of plum to maraschino cherry, and then to baby pink. With the help of Advil and aloe vera, Oregon's air conditioning unit, cold washcloth treatments, and mothering spirit, I eventually bent my arms and legs without moaning.

"I can't thank you enough. If you ever want to come visit me, wherever I am in the world, just holler. Free stay. Free food. Free everything," I said.

"I think I'll take you up on that. Where you headed from here?" she asked.

"Remember? I'm still in Fiji for three months. I think I'll go to Waya. It's an island in the Yasawas. A Fijian woman at the airport told me it's real nice, and I'm over cowboy Kool-Aid cocktails, touristy breakfast buffets, and British dudes trying to dance. It's just not what I envisioned for Fiji, ya know?"

I leaned forward from my sitting position on the bed and stretched my peeling arm in the direction of a Fiji Water bottle. I palmed it, unscrewed the blue top, and took a giant swig. It felt glorious running down my esophagus.

"Isn't Waya dodgy?" Oregon asked.

"I found a hostel called Bandi's Place in *Lonely Planet*," I said, ignoring her question.

But yes...it was dodgy, or at least that was the rumor.

According to a few travel books and backpacker conversations, Waya was the home of a possible murder. Not too many years before, a backpacker's bones were found in the mountains next to a waterfall swimming spot. The man's skeleton was lounged perfectly on the rocks—totally intact and Anatomy-study ready.

No one understood what happened. It was weird that his clothes were folded in a neat pile next to his osseous matter—apparently he was as tidy in death as he was in life. But, there was a problem with the scene. There was a dent in his skull, and most people don't mix relaxation with head trauma.

I'd read over the island description twice and the warning three times. The tale worried me a bit, but I figured I'd at least go and check it out. I was learning not to trust everything that I read and heard. I wanted to form my own opinion.

I closed my eyes and took a deep breath.

"I don't know. The nice woman at the airport told me to go there. She seemed cool. Why would she send me to a death sentence? I mean it might be dodgy, but something about the story stinks. It seems like an urban myth. Even the books are vague. I'm gonna at least head that way, and if the workers on the yellow boat seem nervous for me to get off, I won't. If I do get off and it's weird, I'll leave the next day."

With her legs draped off the corner of the bed, Oregon scowled.

"Well good luck. I'll be thinking of you while I'm in China—I mean Va-China."

Va-China triggered a memory of our drunken state, me rolling around on my beach towel telling Oregon that she was going to get a bad case of China Vagina in Beijing, which quickly turned into Va-China.

"Ha! Totally. Well, I'm catching the yellow boat this morning, which means I should probably go pack. I just can't thank you enough for everything. You have my email. Promise you'll use it?" I asked, standing up to leave.

Oregon smiled and stood up too.

"Sure. Get outta here and be careful. I don't wanna read about your skanky skeleton being found all propped up reading John Grisham next to a swimming hole. I still don't know why you're going there."

"Sfine," I said, leaning and wrapping my arms around her neck.

She cringed.

"I don't do hugs. Take care."

CHAPTER 18

On the yellow boat once again, I chugged from the Mamanuca island group toward the Yasawas.

The ocean churned hard. It was different than the first ride. Within the Mamanucas, enough land mass existed to break up the natural rowdiness of the water, but once we were out in the open it was a different ballgame. It was rough and swollen.

The eleven a.m. sun was bright and hot as usual. I sat in the shade, wearing sunscreen on my already peeling skin. There were about fifteen passengers on the lower deck. None of us talked. We just stared beyond the boat.

I locked my eyes on the horizon. Seasickness and I are good buddies. Normally, in as rough of water as we were in, I would've felt the first stages of hurl brewing in my stomach, but so far I was fine. I actually felt great. I was confident in my decision to go to Waya Island, even though the rumored skeleton femurs and clavicles rolled around in my head.

I resolved to be safe. I didn't have a death wish—never have, never will. Quite the opposite actually, so I've always traveled thoughtfully with a finger wag and a tisk-tisk of the tongue to those who embrace carelessness. I always considered options and weighed risks, even when it meant bungee jumping off bridges or nighttime scuba diving into black waters.

My decision to go to Waya wasn't any less considered. Murder mysteries and all, I decided to go there based on four things:

1. The incident was years ago.

2. The stories I'd heard about it sounded campfire-ish, at best.

3. I was salivating to see the natural, less-traveled part of Fiji—no more resorts, no more Nelly or Michael Jackson, and no more tourists for the most part.

4. The airport lady had told me to go there. I trusted her, because she worked behind a desk, had a pencil, wrote stuff, and pointed to things on maps. Her opinion, to me, was relevant.

I switched my thoughts to Oregon and her Va-China travels. She was a cool girl, and I hoped the best for her—a sandwich break on the Great Wall, a chat with a hot boy in the Forbidden City.

A year after that moment on the yellow boat, when I was thinking about Oregon and her trip to China, I found out that she had a lot more to worry about than I did. Her travels turned out to be way more dangerous than my Waya trip. She'd kept her word and emailed me one short, to the point email:

> *Hi! How was the rest of your trip? Mine sucked balls. I left Va-China early because I contracted SARS. I'm fine now. Talk to ya later.*

I called her immediately and yes, she'd contracted SARS. She'd been isolated in an American hospital until recovery. It all turned out just fine though, and we even laughed about it.

We were reminded of how neither of us on our very separate and unique paths knew what we were getting into. We'd assumed my path was more treacherous, but you know what they say about assuming.

On the yellow boat with my face tilted toward the puffy clouds, I took a deep breath of the briny air and relaxed. I didn't care to assume. I didn't want to think about the future anymore, because I had little control over it anyway. So, I chilled out. Time passed quickly in my semi-daze until a garbled announcement ripped me back into reality.

"Waya," it squelched through the speakers. "Bandi's Place."

I opened my eyes and stared at an island in the distance. About a quarter of a mile beyond the yellow boat curved the graham cracker shore of Waya. It was bigger than I'd expected. It sprawled against the

blue backdrop, overflowing with greenery—bushes and trees.
Mountains crawled into the sky.

Rugged Fiji.

I stood, wobbled on sea legs, and grabbed my bag. The boat was
barely rocking though, it was just my sea brain. In the bay that we'd
pulled into, waves were almost non-existent. It was nearly as flat as a
giant, salt-water swimming pool. Dainty ripples slapped the boat
wearing kid gloves.

A dingy motored from the shore toward us, but this dingy was totally
different than Beachcomber's. The MTV island dingy had been polished,
bright, and ready to rock, just like the island's reputation. Waya's dingy,
on the other hand, looked like something you might find in your
grandpa's shed hidden under a moth-eaten cover and filled with five
sets of *Encyclopedia Britannica.*

I scratched my head with one hand and tightened my grip on my bag
with the other. *I trust the airport lady and her man-hands. I do. I really do,* I
repeated to myself.

"Waya?" a slender-ish Fijian man asked as I neared the disembarking
area of the yellow boat.

His shirt was the same canary color as the boat. It made me want a
dress in the same shade.

"Yes," I answered, "Bandi's Place. The front desk worker at
Beachcomber made a reservation for me…supposedly…I hope."

He extended a long hand toward my luggage, but I hesitated. In the
water below, the dingy sidled up to the yellow boat.

"Bula vinaca," an old man coughed to us from the dingy.

I froze.

"Bandi's Place?" he asked through tired eyes.

"Um…" I stalled.

I swiveled my head on my neck like a hunting owl. I was trying to
buy time. When you travel alone your instincts get cranked up to
eardrum-busting level, and right then my gut was giving me the raised
index finger signaling my brain with the "Caller, please hold" message.

I didn't like it. It seemed shabby. It felt off.

"Yes, she's going to Bandi's Place," the yellow boat worker answered for me.

"Well..." I started.

The yellow boat worker stared at me, patiently waiting. He didn't seem bothered by my delay, and neither did the old man in the dingy. The old man in the dingy actually looked like he'd fallen asleep.

"I'm not sure that I..."

All of the sudden, I realized what was bothering me. It was the lack of other people departing. When I'd arrived at Beachcomber, hordes of humans had herded toward the exit rail. All the stops between there and Waya had been the same, at least five people always got off. But at Waya, it was just me—Han Solo.

"Am I the only one getting off here?" I asked the yellow boat worker.

He stared at me for three years. I stared back. We stared some more until I finally felt awkward about the best staring contest I'd ever entered.

"Okay," I said. "I guess I'm getting off here."

XXX

I took a deep breath and climbed down into the toy boat where the old man snoozed.

"Ugghh, b-b-bula," he stuttered, waking up and bolting upright against the rocking dingy.

"Sit, sit," he motioned for me to take a seat on a wooden plank across from him.

"Thanks. Vinaka," I replied, lowering myself with concentrated care.

The old man twisted the throttle on the long board engine. It grumbled, shoving our little dingy in the direction of the beach. I watched the yellow boat get smaller in the distance until it disappeared and Waya was all that was left.

We moved toward the shores, but instead of being transfixed by the clarity of the water, I was in love with the grandpa driving the dingy. He'd gone from totally asleep to crackhead alertness with the transition skills of a person half his age. Without his grey highlights and slight hunch, one might call him a beacon of youth. His flawless epidermis was the color of mocha butter and it was clear that his cells were the kind that had been nutritionally binging since birth—rich with fish Omega-3, papaya antioxidants, and fiber-filled breadfruit.

I watched him make small steering adjustments. He smiled. I returned it. His glossy eyes looked like someone poured a bottle of topcoat fingernail polish into them. Indo-Fijian, he possessed a face similar to Gandhi, a very refined bone structure.

"Hi," I finally said.

"Bula," he said back.

He was beautiful. I wanted to give him a giant bear hug. I really like old people, and this man seemed ultra-special. But before I could hug him, he wagged a finger at the clear water.

"Ika," he said, nodding at the surface. "Fishy."

His voice was high in range and gentle in delivery—trustworthy.

"Ahhhh…" I exhaled a soft breath of wonderment.

I could see perfectly at least fifteen feet below the surface. We were floating on glass. Below us swam three shoebox-sized, iridescent fish with pastel pink beaks.

The sun was soft and the temperature mild. I smelled vanilla on the breeze. The old man killed the dingy engine and we drifted onto the beach. It was empty. He leaned toward my bulging bag, but I waved him off.

"It's okay. I'll get it," I said, hoisting it onto my shoulder.

I slung one flip-flopped foot over the side of the dingy and into the shallow water. It was a sexy temperature—robe warm.

"Okay," the old man laughed, climbing out after me. "Mani," he said, extending a weathered hand and smiling a white-toothed postcard for dental excellence. The Fijian teeth were killing me—it should be illegal to have such naturally gorgeous chompers.

"Shelby," I said, giving my hand back.

I locked into Mani's black pupils, and from that second onward I knew we'd be pals. He had a kind soul. Together we walked across the pale sand and, unlike Beachcomber where the island was made of broken seashells and particles of reef, Waya was powdered sugar. I left behind deep imprints with each footstep. The old man was barefoot. He strode next to me, still smiling as he led me up from the beach and into a clearing that was well manicured and dotted with huts.

"Bula!" a woman hollered from an open-air breakfast nook.

She set down an apple she was washing in a tiny basin and wiped her hands on her t-shirt.

"Come! Come!" she demanded.

Her gold tooth twinkled in the sun. She was nothing but wide hips, island attitude, and a massive fro—the kind that looked like the world's best trampoline for ants.

"Welcome to Bandi's Place. You are Shelby?" she asked, jutting yet another huge hand toward me—her English was damn near perfect.

"Yes, I'm Shelby."

"I am Silvi. I am the owner." She straightened her spine and touched her hand to her chest.

"Nice to meet you. It's gorgeous here," I replied.

"Good. You will like it. Your room is over here. Come."

She led me through a freshly mowed lawn, past a covered porch attached to a wooden building, and toward a tiny shack—all of which hugged the entrance to the forest and mountains beyond.

Inside the covered porch we passed sat a couple. They stayed silent—eyeballing us from behind the chicken wire as Silvi and I walked by. They looked young. The guy was white and the girl looked kind of black, but I couldn't quite tell. We made eye contact but exchanged no words, I was busy trying to keep up with long-legged Silvi. She finally broke stride in front of a small, shack-ish building.

"Here, this is your room. How long are you staying?" she asked, pushing open the rickety screen door.

It whined against rusted hinges. We walked in together.

"You stay four weeks? Eight?" she asked, reaching over and removing my bag from my shoulder without asking.

She laid it next to the single bed with clean sheets. The room was almost bare, with one old side table, two little windows—also covered in chicken wire—clean wooden floors, and a fresh cut hibiscus lying on a single pillow. The space smelled slightly musty, dabbed with a hint of honeysuckle.

"I'm not really sure how long I'll be here. I figured I'd see how I like it," I answered.

"You'll be here at least a month. Lunch is in an hour," she announced.

Then she turned and left. The old door banged shut against the frame behind her. I stood in the middle of my shack wondering what the hell had just happened—*did I just sign up for a month at this place? Is this how the waterfall skeleton started his days on Waya?*

"Okay, thanks Silvi," I yelled through the screen to no one.

CHAPTER 19

"I'm Tara. This is Jason. We're from Canada, here on our honeymoon," the girl said.

Her emerald green eyes offset her light black skin in a way that made me feel ugly. Jason nodded at me. He was your average white boy traveler, shirtless, tussled blonde hair with tired blue eyes, and a guitar propped against the left side of his chair. I put money on a bottle of patchouli tucked somewhere in his travel kit.

We gathered as a threesome inside their room, the porch enclosed with chicken wire, and played the *getting to know you* game. It wasn't the first time I wished I had a travel resume that I could just pass around—bullet points of backpacking objectives, chronologically ordered countries of visitation, and gained education highlights.

Tara and Jason had quite the pad compared to my shack. Without solid walls, the soft breeze was as good as aircon, and the chicken wire kept the big critters out and made you feel like you had a bit of privacy.

They had a tent set up inside along with an old cable spool they used as a table, three plastic chairs, and clothing line they'd strung from one wall to the other. Various clothes were folded and stacked around the edges of the rectangular space. A stack of playing cards sat next to a half-burned candle alongside a copy of *Harry Potter and the Prisoner of Azkaban.*

"How long ya been here?" I asked, leaning against the door.

"Six months. How long ya been in Fiji?" Tara asked.

"Wow! That's a long time. I got here a couple of weeks ago. I'm kind of island hopping, ya know. I have three months total in Fiji, but I don't have a three-month plan. I'll probably just keep moving around, try to fit it in as much as possible."

"Cool," said Jason.

"Yeah," I replied.

Awkward silence. So, I shattered it with the only real question I wanted to ask.

"Hey, did a backpacker get killed on this island?"

"Yeah," Tara said, leaning forward to pick up a nail file off the giant spool table.

She started shaping her perfect nails—not too short, not too long, half-moons.

"He slept with a village woman that he shouldn't have. He was here a long time, mingling with the Fijians, poking around in all the wrong places. Pun intended."

"Danger sex," said Jason.

"High voltage," I added, having no idea what I meant by it.

Silence again. I scuffed my flip-flop on the wood floor—looked around some more.

"Wanna smoke a joint and go snorkeling?" Tara asked.

"Yessum," I answered, pulling up the spare plastic chair and making myself at home.

XXX

I was becoming island wild.

Tara was becoming my bestie.

Jason sat back and watched.

The hours of our lives were dictated by nature. We rose and fell with the sun. The island had no electricity, no running water, and only a Fijian tribe that lived about a fifteen-minute walk to the east of where our hostel existed—they were our only human counterparts.

Not many, if any, tourists came to Waya at that time. It was weird, I don't know if it was the rumors about skeleton boy or what, but whatever it was, our magic depended on them staying away. We demanded few, to no, gatecrashers. It was our private paradise. Our toys—*go away, you*. I wanted to put a colossal DO NOT DISTURB billboard on the mountaintop.

I couldn't handle other people. I'd gone feral, armed with jungle powers, beach swag, and reef juice—Jason, Tara, the Fijians, and I patrolled that motherfucking island. Whenever I'd see the yellow boat in the distance, I'd growl and bare my teeth in its direction, daring it to come into our bay. No way Jose.

In my head, it was turf war. I wanted to make gang jackets for us out of palm leaves. I planned on painting *Sea Snakes 4 Life* on the backs and wearing them while we shook down other tourists who dared enter our beaches, forcing them out of our territory with coral shanks and assault reeds.

I never made our gang gear, but I did figure out how to make dried up seaweed into a beard that made me look like the old man under the sea when I wore it. It had weak intimidation factor, but I wore it in the evening sometimes after a joint to heighten my storytelling.

Our days consisted of going for a run, eating breakfast, and then snorkeling. We were snorkeling freaks, swimming in our private lagoon at least three times a day for an hour or more at a time. I was developing gills and a prison-jacked body.

Lean muscles, smooth brown skin, and a clean glow.

I was in fighting shape—the best shape I'd ever been in. I felt and looked beautiful. I felt especially gorgeous in the evenings after using rainwater to shower my salty body. Inside our "shower hut" was a rain barrel and wooden bowl for scooping. The water was cold and fresh, and it made my skin soft and clean, my hair shiny and full. Fijian rainwater…better than anything on the market.

During the day in between snorkel sessions, we'd have teatime and smoke breaks. We sometimes used the afternoons for any "plans" we'd conjured up the day before—like a possible mountain hike if we weren't too stoned, or sand castle construction if we weren't too stoned, and basically anything that took more energy than we'd had the day before, due to being too stoned.

At night we talked and relaxed in the warm glow of lantern light. We'd fall asleep early, and if we stayed up past ten it was like we'd been out all night partying. In the morning, we'd start the whole process over again.

Some days were tough, like when I'd smoke so much that my legs became Jell-O barbells that refused to make it the fifteen feet from our sleeping areas to the beach. But, with hard work and perseverance, I always pushed through.

The weed was our fourth player, and just like in most countries, it was illegal. We had our ways, though.

We'd met a Fijian man on Waya who partied, so about every three weeks we rolled dirty with him into the mainland. He had a mini-tug boat that took about three hours to chug across the sea. Once on land, we'd purchase bushels of the bunkest weed ever from a village full of leaning shacks.

It was a super dodgy deal. We would tie up at a dock that had been ravaged by years of storms. It rolled like a heartbeat image, sideways and slanted, up and down, so we tiptoed across it, watching for rusty nails, until eventually hitting a dirt path. The path led to the other man we needed.

The path was my favorite part. It took us past wild pigs, chickens, goats, discarded cars, mountains of empty Coke bottles, and sometimes a random couch or workout trampoline from the eighties. It was different, and the weed was even more unique.

Literally, it was bushels—three-foot sticks that were thick with green fur and wrapped in yesterday's newspaper. It seemed someone had walked out into a field with a machete, cut down the entire plant, and folded it into the Sunday Funnies. And it was cheap schwag, that's how the Fijians got down—schwag schentral. Nothing but the weakest, but it did the job. It got us plenty high, and so we flew over the beach and water most days— dazed, glazed, and soft around the edges, but definitely having the time of our lives.

At some point, I'm not sure when, my brain stopped being American. What I mean by that is that I didn't feel worried anymore, or like I needed to stay busy, or was lacking entertainment. Everything slowed and focused.

Compared to when I first landed in Fiji—when my mind would constantly drift toward worrying about future bills, job stress, past and future love life, and more of the future-future-future bullshit thoughts—I was incredibly chill. I'd become the gentle animal a human can be when they are set free of stress and burden. I was present.

Without technology, artificial sounds, scheduled must-do's, and built-in entertainment, I found a new place inside my brain. That place is labeled "CALM". Inside that space is unmeasured creativity, and answers to deep emotional and silly surface questions that I never had time to ponder before.

Sure, there were times in Fiji that freaked the fuck out of me, and I wondered if I might wake one day to a cockroach buried in my inner ear canal or if I'd accidently rear-end a sea snake during one of my daily snorkeling sessions, provoking it into biting my ass and ending my life simultaneously.

But, somehow the thought of the bad things on Waya were more okay with me than the bad things I'd thought about happening to me in other places. The only explanation I have for my ease was this newfound relaxation. I was primitive.

Out on the island, I realized that I was born to die. One day it will happen—no sense in getting all upset about it. I decided that maybe death is less like the feeling a whale might have in the middle of a net and harpoon fight, and more like the feeling a nature lover might have in the middle of an afternoon cup of tea, swinging in a hammock. It's not scary. Dead is dead. I came into this world alone and I'll go out the same way. The end of my story will be the same as everyone else's—none of us get out alive.

Once okay with my living, breathing self—me, the hunk of meat that really doesn't mean much to the plight of things—I could stare at the clouds for hours. The birds. The waves.

I felt lucky to get the chance to behave like a real human; someone without any answers put here for probably no reason, but luckily dropped into the middle of one hell of a playground—Earth. I was starting to understand how tiny and insignificant my existence is, and I loved it.

But then I got antsy again, and it was entirely my crotch's fault.

XXX

"I know. Let's start a shell contest," I said to Tara, passing the tri-forked blunt to her that she'd rolled earlier that morning.

Tara was a spliff ninja. She owned a book that taught her over thirty different rolling techniques, all of which she had mastered, and she put them to full use in Fiji. Jason and I reaped the benefits. Her latest creation feat smoldered from three prongs and caused a massive haze inside the chicken wire porch. I couldn't decide if I liked it or was freaked out by it. I felt like I was smoking the male end of an AC plug.

"What do you mean seashell contest?" she asked, squinting her emerald eyes against the endo cloud.

I passed her the tripod.

"I mean like a shell contest, foolio. Best shell wins. We'll have different categories—like coolest design, and nicest colors, and best muzzle and coat, and stuff."

Tara took it, puckered her lips for a drag.

"Muzzel and coat are for dogs," she mumbled mid-suck.

"Semantics. I think there should be either a weekly or bi-weekly prize." I said.

"Totally, like a Snickers or Oreos," she said, releasing a mushroom cloud from between her lips.

"YES!" I clapped.

"A contest might be good," Jason added. "Oreos are delicious. Hey, do you guys think Tori Spelling looks like an iguana?"

He strummed his guitar next to us, staring through the wire squares at nothing in particular.

"Yeah, I could see that. Her eyes are bugged and set far apart. They look like they might move independently of each other," Tara replied, passing the joint to him.

He reached out toward it with one hand and cradled his precious guitar in the other. His and Tara's fingers met in mid-air, and she pushed the joint into his grip with the loving finesse of a newlywed.

My sight faded to a pale green, airbrushed with jealousy.

"So, are you two in on my shell contest or what?" I huffed.

"Yeah, maybe," Jason answered.

He slid the joint in between the A and D strings on the neck of his guitar and returned to strumming. Three thin smoke trails floated toward the ceiling. He leaned and inhaled only the one closest to him.

"I guess we could give it a go tomorrow or maybe the day after," said Tara.

"Uggggghhhh. Let's start today! Let's do it now!" I demanded.

I stood and howled at the walls. I paced back and forth, and baby kicked our coconut ashtray with my papa toe. It slid two inches before hitting a nail and spinning in a circle like an ice skater.

"Calm down project manager! Don't poo your britches," said Tara.

"Sir Touchy McMoody the third," said Jason. "Are you seriously fit-throwing over a shell competition?"

I glared at them then flopped down into my chair, defeated and exhausted. I dropped my head into my hands.

"Pleaaaaassseee," I muttered into my palms.

"For real Simpson, what's the problem?" asked Tara.

I moved my hands away from my mouth but still covered my eyes.

"I don't know. I think I'm PMS'ing. Or no…I think I'm just bored. No—I totally take that back. I'm not bored. I'm having the time of my life, but when I see you and Jason sharing this amazing experience and touching fingers while passing a joint, I just…I….I dunno…I wanna share it too damn it!"

I bent and snatched the flashlight off the spool table and held it up to my mouth. I tapped the top with two fingers, testing my homemade microphone.

"Is this thing on? IS THIS THING ON?"

"Could you just turn up the volume a bit?" Tara asked.

I held the flashlight closer to my lips.

"Here ye, here ye homies! Fiji is for lovers. It's hot. It's sweaty. It's become quite the little feel-good spot for me, and I've been fighting it with all my might, but the other night, I think Fiji finally won. This island is making me really horny!"

Tara and Jason gawked at me with red eyes.

"I'll admit, there was a part of me that thought I might just waltz into the village next door and find me a nice Fijian boy to play with, but then I thought about the waterfall skeleton and decided against it. So, now things have gotten so bad I'm about to straddle a palm tree. Hell, sometimes when I snorkel I see coral that's smooth with a round tip and I..."

"Stop!" Jason stopped me, raising his hand to my face.

He plucked the joint from its resting place between the guitar strings and passed it to me. "Dude, do not get freaky with coral," he said.

"No way, do not do that. Tons of bacteria," Tara backed her husband's sentiment.

"I'm not really going to go to town on a piece of coral, you guys," I coughed.

"Good. Maybe make something out of bamboo and leaves, or try a dead starfish," said Tara.

"What the fuck, Tara?" Jason spat.

"Well, I don't know. I was just thinking about their multiple arms. Options..." she said, staring down at her feet.

"They're spiney, like sharp bumpy. I just threw up a little in my mouth. You caused me to bile up." Jason turned his head and mini-gagged.

"Okay, Shelby. We'll do your little shell competition or whatever. Just don't go getting too friendly with the village people or any sea cucumbers. Just use Handrew while you're here. You know, churn your own butter," he recommended, doing a hand motion to represent what I imagined was an Amish woman rapidly mixing whole milk over her crotch.

"Yeah. Pat the Sasquatch. Spelunk your cave," Tara chimed in, air-tapping her love mound.

"I don't want to touch type my own essay anymore. I'm over it. I need an actual, live human up in this bitch. No more double clicking my own mouse."

"Well…" Jason said, leaning back and rhythmically drumming his fingernails on the body of his guitar.

"Well…" Tara followed.

"Well…" I joined in, then gave a sad face-pouty mouth.

But then a glorious thought hit me out of nowhere—there was a boy I'd been seeing in New Zealand who was only a plane ride away. Being a contractor, he was quite possibly finishing a job, which meant he'd be available and maybe needing a vacation.

I crunched the cost of his ticket in my head and weighed it against what I believed I had in my savings account. The numbers seemed good. No—they seemed likely, great, and very doable.

"I've got it!" I shouted, jumping to my feet and pointing toward the sky like Foghorn Leghorn. "I say, I say, boy! I tell you what—I've got it! I'm going to import cock!"

"Good for you," said Tara.

"Bring that dick," said Jason.

XXX

One week later, I was on cock detail. It took me two very long boat rides across choppy ocean water, a kinda-long taxi ride across bumpy roads, and one semi-expensive long-distance calling card to even get ahold of the boy attached to the cock. But when I did, he accepted my offer with only the tip of hesitancy.

"Are you sure? I mean, are you for real? You're going to fly me out to Fiji, and all I need to bring is a tent?" he questioned through the staticky phone line.

"Yes, I'm sure. I want you to come. I really, REALLY want you to come," I pleaded, hoping he couldn't hear the sexual desperation in my voice and spot the double entendre.

I wanted him to hurry up and accept my offer, so I could hang up the phone and get back to my comfort zone. At that point, seasickness was feeling better than the city sickness. My few weeks in Fiji had already transitioned me into a more natural version of myself than I ever thought possible, and it was whittling away at my toleration for gathered populations. Through my new island eyes, the city was abysmal. Actually, the whole mainland seemed sickening. Sagging phone lines and faded storefronts lined trashy streets and stinky gasoline, hot sewage, and steamy tar singed my nostrils. The noise pollution cut into our conversation, splattering horn honks and hacking mufflers over words.

"Are you still there?" I yelled against the backfire of a passing scooter.
"I'm here."

"The owner of the hostel said she'd only charge me $300 rent for each month if we stay in a tent. Tara and Jason stay in a tent. It's cool. It's actually better than the rooms…shacks…that they have.

"Plus, they feed us three times a day with food they've grown on the island and fresh fish they've either caught or that we catch. They have beef and chicken dishes too. It's pretty outstanding."

"Do I need to bring anything else?" he asked.

"No, it's super uncomplicated. There's no electricity on the island. We use gas lamps at night to hang out, sometimes play card games and shit. Just get here. Will you come, please? Say yes…"

A hoopty passed by, farting in my direction. I flinched. A pregnant pause nestled into the phone line.

"Yeah I'll come. I feel weird about it, but okay. Shelby, no one has ever done anything like this for me."

His voice was tender. He seemed genuinely touched.

"Yay! Well I'm happy to give you this gift. I'll book the flight, just look in your inbox in a couple of hours. See you Friday?"

"Yeah, see you Friday, babe."

I hung up the phone.

Babe.

I liked it when he called me babe.

He'd just started dropping "babe" right before I left New Zealand to come to Fiji. Through the dust and chaos, I saw a small sign that read "Internet" and stepped off the curb in a hurry. I wanted to get that ticket booked and get the hell out of dodge—pronto.

CHAPTER 20

"Hi," Andrew said, stepping off the same old dingy I'd ridden onto our pristine beach a month before.

He was already barefoot—in true Kiwi style. His shirt was open and ball cap tilted. He looked hot.

"Hi," I said, jumping into his arms and giving a hug for the *Guinness World Records* book.

Tara and Jason did the mandatory meet and greet—handshake, hello, how's it?

"Phew wee," Tara whispered to me. "Hot." She shook her wrist like it held a Polaroid picture.

"So, where do we set up camp?" my man asked, looking around.

"Come on. I'll show you 'home' for the next month," I said.

The four of us walked the beach and chatted. He admired the view.

"Over there," I pointed further up-shore and into the grassy clearing. "That's camp."

"Sweet. Well, let's get set up and then let's have a swim, shall we?" he asked, flashing his Hollywood grin and wrapping an arm around me.

My knees slightly buckled.

"Yes, let's—after some tent time."

It was what people talk about when they say they want to run away to a desert island. This was paradise—a warm existence decorated with tropical fruit, pristine reefs, and mountains wrapped in a rainbow of flowers, plants, and trees...and love.

It was the stuff of storybooks.

With an island partner, my tropical existence shifted. The days that had been beautiful but long became gorgeous and too short. I felt like Brooke Shields in *The Blue Lagoon.* Our alarm was the sunrise—shrill bleeps replaced by bird chirps and a tender increase in temperature, industrial soundtrack swapped with wave splash.

And we were ripped back to basics. I wasn't sure anymore where I stopped and Fiji began, but it felt right.

Sex.

Swim.

Eat.

Repeat.

We held hands entering the surf, and continued holding hands while snorkeling—lovers wrapped in fantasy. We pointed at pulsing anemones, candy-apple red crabs, schools of striped fish, and frowning eels that poked their heads out of black holes.

If we felt particularly naughty, we'd remove our swimsuits. Fijians tend to lean toward the modest side, so we had to be incognito when skinny-dipping. Plus, we had to be ready to re-suit with the same speed as Superman's costume change. To be ultra-safe, we'd only take our bathing suits off once we were quite a bit offshore, but once they came off, it was ecstasy.

With arched back and tanned skin that sparkled diamond droplets, I was a mermaid goddess. I'd perfected my dolphin kick, which meant I could project myself through the ocean without hands and with the smoothness of Flipper. In my mind, my man and I were aqua deities. We shimmered sun dust and bathed in the blue silk.

One day, though, he made a comment that when I swam underwater my boobs vacillated between looking like slow spinning propellers and meteor craters. After that, I decided daytime skinny-dipping with masks wasn't so sexy. Turns out, real boobs are so malleable that they cave, dimple, twist, and squish with the Earth's forces. Google any "naked skydiving" pictures and you'll see the concave catastrophe that, on the ground, was a plum hump of breasty-goodness. Just like falling through space, the ocean treats boobs with equal disdain. It mashed, thrashed, and twisted my titties—not very sexy. I just didn't know that was what the water was doing. Once he explained it to me, naked time was reserved for the tent.

But, barely clothed was how we spent most days either way. It felt right, and there really wasn't a big need for clothes. Being one with the outdoors all day every day, you start wondering what cloth, thread, and buttons are for. I got to the point where I felt like the only clothing that might suit my emotional state was a well-oiled animal pelt or a precisely placed strand of flowers.

Even the beach crabs wanted us naked. Every night, we'd hang our bathing suits, shirts, shorts, towels, and sulus on a line to dry, and without fail, the sea breeze would blow them off onto our lawn. That meant that every morning we'd wake to find our various t-shirts, shorts, and bikinis pulled halfway into different holes in the clearing.

The crabs actually tried to take our clothing underground with them into their holey homes. So, each morning was spent unearthing our clothing and wondering why the hell the crabs needed human wardrobe.

Were they fashionistas?

"Oh, look Harry, these boxers are fab. They're Massimo's!"

"Massimo was cool in the 90s, Steve. Go get those Victoria's Secret string bottoms."

Were they making polyester and nylon blend couches for their billiards room? Was my beach towel a late lunch?

I didn't think their staple diet consisted of fish, worms, squids, snails, dead animal matter, and thread—but I wasn't sure. Everything was educationally perplexing in Fiji.

We had a circus mouse with big round ears and a plump body who'd get inside our coconut shell ashtray and rock back and forth like it was his personal seesaw. He loved listening to the guitar. I think he belonged in Hollywood.

We found an unidentifiable cricket alien with too long antennas and spiked skin that used mouth-goo to bind together a fold in Jason and Tara's tent. Inside its hiding space, it made plans to destroy us.

The bugs in Waya sucked, but the food was awesome.

XXX

We learned that you don't need an amazing kitchen to make amazing food. Silvi and Mani were the cooks, and although their kitchen was nothing more than a burner, a cutting table, and a plastic bowl doubling as a basin, their culinary masterpieces would make Bobby Flay blush. We dined like kings and queens at our peasant's table situated under a bamboo and lumber scrap eave.

Tara and I raved about the juicy pineapple chunks with French toast, Andrew loved the banana crepes drizzled in honey. Jason lived for the island scramble—eggs, breadfruit, and diced onion.

Our stomachs thanked us for our time in Fiji. It was the season of freshness—organic goodness. Homemade buns with minced papaya and sugar sprinkles. Fresh white fish sautéed in coconut cream and garlic. Crisp peppers. Crunchy malay apples. Lemony vinaigrette dotted over zesty greens. And sometimes we were served dishes that Silvi and Mani knew that we loved, but had nothing to do with our latitude and longitude. Spaghetti Bolognese of the freshest beef and tangiest red sauce ladled over al dente noodles. Crumbled bacon sandwiches dressed in rich, homemade mayonnaise.

The best was when the Fijians invited us to catch our dinner. On those days, our quartet ventured into the ocean armed with spears, goggles, and fins.

We'd hunt aquatically. My incisors sharpened against my rubber mouth grip, turning teeth into fangs that accepted the crude challenge of killing my dinner.

One hunting expedition, our Fijian friend found an octopus. I followed him down to it, a shallow dive to a rock where he grabbed hold of it. It squirmed against the Fijian's grasp, unsuccessfully. When he ripped the octopus off the rock, he held it out to my mask for a shared underwater-celebration. Then, it inked in my face.

That octo-asshole projected a purple ink cloud around my entire head. I screamed underwater, backpedaling and thrashing against the current. Later, I ate the shit out of him.

The same Fijian friend taught us how to wrangle prawns out of a waterfall pool up in the mountainside. We hunted them with lassos made from reeds that were bated with morsels of coconut meat.

When our catch of the day was featured as our feast for the night, the heavens celebrated alongside our growling stomachs. There is nothing like ocean to table, especially when it's coupled with vegetables straight out of the soil. The way I ate in Fiji changed my life—it changed my relationship with food, with freshness, and with the eating process. I started really thinking about where the stuff I put in my body comes from. I learned what real food—homegrown food—should taste like.

Because of Fiji, I also learned about art and its reflection of nature. That shell contest I got so mad at Jason and Tara about—well, we started it.

Every day that I dove to the bottom of our lagoon to scoop a new shell out of the saturated sand, it was later that evening that my treasure would blow my freakin' mind. I discovered that every geometric design originates in nature. Every pattern. Every angle. But, it was the logarithmic spirals that heightened my appreciation for nature to a level of worship. I spent many nights staring at those spirals on shells—those perfect, impossible to create without tools, shapes.

So defectless.

Too expert for divine creation, yet there they were.

The spirals ran the gamut of the color spectrum too—plum to canary yellow, gunmetal grey to tangerine.

My absolute favorite, though, and the one that I claimed as the champion of the shell museum, looked like it had fallen off the set of the movie *The Nightmare Before Christmas*. I named it Dr. Finklestein. Its spiral was midnight purple and it curled into a wicked cartoonish swirl.

All it lacked was a full moon and a skeleton wearing a top hat in the background.

I was good at finding great shells, able to zoom in on the tiniest masterpiece buried in the sand, but my man was good at clown fish. He located a particular sea anemone on our reef that housed a grumpy clownfish. In the afternoons, I'd follow him out to the spot. Once there, I'd watch him bob in the waves just above the coral—his face three inches from the swaying terrestrial flower that homed the fish. We'd wait patiently for the angry fish, and without fail he'd pop out ready to rumble.

Little Nemo was all fire in his britches and a growl on his tiny fish lips. He'd ram my man's mask with authority.

BAM!

BAM!

BAM!

It was like a cotton ball tapping a fish tank, but the irate fishy didn't care. He was nose to plastic, fish to human battle.

Reverse forward, reverse forward.

BAM!

BAM!

BAM!

The little guy was fierce, and we'd just float there watching his fury, but after a few seconds he'd stop and just hover. He'd stare at Andrew, all googly eyes and confusion, and then it was like they became frenemies or ex-lovers who'd found amicability. That tiny clown fish held still while my man tickled his belly with his pinky, not once, but every day. It was Clownhog Day at Anemone Number Five on Reef Street, and I can attest to this strange, repeated-belly-tickle phenomenon.

On Waya, like sand through our toes, these were the spectacular days of our lives.

XXX

Waya taught me things. It changed me. It took me to a place I hadn't been since I was a child and free of burden, scouring the pasture during the summer with a backpack full of imagination, free time, and obsession with nature.

But for me, life on the island wasn't forever. It was for then.

By the end of the three months I'd spent in Fiji, I actually wondered if I could return to the nine-to-five grind. I was unsure if I could hit the pavement sprinting. It seemed unlikely—I'd gone too far. Toward the end of my stay in Fiji, I found myself mentally preparing during my swims for gridlocked freeways, competition, starched shirts, and cheesy interview questions.

I wasn't only confused about leaving paradise, I was also all messed up in the head over leaving my man. I had accidently fallen deeply in love with Andrew. At the airport, my tummy was a hurricane.

I didn't want to go.

CHAPTER 21

It was midday on the mainland. Waya seemed like a dream I'd had
the night before that was quickly dissipating—a blurry mirage of blue
and green. The airport stunk, but it was all we had. Andrew and I held
each other at the passenger gate.

"S-s-so, I'll…um…" My breath caught in my chest. "I…I…I love you."

He stared down at me with eyes of blue crayon. I'd never seen a shade
so vivid embedded in someone's iris. My heart thudded.

"I love you too," he finally said. No flinching—all gravity. "You're
unfinished business."

We kissed and I left.

I didn't want to dwell on what was behind me, metaphorically or
physically. He'd mentioned a future with our paths crossing—"You are
unfinished business." That was a trinket of excitement I could put in my
pocket. He was magnificently succinct like that—a demon of brevity. It
was that little sentence that brought us back together one year later. That
pathway was the one that took me back to Fiji and also provided the
second most embarrassing moment of my life.

I'd gone to San Francisco from Fiji. A year went by without a word,
and then he called. He'd come to visit me in San Francisco. We were just
as much in love as we were in Waya, so he asked me if he could return
the Fiji favor.

"I want to pay you back. Come to Fiji. It's all on me, but this time,
you'll stay in a swanky private resort in the northeast," he said. "You can
snorkel until you turn into a prune."

He'd taken a job in Fiji designing and building river stone showers for a resort. It was the kind of resort that catered to the wealthy, and he was paid well. He could afford flying me out. Plus, it was his perk as a worker. All the workers were allowed to bring in a partner to stay for free—the owners' way of keeping their workers free of island fever and mid-contract freak out.

"You had me at swanky," I said.

Two months after that conversation, I'd quit my job and was back to functioning in the name of love. This part of my life was very impromptu.

Also, it was super fucking exciting. Everything was love jittery and steeped in anticipation.

As the days up to my departure date carved away, I prepped hard. I worked out like a beast and got my body fit. I waxed my love muffin, deep conditioned my hair, bleached my teeth, and bought a new bikini AND new undies—it was on.

About a week before I was set to leave, I got a phone call from Andrew that was a bit strange.

"I feel horrible asking you this, but can you please bring some porn magazines?" he asked.

"Um…why?" I asked.

"You know how porn is illegal here? Well there are some other Kiwi boys on the building crew who are going insane. They need some…something. They've been here too long, and they'll be here a bit longer," he said timidly.

"Oh, okay. I understand. No problem."

"Really? Awesome! I can't wait to see you. Just a few days now!"

"Yup, just a few days. I can't wait either. Take care," I said, hanging up the phone and staring blankly at my bedroom wall.

Porn.

I knew what he was talking about—island fever is real. If these guys had been out there too long without getting any or having anything to fantasize about, they were dipping a toe in the insanity pool. I had no problem relieving their stress with a few mags.

XXX

When I was packing the night before I left, I thought about the mags. I glanced down at the duffel bag I was using as a carry-on. It was a precisely packed love kit. In it, I had:

1. My jam-box already loaded with fresh batteries and ready to play baby makin' music.
2. Extra batteries for when the heat and salt air drained them dry.
3. A t-shirt for my man.
4. Some new sulus for both of us.
5. A couple of books.
6. My flight pillow.
7. And a brand new leopard print vibrator.

The vibrator was also loaded with new batteries, and I'd bought plenty of back-ups, just in case things got crazy. For the minimal area I was working with, I'd done an amazing job utilizing the space in my carry-on. I was Tetris master, and the porn magazines wouldn't spoil my masterpiece. As a matter of fact, I thought they'd fit perfectly on top of my stereo.

Nice, I thought.

I flew to L.A. a day earlier than my actual departure date, because my flight to Fiji was a mid-morning one. I like to be relaxed, not fussed or rushed.

So, for my one night in Cali, I got a room next to the airport at a cheap hotel. It was fine for one night—the semi-musty carpet and lingering tobacco whiff of bygone days was manageable enough for a short time.

I had friends in L.A., and I was tempted to call them and hit a bar or three, but I was too excited about seeing Andrew in a day. Instead of partying all night, I opted for relaxing to any movie HBO offered and doing some last minute primping.

To the drone of the air conditioner and a retro throwback on HBO— *Top Gun*—I dug through my main suitcase for my tweezers. I hadn't had

time to pluck my eyebrows before I left, or in this case, take the
caterpillars off my forehead. I had some serious work to do. I couldn't'
show up to the swanky side of Fiji looking like Burt Reynolds.

"What the hell? Damn it," I fussed, rummaging for the tweezers.

I shoved peach body lotion, copper eye shadow, deodorant, and other
personal hygiene and beauty products aside, but it was a pointless dig. I
knew I'd forgotten them.

"What the pluck?" I complained. "This sucks."

I plopped down on the squeaky bed and considered my options. I
didn't want to pay for a taxi ride to the closest Walgreens and I still
needed to buy the porn magazines for Andrew's friends, so any old
convenience store was surfacing as the best choice. I hoped to kill two
weird birds with one 7-Eleven stone.

"How convenient will the convenience store actually be?" I muttered,
grabbing the remote control and hitting the red power button.

I needed silence to think. I walked to the window and pulled the
heavy curtain back. The L.A. sun choked through the smog and warmed
the glass. I squinted. Down below, the street was busy as expected, and
right across from the hotel—a 7-Eleven.

"BINGO."

I grabbed my purse and left, giving Tom Cruise and his shirtless
volleyball team full reign of the room. Those tweezers would be mine.

XXX

"You don't have any tweezers?" I asked the man behind the counter
who was pimpin' a big, white-ish turban.

His black chin bush barely moved when he talked. Long fingernails
tapped the side of the cash register.

"We have hair remover. Next!"

"Well, is there like a Walgreens or something close?" I asked.

Someone behind me moaned. Turban man shifted his eye line above
my head.

"Please, I need them really badly," I sighed in resignation, moving
aside.

The woman behind barged up to the counter where she threw down a Kit-Kat and a pack of Dentyne. They slid toward turban man and he stopped their skid without even looking down, rapidly clicking their prices into the register.

"Three nineteen," he spat.

He was done with me, so I turned and went to the "stuff you might randomly need" aisle. Turban man was right, there weren't tweezers, but there was a bottle of Nair. I picked it up and glared at the pair of Vegas showgirl legs featured on the front. They looked nice and shiny— smooth like I wanted my eyebrows to be.

I flipped the bottle around and read the back.

Blah blah blah….shmuh shmuh shmuh…not recommended for facial use.

I contemplated then set the bottle back down. I sauntered over to the magazine rack and began scanning across any options wrapped in black plastic. Trying to think like a man-boy, I decided on a *Barely Legal*, *Juggs*, and *Swank*.

With half my errand solved and three adult magazines in my grip, I strolled back toward turban man. About three feet from the counter, I changed my mind and dipped back over to Nair Land. I grabbed the leggy bottle without anymore analyzing.

I had to at least try. The effort was worth the risk, considering the alternative would be showing up to greet Andrew looking like I'd glued two chinchillas to my eyelids. Most people don't want to make-out with Cousin Itt.

Back in my hotel room, I packed my naked-lady mags perfectly on top of my seamlessly organized carry-on. They fit just right, which was lucky, considering my bag's capacity. Zipping it shut took a bit of effort.

After packing, I went to the bathroom with my Nair and climbed onto the counter, took a seat, and pressed my nose against the mirror.

I examined.

I scrutinized.

I decided that, beyond my eyebrows, I could do with a little removal of the tiny blonde hairs above my lip too.

I opened the Nair bottle and sniffed.

"Whew!" I snorted, drawing back from the acidic whiff.

The aroma was anything but organic, so I switched up my plans. My new strategy was to leave the cream on for one to two minutes instead of the recommended four to five. I understood I needed to be careful with this shit. It was chemical, and I'm sensitive.

"Here we go," I sang at the bottle.

I applied the cream lightly, just under my eyebrows, and in a last-minute decision, in between my eyes too. Then, I spread a thin layer over my top lip.

I sat back and marveled at my creation. It looked like I was getting a fancy spa treatment. The chemical shmear gave off a nice, burnt toast smell.

I climbed down from the counter and walked to the bed to catch some news. My phone showed five minutes 'til ten in the evening—it was wind down time. Right as I reached for the channel changer, I felt the first pang of danger. My lip felt like an ant bit it.

"Ouch!" I hollered, drowning out the news anchor that talked animatedly about a bear found in a L.A. neighborhood.

I raised careful fingers to my lip area and gave a gentle touch-test. It was equal to a hot poker stabbing.

Five minutes, an entire bottle of lotion, and a hefty dose of pain and regret later, I stared at my circus reflection. I looked like I had a cherry Kool-Aid mustache and applied fire engine red lipstick as eye shadow, not only on, but also between my eyes. I'd accomplished freak status.

"Shit! Fuck! Damn it, damn it, damn it!" I cussed at my image.

Burned into a corner, all I could do was go to bed. If I stared at myself or thought about what I'd done any longer, I'd be up all night crying. I didn't want to add "swollen" to my already mangled features, so I climbed into bed hating myself just to the brink of tears.

Maybe it will calm down by morning, I optimistically thought.

CHAPTER 22

"Which terminal?" the taxi driver asked.

It was early morning and the airport streets were already bustling. I was more focused on the taxi man's hair than the cars whizzing past. It was curly red and sprang out of his corduroy hat in cauliflower bushels. The vibrancy of it suited his driving technique, he was all maniac. I didn't mind though, I'd overslept.

"International. I'm flying Air Pacific," I said.

My voice sounded tinny in my ears. I was exhausted from a restless night. The facial burns and personal anger refused to let me reach REM.

"Okay, international it is," he shot back.

We weaved and braked, gunned and coasted. I rolled down the window just a speck and the caustic smell hit me hard. L.A. gags on its own emissions.

The driver looked in his rearview mirror and we made eye contact. I was worried he was going to mention my clown face, but he didn't. L.A. is full of weirdos, and my burns were minor in more ways than one, but they were still noticeable.

Neon red mustache.

Neon red unibrow.

"Your stop is just around the corner. Where you…" he started, but his question trailed off.

In the rear-view mirror I saw the skin between his eyes pucker.

"You hear something?" he asked.

"What's that?" I asked back, leaning forward.

"I said ya hear something? I think it's music, but my radio is as dead as Elvis."

He braked hard and jerked right toward the nearest chunk of curb.

I fell back, swinging my head from side to side trying to locate the noise. I did hear it. It was nearly inaudible Michael Jackson, and I knew exactly where it was coming from.

"Oh, wait! I know what it is! I have a radio in my carry-on. You can keep driving. I don't want to be late," I said, leaning over the seat into the hatch where the driver stored my bag.

He accelerated away from the curb.

"You better get Michael under control before you check your stuff. You know how security has been going lately," he barked, crisscrossing over the pathways of Fords and Chevies.

I grabbed the leather handle of my carry-on and hoisted it toward me. It was kind of heavy, but my gym nights had paid off and it landed in my lap with a dull thump. *Billy Jean* was clear as a non-LA day. Unzipping the bag, the music heightened. The taxi driver glanced over his shoulder.

"I know. I know," I said.

I was starting to panic. I only had a few minutes to get this situated, and my carry-on was packed so perfectly that there was no way in hell I was going to pull out my radio to take the batteries out AND get it all re-packed in time. Time was of the essence and my bag was too difficult a puzzle for the minutes remaining.

I bit my lip and thought hard.

"Yes!" I said, grabbing my purse.

I unzipped it and dug for my answer. Sure enough, right there in the side pocket was a brand new feminine pad. It was one of the good ones—with wings—a great backup for heavy days. I ripped it free from its plastic wrapping, removed the paper strips to reveal the sticky layers beneath, and returned my attention to my carry-on.

With cautious dexterity, I rummaged through everything that was on top of the radio, sliding each item carefully out of the way until I located the ON-OFF button on the ghetto blaster. The stuff packed on top of my radio had pushed the button to the ON position as the bag got tossed left and right during the taxi ride. No doubt the same would happen during flight, so I needed the power button to stay in the OFF position—hence the winged pad.

I slid the button to OFF and stuck the pad lovingly over it, pressing the "wings" down onto the sides of the radio to ensure optimum adhesion. I tested the button's ability to move, trying to wiggle it from side to side through the pad. It didn't budge.

Fuck yeah—freakin' MacGyver.

"All good. I fixed it," I gloated to the taxi driver, smug with my last-second ingenuity.

"Good timing. We're here—Air Pacific," he said, pulling under a shiny sign that read the same.

He slid the gearshift into park with a noisy *clunk*.

I grabbed my carry-on and purse, and climbed out. Back at the hatch, the driver fumbled with my big bag. He set it down next to me and extended his palm.

"Twenty-two fifty."

"Keep it," I said, offering twenty-five.

"Enjoy your trip. Use sunscreen wherever you're going. Looks like you should have used it here," he threw in, just before climbing back inside his taxi and racing off.

Asshole leprechaun.

I grabbed my stuff and marched toward the check-in counter, trying to forget his comment. Security at that time was on high alert, so I knew it would take a while for me to check-in, plenty of time to forget my face burns. Plus, I also knew there would be a double check of my carry-on at the gate; more time to forget my face burns. Airports were doubling down on everything due to terrorist threats.

That meant I had time to chill.

I'd made it.

I was happy, but my happiness wouldn't last long.

XXX

Almost two hours later, I was standing in yet another line. Security was extra beefy—swollen beyond normal precautions (more than my face). There were checkpoints to check the checkpoints. Terrorists are truly a pain in the ass. My bicep was achy from the weight of my carry-on and my purse was cutting into my shoulder. I was ready for the long-haul flight, just to get some sitting time.

I'd made it through the hour wait at the ticketing counter, where I handed over my big bag. Then I made it through another hour and a half security line to get to my gate. I thought the boarding area would be a reprieve from the standing and waiting, but when I got there my stomach dropped.

At my gate, there was yet another security line. All three hundred-ish passengers stood, waiting to get one last bag check. That's how bad the terrorist scare was at that time.

"Oh my God," I groaned.

I had no choice but to wait. I took a deep breath and resigned to my last security check, slinking into the line, crabby and irritable. I yawned and scanned with half-mast eyes ahead and behind me—happy couples everywhere, hundreds of them. I was the only one traveling alone. I would have envied them, but I knew I was meeting my man on the other side. My love was only an ocean away. The thought perked me up a bit, and I straightened my posture and my attitude.

At the front of the line stood one lonely security guard at a pathetic card table.

No wonder this was taking forever. Of course TSA would leave it up to one person to take care of hundreds, I thought.

Completely sick of carrying my bag, I kicked my carry-on along the ground as we progressed toward him. Thirty years later, it was finally my turn.

"Bag please," said the friendly black man in a crisp TSA uniform.

He was cute. His looks almost made up for the wait.

"Sure thing," I said.

I leaned down, grabbed my bag, and held it out to him. When my fingers wrapped around the handle, I felt it. My bag was vibrating. Unfortunately, my grey matter was too sleepy-slow to connect words to my mouth in time, so I didn't get a chance say, "Wait" or "Oh shit."

Instead, I zombied in front of the good-looking security man while he took my carry-on out of my hand. He frowned and set it precariously on the table.

"Ma'am, I need to go through your bag."

Then things got serious. He snapped on a pair of blue, rubber gloves.

"Uh...uh...okay," I stuttered.

He unzipped my carry-on with caution.

I swallowed cotton, and my fizzled nerves made me forget my strawberry-colored upper lip and rashy unibrow.

XXX

There I was—single, human mutant with a fire engine red unibrow and burn mustache. The TSA dude first pulled out of my bag three REALLY smutty porn magazines—*Juggs*, *Barely Legal*, and *Swank*.

Giggles came from behind me in the line.

Next out, my jam box....with a giant feminine pad stuck to the top. Wings wrapped lovingly over the sides.

Laughs from behind me.

Last, Mister TSA pulled out my leopard-print vibrator.

It buzzed in his palm on its highest setting like a washing machine on spin cycle, and the TSA guy mouthed a sad-faced "sorry" to me.

Hysterics from behind me.

It sounded like the whole goddamn line was rolling on the ground peeing themselves.

I wanted to implode, and also explain at the same time. I felt like screaming, "Yes, me and my cherry Kool-Aid mustache with matching monobrow are flying solo to Fiji with the world's wackiest sex-kit, but I swear there's a good reason!"

I contemplated turning and busting through the wall at full-speed, just like the giant cartoon Kool-Aid pitcher would do. I mean I couldn't possibly fly across the Pacific Ocean with these people—who was going to sit next to me on the plane?

Standing there sweating through my clothes, I could hear their imaginary thoughts. I pictured myself walking down the aisle of the plane, clutching my sex party carry-on.

"Oh great, here comes that horny girl with the burn-stache. I hope she doesn't have the seat next to us. She'll probably try to masturbate with the seatbelt," or, *"Oh my God, that thing is going to sit here. She's probably looking for someone to impregnate her in the bathroom while she eats honey roasted peanuts."*

In the end, I shut my eyes, took a deep breath, and took back my perfectly packed carry-on out of the hands of the apologetic TSA hottie. I was going to Fiji damn it, whether everyone on the flight thought I was into plastic ponies and hooking my nipple clamps up to a car battery or not.

If I could deal, they could too.

During the flight, the guy next to me never said a word—not a single peep for the ten hours it took to get there. Maybe it was the feminine pad I'd taped over his mouth…with wings.

PART IV

"Only when we are no longer afraid do we begin to live."
Dorothy Thompson

Long-term Travel Possible Gain List

1. THAT story. The one that's too crazy to be true. The one that blows minds, even your own.
2. International work experience.
3. An island life.
4. New ways of thinking.
5.
6.
7.

Long-Term Travel Possible Loss List

1. Your naivety.
2. Confusion about what you really want to do with your work life.
3. Weight.
4. The urge to surrender to fear.
5.
6.
7.

Death and Vomit

CHAPTER 23

Mr. Death.

He wears black sometimes, but not all the time like a lot of people might imagine. Black doesn't always suit him, so he switches it up based on how he feels. Basically, he's an average guy who likes all types of gear—hoodies, t-shirts, jeans, and sometimes a slick GQ suit that makes him look smokin' hot, but his favorite outfit is a warm robe paired with fuzzy slippers, the Sunday chillin' duo. He's sensible like that...most of the time.

He, or no, wait...*she*...is actually really interesting.

Ms. Death.

She's mysterious, the kind of enigma you wish you could decipher. I've bumped into her twice while playing in the ocean and once on a drive to Denver, Colorado. Actually, I've run into her more times than I like to think about, but I forget because we never really sat down, hugged, and exchanged pleasantries. Instead she blew by me—flashing a grin that said, "We'll catch up later."

I don't miss her, because she's not the missing type. Plus, I don't need to worry about never getting the chance to properly hang out. I'll definitely get my time with her. She's coming over for dinner one night—maybe soon, or maybe not so soon. I don't know which night she's available, and I'm not sure if night is exactly right either. Maybe she'll come over for breakfast.

She's confusing.

Anyway, dinner…brunch…a get together next week or in 2051—she's positively coming to my house at some point. I know this, because I sent her an invite the minute I was born, and when I took my first breath she accepted.

Death is waiting to dine with me and with you too—with all of us, actually. Here's hoping the doorbell doesn't ring tomorrow. Pass the butter.

CHAPTER 24

Traveling to exotic locations can kill you until you die from it. There are many things waiting to stop your beating heart—land animals, water animals, land, water, all forms of transportation, disease, a bad decision, and/or a mildly under-chewed, undercooked sausage. I'd heard about all the death possibilities, in loop, before I went overseas.

Doesn't everyone have hep-AIDS-bola there?

Some chick drank the water there, and her stomach burst open thirty minutes later—just like in the movie Alien. She died with her large intestine draped across her purse.

There are insects there that like to sleep in vaginas.

They have plants that blind you. The sap disintegrates your cornea, and it even floats in the air. Weird, huh?

Don't they get a lot of earthquakes, like the ones that open into a massive canyon that swallows people?

My uncle says that's where people go to suffocate in mudslides.

It didn't matter the city, village, country, or continent—all were deadly if they weren't part of the United States. So, I started to wonder why anyone went overseas if death was waiting for them at customs.

Then I realized it was a timing thing.

If you were just going somewhere on vacation for a short time, like Mexico perhaps, then it was totally sweet. The all-inclusive poolside sloth/drunk-skunk package waited with open and safe arms.

But, if you were moving somewhere overseas long-term, like say...Mexico, then it was not totally sweet. The food poisoning and

Cartel human trafficking experience was waiting to give you your esophagus burn and bullet massage.

When people made comments about my imminent death overseas, it bothered me.

I didn't feel like dying. I didn't want AIDS as my tour guide, and who would be blasé about great white sharks hanging out at a city beach? You got your sunscreen, your beach towel, your good waves, and your giant ass shark waiting to eat your mid-section when you go in for a dip—nobody is okay with that, and I certainly wasn't.

So, before I left the United States for the first time, I had some thinking to do. I actually had more than the average grasshopper, because something very momentous happened two months before I was getting ready to pull out.

Back, back, back in the day when I did my first long-term trip by myself overseas, I wanted try living in India. Then I heard on a travel show that Bali, Indonesia was a magical place filled with exotic animals, great food, lovely people, badass beaches, and quite high-end living for an extremely low price. Literally, at the time they quoted the price tag for three meals, a spa massage, accommodation, and a temple tour at about twenty USD a day. BOOM.

That changed my mind.

I decided I would make a life in Bali for a year, because I could stretch my minimal dollars into a really nice existence, and if I could find work there, then it was really on.

Right before I was set to leave, however, the 9/11 attack on the Twin Towers happened. From there, my delicately knitted sweater of Bali dreams unraveled.

The highest Muslim population in the world exists in Indonesia, not in Bali, but in Indonesia. Because of this, I didn't know if it was the right place for me to be traveling to on my own. I had no idea if Bali would be an unsafe place for an American post-9/11.

I didn't understand what was happening, not only overseas, but on American soil as well. It seemed no one did. It was unsteady times. Most people smelled war on the horizon, but no one knew where the battle would take place. It was a toss-up. It could be bombs in Baton Rouge, Bali, Fallujah, anywhere, or everywhere.

I was scared, but I still wanted to travel. Waiting wasn't an option, and I thought if I delayed, I'd never go. I'd settle into my ways. Get comfy accidently.

So, I switched up at the very last minute and applied for a work visa in Australia. I figured that if I at least spoke the language I'd have a better chance at understanding where I stood, and guess what? My little plan worked.

I got my Australian work visa, threw fear on the ground, and squashed the shit out of it instead of letting it keep me at home. It could have though, very easily, because there were other fear contenders barging their way into my travel life. There always are.

Beyond average political paranoia and nervousness about the unknown, I have aviatophobia— a morbid fear of flying. This was THE MAJOR contender threatening to knock me out of the travel game before I got in the ring.

XXX

I've had this fear since I was twenty-one. I know exactly how it started, and I can relay each slight escalation of my sickly terror down to the year, location, smell, and heart palpitation that it grew worse, and finally into a mutant that made flying nearly impossible.

Contrary to what one might guess, it wasn't an air scare that sparked my problem. Instead it was a television show called *Why Planes Go Down*. I would say that this show was like watching a train wreck, but the metaphor is obviously wrong and unneeded. This show was watching a plane wreck—one, two, three, thirty-two plane wrecks—one right after another. It was like it was the fucking *Benny Hill Show* of crashes or something.

Smash. Flames. Smoke. Melted panty hose adhered to snapped bones.

Sometimes the wrecks were computer-generated, matched to the hyper-breathing, panicked words, and eventual hoarse scream of the captain as the plane nosedived. Sometimes it was photos of mangled wreckage. Sometimes it was video of blurred-out bodies floating in the ocean, their limbs bent at unnatural angles that made my stomach do back handsprings.

I couldn't hack it.

After watching that show, every plane I boarded was a casket.

At first, I started having what I truly believe were mild heart attacks, then those led to full blown freak-outs. By the time I was in my mid-twenties and treating the world like my playground, flying sometimes five very long hauls a year, I was an unhinged passenger.

I actually sprinted off an Air China flight one time, shoulder barging the flight attendant out of the way seconds before she locked the hatch in preparation for flight.

The cause of that spaz attack was my secret number game. Because I'm truly demented in some ways, just like every other human, my cray-crazy brain decided to use a made-up number system to determine whether or not a flight would crash. It's this stupid OCD thing I do in my head that's supposed to equal good luck or bad luck based on the total I get from adding each digit of the flight number to my seat number. Then, I decide if the total looks good or not.

I have no lucky-numerology background. I based the good or bad luck total on nothing rational. Basically, my system was nuttier than squirrel shit. But on this particular flight from Bangkok to Taipei, the total came to a number that had too many sixes in it for my taste, and I flipped the fuck out.

At the last possible minute before taxiing to the runway, I decided I needed to sprint my way off the flying death trap like Flojo—a blur of churning legs and creatively painted nails.

I made it as far as the check-in counter before security mobbed me. They circled me, shark teeth bared. They said I had to get back on the plane. It was law. My bags were on it, so my ass was too.

Bangkok jail seemed less appealing than my upcoming death, so I forced myself to get back on the plane. I white-knuckled my way back to Taiwan with new gray hair as company.

After that flight, I discovered pharmaceutical drugs.

I made this discovery by relaying the Air China story to a friend. She listened while making a face that someone might make if a homeless person were telling them about Taco Bell being a spaceship bound for Narnia. Then she asked me, "Why don't you take a Xanax when you fly?"

And I thought, *huh....why don't I take a Xanax when I fly? Brilliant question.*

The answer was, "I don't know."

And after that, the new question was, "Why is the girl in seat 17B so damn happy?"

The answer was two Xanax.

My problems were sssshhhhhooooollllvvveeeddddd (to be said out of the corner of my mouth with a bit of spit bedazzle).

And after that, the best question was, "Why is the girl in seat 17B warning the guy in 17A that she may later sleep talk, sleep walk, sleep sex, sleep dance, or sleep conduct business on a brownie she's using as a calculator?"

The answer was Ambien.

Problems double solved.

For the record, I have never tripped-out on Ambien mid-flight, but I know it can happen, so I warn the lucky passenger next to me to shut me down if I start acting kooky.

I do this because one night, the mom of a guy I know—a classy woman who prides herself on being slightly bourgeoisie and floating in the crème caste of the city—put on her nightgown, popped an Ambien, and drank a nightcap in her home.

When she awoke in the police station, she was told she'd driven to the gas station, parked INSIDE the gas station—as in parallel to the counter—got out, grabbed some Cheetos, Ding Dongs, and Doritos, then got back in her car. She got in the backseat, mind you, and once comfy, she started munching down.

Needless to say, she was horrified. She hates Cheetos.

So, even though I realize the potency of Ambien, I still take it to knock me out on a flight. It's the only time I take pharmaceuticals—I'm a vitamins-when-I'm-sick kind of gal. Netty Pot to the rescue. Natural as much as possible, but when it comes to flying, give me the hard shit. No apologies. I'm tellin' ya, it changes long-haul travel like a mug.

XXX

Since welcoming prescription drugs into my flying life, I have never been afraid of flying or dreaded any flight over ten hours in length. Sometimes you have to seek extreme measures to make your dreams work.

For me, this is one of the things I had to do to not let fear roadblock me from accomplishing things. The rest of my fear has been stifled by rationalization and a forced stop to "what if" obsessing. I learned to put my bad thoughts in a box, lock that box, and toss the key in a river. "When you're feeling certain feelings that just don't seem right, treat those pesky feelings like a reading light and turn 'em off," Mormon style (thank you to *The Book of Mormon*).

But, stifling fear isn't easy. Fear has tried to spin kick me out of service many times—it continues to. My fear of flying, my fear of political unrest, my fear of disease, sickness, bad people, natural disaster, fake demons—none of these fears have stopped me, because I'll be damned if I let a "what if" take the steering wheel.

So, all those years ago, with the Bali incident and ever since, with each adventure I embarked on, I've figured out how to travel in spite of things. No one gave me advice on how to do it, because I had no one to give it to me. There was no "how to" guide that I knew of then.

The way I was able to move forward, despite my fears and wiry nerves, was to analyze my trip for a while, then quit analyzing, book a flight, and go. I put fear in my back pocket and sat on it.

Then, I replicated that recipe around the world. That's how I've been to or lived in so many places. And here I am writing about it.

Not dead.

Not sick, same as thousands of world travelers.

Since framing that state of mind, I've been to all kinds of places that most Americans fear, some that were actually red-flagged on the Department of State travel warning website. Others, not so much.

By no means do I recommend going to a place that's been labeled as dangerous, but I also don't believe in taking one person's word for it.

Shop around. Read, ask, listen to dialogue about a location, and decide what is rhetoric and what isn't. Think. Be sensible, but remember that life is a risk no matter where you are—some places are just riskier than others.

I will say now, ten years down the line of world traveling, I understand something very well. You are only as safe as you try to be, and as luck makes you.

Nothing is certain.

Exacts are rare.

Just because a place is hosting a coup doesn't mean you'll die if you go there, and just because somewhere has a staff member whose only job is to clean guests' sunglasses doesn't mean you'll survive if you go there.

Your time, date, and reason of death is unknown, whether you're in the backyard of your house just off Serene Street or visiting the Congo. There is definitely a higher percentage of danger in certain places, but you can choose to put yourself in those places if you want to…or not.

Also, just because one part of a country is in turmoil does not mean the entire nation is. Two blocks of a town can be a riddled battle zone while the outskirts resemble Disneyland. That's life—insensible, unpredictable, and ready to be embraced, if you're ready to accept a certain amount of peril.

And of course there is peril.

There's danger, Will Robinson.

I've been around death overseas. My heart shrivels from the things I've seen and heard, and my condolences go out to those who have lost their lives in the midst of their world travels. But, I'm guessing they were happy to take those risks, because the reward would've been worth it. Maybe now they look down from the heavens and applaud their departure, thrilled to exit mid-jungle hike, instead of choking on a grape mid-conference call or being plowed down during the seven a.m. commute to a job that was a real wrist slitter. Maybe they regret nothing.

They died living, and there's nothing nobler than that.

CHAPTER 25

The biggest death scare I'd heard about was in South America.

"You saw this? The guy had photos?" I asked my friend, unable to hide my disgust.

I sat down slower than I would have without the new information. The imagined atrocity froze my central nervous system—snail-paced my movements.

"Yeah, he showed them to me last night. It was horrible," said Cam, dazed by the nightmare and staring blankly at the wall of our new hostel room.

He delivered the story from a simple wooden chair in the corner. The bare concrete walls matched my feelings. Cam looked more solemn than I'd ever seen him, and hanging out with Cam is usually like attending a hip-hop concert featuring a Tekeshi's Castle competition every half hour. His news was killing his euphoric spirit. It did more than that, it scared me too.

"So, what exactly were the pictures of?" I tiptoed my way through the sentence.

I wasn't sure I wanted to know, but curiosity beats me every time.

"It was bad. Didn't you hear? You had to have been there when it happened. It was a major wreck. Bad drivers. Bad deal..." he said, passing his hand over his bald head.

"No, we didn't hear. You know how it is out there. Our drivers didn't even know if we'd get off the plains. Some uprising bullshit, guns and stuff. We had to take a new route, so at one point our guides actually

thought we were lost. I guess we took roads that they don't usually take
to avoid some blockades. That's what they told us anyway. I dunno," I
said to my feet, my words scrambling away into pathetic silence puddles
on the floor.

I thought about it a minute. I did want to know, and I wanted details.

"So, what happened?" I finally asked with intention.

Ears ready. Brain scrub brush prepared.

XXX

As told earlier in the prison story, the Salt Plains of Bolivia are a
bleached infinity. Empty; weird and amazing in the same breath. No
marked roads. Sky and land stretched into spooky vacancy, but then
sporadically occupied by a hostel made of salt, a lake full of pink
flamingos, a cactus island, and lastly, a natural hot pool you can defrost
your bones in. Nothing makes sense there, but the locals who run the
tours seem to have a grasp on the stark landscape—somehow.

They make a living driving tourists around in overstuffed Jeeps for
days, sometimes weeks at a time. They load the Jeeps with everything
you'll need for your trip into no man's land—food, extra blankets, warm
gear, potable water, shelter accessories, and fuel. All of it is strapped to
the top of the Jeep as it rambles over the vast countryside like an
overladen camel.

And, it's cold.

Let me rephrase that—it's fucking freezing. It is paralyze-your-
fingers, numb-your-organs, ice-your-activities freezing. The best you can
do is sit, or better yet, cuddle with travel mates like a rookery of
penguins while you view the sites, walk around a bit when told to do so,
and then wrap back up again. That's how disabling the temperature is at
that altitude.

So to get through it, to live day after day in those bitter temps, the
tour guides have a little helper to warm the heart cockles—good ole
alcohol. They drink the hard and good stuff.

Our drivers quietly sipped at a potion that smelled similar to a drink
I'd made when I first discovered my parent's liquor cabinet—a suicide

concoction comprised of one tip from each bottle—the infamous whiskey, tequila, vodka, sherry, gin, and rum smoothie. Hurl.

Our drivers handled their moonshine buzz with steez, and dare I even say, semi-drunken *care*.

First of all, we barely witnessed them sipping at their home brew. Secondly, they didn't act drunk. Our tour guides were cautious with our well-being.

Other drivers, though, weren't so responsible. A girl we met asked how our driver was. She asked because she'd had to take the wheel when their driver passed out, the Jeep careening off into nowhere-ville. She said she'd actually had to reach over his sleeping body to take the wheel, pressing her foot into the resistant brake to eventually bring the Jeep to a stop.

Once stopped, they realized nobody was around to help. With a party corpse as a driver and their truck burping white clouds of exhaust into empty space, they needed to figure shit out quickly. All alone and flustered on Mars, the young tourists ran through their options.

1. Drive the Jeep themselves into a vast wilderness that had no road signs, food, water, or shelter, unless you know where to find it.
2. Stay there and wait for…hopefully…help.
3. Get the drunk guy to sober up and drive them the hell out of there.

They decided that they had to wait for the guy to sober up, because no one knew where to go. Driving out there would have been like driving into the matrix maze—a streaming code of white grains and blue skies fuzzed into impossible duplicates. To get out, they needed their drunk driver.

So, because Cam's story involved bad driving, I wasn't surprised.

Cam learned the story because he'd been talking to a Euro boy who'd just come from the Salt Plains, as most travelers in the area had. Most backpackers in La Paz were either going to or coming from the salt flats in Uyuni. It's a common route.

This was the story; after a few drinks, Euro told Cam he had photos of people burning alive on those Salt Plains. Cam saw the photos.

XXX

The cause of the wreck: two very drunk Bolivian tour drivers somehow crashing into each other. Without marked lanes and astute attention to what is happening, this is very possible.

There are lots of Jeeps out there, it's just that you don't usually see them. If you do, they're taking their own path, crisscrossing their way across the frozen tundra toward whatever destination they have in mind. Without marked roads, they just go where they want. It's just salty tire tracks woven together. As a rider, you're too busy trying to stay warm to think about it.

One Jeep was full of Chinese backpackers, the other full of Israelis. Everyone most likely in their twenties.

When they crashed, the fuel on top of the Jeeps exploded.

"The photos showed bodies on fire crawling and collapsed on the salt," Cam said. "The Jeeps were engulfed in flames. People were running away...on fire."

No doubt the backpackers were too sardined inside to make an escape. I know we were packed tight enough inside our Jeep to produce a human diamond at the end of each day's drive. So, I'm sure those Jeeps were the same.

The poor travelers were trapped.

"Why would he take pictures of that?" I scolded Cam as if he'd been the photographer himself.

He recoiled.

"I don't know. It was gross. I couldn't look at them really, but I guess humans, they're, ya know...abhorrent. There was nothing anyone could do. The Euro guy said that it was too late when they got there. I guess there was no help to give—they were goners. They'd pulled up just after it happened, but everyone was on fire. They had no way of putting it out."

"Oh my God. That could have been any of us," I whimpered into shaking hands that cradled my cold face.

I was blood drained.

"I know, but it wasn't you guys, or us. It's horrible. It makes me sick. I can't talk about it anymore. Can we just do something else—anything? Want a beer?" Cam asked, his voice a kilometer away in my mind.

"Yeah, sure," I finally gulped.

"K. Let's go. Oh, and a guy from Canada fell off the balcony in our hostel in La Paz the same night I met that Euro guy. Died. Guess he was all coked up."

"Lovely," I croaked.

We locked up the sad little hostel room and walked down the narrow hallway toward the bar.

It had never been more beer o'clock.

XXX

Bolivia wasn't done being creepy.

Mon and Cam told us that when they arrived in La Paz, they'd attended an underground party for backpackers. The piece de resistance of the evening was a piñata that hung from a rafter above the dance floor. To get the fiesta started, a lucky backpacker was given a stick and a thumbs-up to destroy the piñata.

As the tourist bashed its teddy-bear-piñata brains in, a hundred baggies of cocaine rained onto the floor. Crazed foreigners scrambled for the precious powder. Mon and Cam left shortly after that.

They said things got weirder, and I'm sure that's an understatement. The next morning on their way to breakfast, they found a guy they'd met at the piñata party T-Rexing his way home. It was ten a.m. and he had no idea where he was. He was a swamp donkey—frail, shaking, geeked out to the point of rolled eyes and crippled legs. He was scrambling along like one of those marathon runners whose muscles have failed—limbs contorted, tongue licking his dry eyeballs. Sexy. Fun, ya know.

Mon showed him to his bed. She reckoned that he was close to dying.

Also, you may or may not know that Bolivia hosts the most dangerous road in the world. This forbidden road is called Yungas Road, and it runs from La Paz to Coroico. It connects city to rainforest—La Paz to the Amazon. This makes it popular with backpackers, but it's also popular as a local highway needed to get important goods from point nowhere to point somewhere.

I'd heard that the men who take jobs driving trucks or buses (not cars, rickshaws, motorcycles, mini, tiny, or smart vehicles) on that road are prone to drinking. Hmmm. Weird.

Supposedly they like to use a million-proof alcohol and maybe a white line or two of powder courage to get through the nerve sizzling adventure they call "just another day at work." I know I'd need a lobotomy, three acid tabs, and a snow shovel to the forehead.

On the daily, these men barrel down a crumbly dirt road big enough for only one vehicle—a raw highway made of sketchiness.

It has no guardrails with parts hovering at two thousand feet—taller than the Empire State Building.

So, imagine riding a tour bus on the edge of the Empire State Building with fog, rain, and mud hindering your careful turns when another bus pulls up and kisses your bumper. It's a standoff. Nobody's going anywhere, but both buses have to move eventually, unless everyone wants to live out their existence on Death Road. Plus, the drivers need to get paid, so if the dollars are callin' then the buses are crawlin'.

It shouldn't be too difficult to get around each other, because this is what the drivers do day after day, right? They're seasoned bad asses…possibly. Or maybe they're veteran risk takers resigned to death; sloppy decision makers with disintegrated instincts—most likely.

Either way, as a passenger you must accept the way the meatball bounces. The buses have to move, so they will either:

    A. Both drive in reverse along the rim of the Empire State building, back to the place they came from. This option basically guarantees death and isn't really an option. Or…

    B. Play the slide-by inchworm game.

Since both have to get to where they're going, all that option B does is win. So, the fun begins.

This is the part where the local road rules state that the downhill driver must take it in the ass. Deep breath—that means the downhill driver must move his truck to the rim of mortality, edging his twelve tons right out to the valley-side of the road and nuzzle against the drop-off. His outer tires eventually sit less than an inch from gravity's invitation to nothingness. A quarter mile plunge. At that point, it's almost guaranteed that everyone inside the bus is signing the cross on their chest, humming prayers, and sweating waterfalls.

The view from a seat in the death trap is nothing but valley—deep, dark valley. No road, it's hidden under the bus. There is basically nothing between that automobile and sure death, and passengers have no choice but to wait. You can't get out, because the bus door opens into the other bus—no room for a human's escape without crushed bones. You can't get out of the windows, because busting out windows on the door side will only bring the same outcome—the passing bus will demolish you. Climbing out of the window on the other side means swan diving into a two-thousand-foot valley with boulders as the landing pad.

Because of these horrible selections, no one is allowed off the buses.

So, back at the WTF party, everyone is asking some sort of God to take the wheel—literally—while the uphill truck eases by on the inside lane.

It scrapes a blemish into the mountainside, trying not to touch its trembling friend that waits in the outside lane, but sometimes it nudges the poor bastard just enough to make a rear tire on the outer bus lose ground. The outer bus sways on three tires while its passengers wait patiently for their destiny.

Will they fall?

Maybe. Plausible.

If so, they'll be only a few of about three hundred that month that screamed their way to the bottom of the valley inside a tumbling, metal coffin.

So, why would anyone ride on this silly road? I have no clue. I'd rather eat a hot tuna fish sandwich in a porta-potty at the county fair.

I do know that taking the deadly road is less costly than flying to the Amazon from La Paz, and some backpackers count pennies instead of notches on their nine lives scratching post.

Cam and his girlfriend Mon rode one of those big tour buses on that evil road. They took it on the way back from their Amazon visit to La Paz, and they are two very sane and reasonable people.

Mon doesn't cry. She's one of the strongest, most optimistic and fundamentally sound humans I know, and she was reduced to Sarcosuchus tears while she screamed helplessly from the back of a bus. It pathetically dangled a rear tire over the mile-high ledge waiting for another bus to pass.

I say, "Gross."

Overall, Cambodia is sketchy, as is all of South and Central America in my opinion. So far, it has been the only area of the world that convinced me it was normal to sob during bus rides, flights, and any road or sidewalk sessions. Don't get me wrong, I loved it. It was one of the best trips of my life, but it was full on. I think the reason it was so freaky-dink was the lack of safety precautions.

The roads and drivers there scared me, and those things are usually the least of my worries. It just seemed overly risky—deadlier than other areas of the world. I don't know if it really is, but I haven't read any statistics, except about the road in Bolivia.

In the end, crashes are accidental. They are unfair, sad, and common everywhere. It can happen traveling to Cancun, Buenos Aires, Dublin, or right down the street from your house.

CHAPTER 26

I heard about a group of hikers in Thailand that entered a cave system on a tour when a flashflood hit. The story was that they were just your average tourist group from various locations dotted across the globe.

A German. Some Swiss. An engaged British couple. Thai guides.

The group entered the cave during rainy season, despite the warnings. Unfortunately, this was the day to take heed. A downpour had occurred up-country an hour earlier, and Mother Nature had already released her ambush. She can be a real bitch like that.

The tourists hiked into the belly of the cave, into the beauty of Thai nature and the excitement of it—and then the roar came.

A massive wave crashed through the rock tunnel.

Out of everyone, only the British couple managed to scramble up on a ledge. The rest were washed away into darkness, swallowed by the liquid freight train. A tragic disappearing act—and then there were two.

The loving couple squatted on the shelf listening to the newly created and raging river surging beneath them. They were trapped inside Earth's anatomy, kept company only by glowing insects. They clung to the slippery rock wall, alone but together. Shocked. Confused. And then, I guess they had to make a decision.

I heard that the man decided he had to get help. He deducted that he could flow with the water and the flood would spit him out into safety. He would save them.

I don't know if she said she had to stay or if she couldn't move, paralyzed by fear. Maybe he told her to stay, I don't know. No doubt, he just wanted to get help and to bring his fiancé to safety.

So, he dropped into the water, disappearing under the unforgiving surface. She perched alone in the inky cave for hours waiting until the water dropped and finally a light bounced off the slick walls. It was people from outside. They were looking for her. I read that she screamed to let the search party know she was still there—still alive.

Help had come, but without her lover. He'd become one of the lost souls taken by the flood, taken by nature. His life was lost to heroic ill-decision.

But overall, it was Mother Nature's fault. Her angry slap left a permanent welt—a mood swing that caused a violent and unpredictable ending, but it could have just as easily brought amazement and awe. That cave trip could have been nothing but outstanding, but that's Mother Nature. She's fickle—an equal opportunist for wonder and terror.

I ran the cave story over and over in my head for years. It's a movie reel that I still replay sometimes. That British girl—someone I never knew and probably never will. I hurt for her. I cried for her. I still get teary when I think about it. I think it will always pain me. Sometimes hurt that isn't yours sticks to you. Adopted ache. Borrowed bruises.

Dear stranger, I'm sorry. Your loss is remembered.

You never know what might happen overseas. Nature is harsh and amazing.

Is it worth the risk? You never know.

Is it worse to die while living your dream, or to live with the regret of not chasing your happiness? For me, I have my answer to that question. I like calculated risk that invests in my contentment. It's the best I can do.

CHAPTER 27

Traveling can be sick—both sick as in rad and sick as in stomach regurge.

The throw-up type of sickness is scary. That type of sick is never fun, and I've seen some sick travelers, but Mike's story was on the next level.

He was a fellow traveler who was currently in London. He dressed the part of travel boy, even though he'd been in the city awhile. His boots were chunky and meant for loose ground, not pavement. He wore them around London anyway. Those boots were most likely his only pair of shoes. I didn't know yet, because I'd only met him the week before—he was a friend of a friend. Kind of weird. Kind of cool. I'd been introduced through *Halo*, the one-on-one shoot-em-up video game. The day I met him, Mike had come over to play a four-way battle.

We were taking a *Halo* break in my backyard, and the rare sun of London spring broke the clouds. We would have gone to a city park, but when the sun comes out in London, everyone goes to the park.

Everyone—it's like a law.

On a gorgeous day like that, we knew that the park would be human soup—a giant entanglement of alabaster legs and arms, a sea of snaggletooth.

I plopped down in a half-green, half-brown patch of grass and watched Mike wrestle to get his boots off. I eyed him suspiciously, still testing the hangout waters, and held a Frisbee I'd found in my closet. He glanced at me between grunts and tugs.

"That dude I was telling you about, the guy I met backpacking through Zimbabwe, he's now tired for the rest of his life because of Zimbabwe," he said between shoelace fumbles.

He pronounced it Zeem-bobe-why, and it made me smile.

"So, wait. You met someone who's tired for the rest of his life due to something that happened overseas? What do you mean tired for the rest of his life?" I asked, tugging at the grass and tossing the natural confetti into the air.

"I mean tired for the rest of his life. What the fuck you think tired for the rest of your life means?" he returned, yanking at his right boot.

It popped free of his appendage. He did the same to his other shoe. The whole process looked uncoordinated. Next, the socks peeled back.

"You get eyes for Christmas?" he asked.

I glared at his feet. They were part-Hobbit, part-vampire. I suspected that he hung from them at night to sleep. His socks and shoes were discarded too close to me. I used the Frisbee to edge them away.

"Well, I don't know exactly what you mean by tired. Be more specific. You mean he sleeps a lot or wants to sit on the couch all the time, or is he just kind of in the doldrums sometimes, or what? Is he like narcoleptic— the sneaky nap king? I was staring, because your feet are unnatural. They're Discovery Channel feet."

Mike laughed and reclined onto his elbows. He took his t-shirt off. A white concave chest reflected the sunrays. It seemed to me that muscles were unnecessary in England. Real shame.

Mike draped the shirt across his eyes as replacement sunglasses.

"Look, I dunno. He's probably all those things if he's tired all the time. I don't have a list of his daily habits and emotions. Why do you need so many bloody details?"

He wasn't the first and he won't be the last person to ask me that question, but usually without the "bloody" part. I'm infamous for asking one million questions to collect the details my crooked brain needs. So, his annoyance didn't annoy me. I pressed on.

"You can't just tell me someone is now tired for the rest of his life from visiting Zimbabwe and not expect me to ask more questions. What caused him to be tired?"

"Uhhhhhggg....fuck! It was like a virus! I don't know if he got it from an insect, or water, or a chick named Oshkosh B'gosh! He's tired. He takes a heap of steroids every day now just to get going. That's what he told me. That's all I know."

He balled his fists and fidgeted his legs, mumbling something under his breath. He flopped down onto his back, letting out a mini-grunt when he hit the ground.

I shrugged, "Well, that's weird. I slept with a guy named Oshkosh B'gosh last month and I've been taking sneaky naps at the bar recently. You know, like extended head nods between Cosmopolitans."

Mike flashed a smile. He sat up and tied his t-shirt around his head. He kind of looked like a nun, and I took note that his smile was nice—unlike his Frito toenails and funnel chest.

"Look Shelby, I told you this story because you claim people don't get sick overseas. But I know people who have. Granted, I haven't gotten sick. You haven't either, but this guy is tired for life. The point I'm making is that it happens."

"I know it happens. I just don't know anyone who it directly happened to, and I haven't heard a story firsthand from another traveler about someone getting super sick," I replied.

"Until now," Mike said.

XXX

I frowned, "Yeah, I guess until now. That would suck, being tired for life from catching something or being bitten by something overseas. When you think about the way things can go wrong when you're traveling, you don't really put *exhausted for life* in the grab bag."

"No, you don't. That's why this guy wigged me out. He was slow, like motion-wise. It was like watching a turtle make pancakes."

"I'd watch that, no matter how long it took. Was he wearing a turtleneck while he made breakfast? That would make it even better.

How'd you meet him? Was he trying to shell you something?" I punned, using the Frisbee to poke Mike's side into enjoying my bad jokes.

"No, but he was eating turtle-cheesecake when he told me the story," he laughed.

"Weak. So, you met this dude in a hostel?"

"Yeah, he stayed in my room. It was one of those four-person rooms, so we got to know each other pretty well over the week that I was in Egypt. Like I said, this chap had come from Zimbabwe. He told us he'd been tired for a few months. He'd traveled back here to try and get some help, but they said it was something he'd contracted for life. Real shitter."

"No doubt. Sad. But at least that's the first person I've heard of getting badly sick. By now, you'd think I'd heard of tons."

I paused for contemplation.

"I have heard about food changing someone's life. Well...drugs. Food drugs."

"Wha?" Mike asked. His nose wrinkled into Shar Pei-ish folds.

"This guy I met in Australia. He's kind of odd. It's like he's socially awkward without being autistic or having Asperger's. There's just something tilted about him, ya know."

"Uh-huh," Mike confirmed, making full eye contact.

"He does things—like if he's handing you a drink, when you put your hand up to take it from him, he keeps his hand on the glass too long while passing it to you. You both stand there with your hands on the drink for ten seconds longer than normal."

"I guess I could see what you're saying," Mike nodded.

"One night, I thought he was being rude and mentioned it to his friend, and that's when I heard the story explaining why he comes off as distant, weird, or even dick-ish sometimes. Turns out, he wasn't always that way."

"Yes, you've got me. Continue."

Mike swished his hand through the air, allowing me continuance. I played it up.

"Thank you, sir. Lovely. Anyway, story goes—he used to be a super chippy-chap. Gift of the gab. Great with the ladies. Life of the party. He and a group of mates went to a Full Moon party in Thailand, drank some mushroom shakes, and had an awesome night. The problem was that the next morning he was still having an amazing night."

"He was still tripping balls?" Mike asked in the same tone a child might ask, *"Did the wolf blow the house down?"*

I got into character—movie trailer voice—velvet pipes.

"Yeeeessssss. He tripped balls for dayyyyysssss. His friends were forced to call his parents to help wrangle him up and get him home. He's still tripping balls, but medication makes him a functioning ball-tripper—hence the weird glass passing maneuver and slightly dick-ish attitude. He's just off. Perma-trippin'."

"Yikes," Mike grimaced.

He pulled his legs up to his chest and removed his urban turban. He appeared to be in deep thought.

"So, this friend of yours, he's brain damaged now from that mushy shake?"

"He's not my friend, but yes."

"But you know him, right?"

"I met him. I've been around him a few times. He's definitely off, and it's because of one bad mushroom trip. Wouldn't that suck—mentally checking out overseas and never checking back in?"

I sighed, flipped the Frisbee around in my right hand a couple times.

"It would be dire. Was it a bad batch of mushies?"

"I don't think so. They sell them at a bar on the cliff that overlooks the beach. All of the guys had a shake that night. They all hallucinated and shit, but they came down just fine, and he stayed high. Who knows what happened. Poisonous things are unpredictable."

"Yeah, well lucky us. Lucky we're not constantly tired or forever tripping. Wanna throw that disc around?" Mike asked, pointing to my Frisbee.

"Sure," I said.

Without standing up, I tossed the Frisbee two inches into his open hand. He tossed it back. We did that for the next half hour and talked about anything except sickness.

CHAPTER 28

I've heard the laundry list of death ploys.

Parasites from a salad.

Tsunami.

White heroine sold as cocaine—the results probably not far from Mia Wallace's mistake in *Pulp Fiction*.

A bombing in a nightclub. Bed bug pesticide toxicity from a mattress. Box jellyfish sting. Malaria.

Someone who looked the wrong way like a dumb-dumb when they were crossing the street—that person was accustomed to traffic driving on the right-hand side of the street, instead of the left-hand side, and got taken out by a city bus.

Oh wait, that was me...and it didn't happen, but it almost happened about a dozen times in a handful of different countries. But, I always caught my step in mid-air right before the bus grill caught my bone structure in its metal teeth. Lucky duckling, or as my Taiwanese assistant teacher Ms. Happy would say—rucky duckring.

A British couple I went with on a diving trip to the Great Barrier Reef told me that a hippo had gotten aggressive with their boat. Not in Australia though, they'd come from South Africa.

It was during their safari trip. They were riding a boat to their campsite and the hippo gave it a hard nudge. Fortunately, the hippo took off and never came back for more bump and grind, but they said their black tour guide turned white as snow during the incident. Hippos kill the most humans out of all animals in Africa—more than lions, elephants, great whites, or rhinos. Two days after the hippo collision, their guide admitted that the run-in was damn close to being the end of their safari trip and their young lives.

A twenty-something year old Asian girl died on a white water sledging trip in New Zealand one week after I'd looked into doing the same trip out of Queenstown.

Sledging is when you get out of the whitewater raft and into the actual water, using a "sled" for buoyancy. The sled is a big, heavy plastic float with handles. While wearing a wetsuit, fins, life jacket, and helmet, you float half of your body on it while you propel down the river with your legs in the river. You hold tight onto that sled, when you can, then you go down a class-three river with as much control as you can pretend to have. It's a crazy adventure, if you can make it to the end.

This girl didn't.

She got trapped under a rock in the middle of the rapids. The tons of pressure coming from the current had a vice grip on her, holding her down under the water. I read that it took hours to pry the woman's body from the river's clutch.

I still went sledging years later though, on a different river with a group of friends. Supposedly sledging is fairly safe sport, but all of us, and I mean two competitive swimmers and some solid athletes, agreed that it was a very messed up experience. We had no business in that river.

First, the guides said that, due to earlier rain, the river was so bloated it was almost undoable, but they were letting us go anyway. Nice guys, eh? They were simply adding an extra guide to keep us safe, so there was that.

Secondly, the guides warned us a few times when we'd pulled over to the shore between rapids to discuss our next treachery.

"Now, be sure to stay left on this next part. If you get pulled right, it gets pretty hairy. You don't want to go there, so just don't." Their faces were stretched into a worried frown that no amount of Botox could ever hide. Ours mirrored theirs.

Lastly, the guides ended our final pre-rapid pullover speech with these verbatim words, "Now, on this last part you need to stay right—hard right. If you get sucked left, you'll get taken into the death cave. In there, you'll get caught in a hydraulic that will suck you down to the bottom of the river, then back up to the surface. This will happen over and over until we can get in there and try to get you out. If this happens to you, stay calm. Take breaths at the surface. Okay, let's go. Stay right!"

And off we went, but the funny thing was, we had very little, if any, control over where we went in that river. It was swollen to the point of a raging serpent, muscular and thrashing. I kicked my feet like they were doing something, but I was a leaf in the middle of a tornado.

"I'm not having fun," my friend Jade admitted to me through chattering teeth about halfway through.

She's the queen of extreme. Her statement was frightening.

"Can we hike out?" I asked, my numb lips fumbling the sentence.

We scanned the steep banks. It was all tangled woods—rock walls. We didn't need to discuss that there was no other way out, we had to finish.

So when the guides said, "Let's go!" —we went.

We swam without belief that we could avoid Death Cave on that Saturday afternoon, but we were damn sure going to try. The effort paid off. We avoided it.

Brow swipe. Never again. Screw sledging.

XXX

From death by water, to death by drinks spiked with DEET, to getting trampled by a bull, or taking a coconut to the noggin—anything is possible. And let's not forget injury. There is always a wave-tumbling surfboard ready to knock your incisors out or a falling boulder ready to remove your right thumb. Shit happens.

There's a website called *Tourist Killed* that will scroll international headlines of tourist deaths, if you're into researching that kind of thing. I don't recommend it though, sicko. They're all what-ifs. I'm just saying, you can. Go ahead, marinate in your fear.

But, please know that when people tell you to be scared of traveling to foreign lands because they heard a story about someone's death or extreme illness overseas, I think it's important to ask the right questions.

Yes, there are mountains of unfortunate stories, but get to the bottom of how or why those people got their numbers pulled. Usually the stupid and statistically unfortunate bite the dust first—the former in that group you can avoid. The latter you can't. Acceptance of reality is important.

Certain things about traveling are a considerable menace.

Be adventurous, not careless.

Be smart-brave, not dumbass-reckless.

If you do that, you should be fine, unless fate feels otherwise.

In the end, life's a gamble no matter where you are, and I want to spotlight that fact. This is coming from the mouth of a girl who started traveling at twenty, behaved intelligently and cautiously most of the time, and has never gotten hurt or sick. The rest of the time I was very stupid, very daring, often times very drunk, and very alone while traveling for ten years—but I didn't die, go to a hospital, or even have diarrhea once.

And all that time, I also was NOT treating myself with kid's gloves. I was sky diving, bungee jumping, surfing, caving, sand dune surfing, jungle hiking, outback sleeping, driving fast, riding faster, drinking and drugging, boating on high seas in questionable vessels, scuba diving with a buddy who was bleeding profusely into night waters, zip-lining, biking, sliding down glaciers, hanging out with people in places that were beyond sketchy, and just moving around on all flavors of terrain— I've done some stuff.

I'm not dead, I suffer no scar tissue, and I own great memories.

I will die one day, and maybe it will be from a gnarly reef cut infection, but maybe it will be on my couch in Oklahoma from an aneurism. Maybe I'll slump off in the middle of *Jeopardy* after asking my boyfriend, "Do you smell toast?"

Who knows? It scares me, but it won't stop me. Shmuh. Shrug. That's life, and the hell if I'll spend all of it in a familiar stomping ground.

PART V

"No, no! The adventures first, explanations take such a dreadful time."
Lewis Carroll, *Alice's Adventures in Wonderland*

Long-term Travel Possible Gain List

1. THAT story. The one that's too crazy to be true. The one that blows minds, even your own.
2. International work experience.
3. An island life.
4. New ways of thinking.
5. A movie-like adventure.
6.
7.

Long-Term Travel Possible Loss List

1. Your naivety.
2. Confusion about what you really want to do with your work life.
3. Weight.
4. The urge to surrender to fear.
5. Disbelief in magic.
6.
7.

Your Personal *Goonies* Moment

CHAPTER 29

"Because it's their time. Their time! Up there! Down here, it's our time. It's our
time down here. That's all over the second we ride up Troy's bucket."

- Mikey, *The Goonies* (1985)

When I was about eleven years old, and up until…well…probably the
day I die, I always wanted to be some acrobatic, super adventurer,
Indiana Jones meets *Gem and the Holograms* kind of girl. Growing up, I
spent many hours using my crawling body to bulldoze spy tunnels
through wheat fields. I climbed tall trees to escape imaginary pirates and
walked the creek in search of mermaids.

I grew up in the country. I was lucky to have the space, time, and
weird farm tools to make my adventure whims pretty intricate. With my
imagination as my best friend and nature fueling the fire, every day was
a new quest that would last until sunset or the dinner holler—whichever
came first. Sometimes the fun even continued after dark, if I snuck out to
have a night jump on the trampoline or attempt to actually sleep on it,
even though the dew always failed my effort.

When I saw the movie *The Goonies*, when I re-watched it, and when I
continued this pattern until I could repeat every line and reconstruct

every scene, I became fixated on the idea of having at least one big, secret adventure in my lifetime.

It's all I wanted.

One of my favorite swimming pool games was pretending that I was Andy from *The Goonies*. I'd walk the plank, holding my pretend-tied hands behind my back while I screamed, "Brand!" and jumped off the diving board. I'd end the scene by swimming to the side and making out with the vinyl wall. I spent a few years obsessed with learning how to kiss boys while also finding them equally repulsive.

As I got older, I adventured around the States. I tracked into the wild. I explored abandoned buildings with dim flashlights, but I still didn't have golden doubloons and that One-Eyed Willy feeling.

It's probably because the days of discovering a hidden map that leads to buried treasure are most likely over. Secrets still exist, but they are few and far between. No one gets lost anymore. It's nearly impossible, plus the modern world is nosy. Everybody is everywhere. All you have to do is click a button to go anywhere in the world, learning about foreign things without touching, smelling, or feeling them. You can circumnavigate the globe from your couch.

Because the Internet allows us to visually try before we buy, the mystery is dulled. Some of the surprise is blown—add that to population growth, and the result is a much smaller world. Every corner is being stepped on. Cultures are melting and molding together.

That's why I believe that, if you have the urge to see nature and experience unique cultures, you should go while rugged nature and distinct cultural differences still exist. Go soon, because although there might not be booty and hidden cities left, for now…there are still secrets.

I experienced a secret destination.

Granted, it wasn't as cool as finding a treasure map in my attic that led to a pirate ship full of gold, but it was still movie-worthy.

When my chance to have a secret adventure FINALLY reared its magnificent head, there was no way in hell a tank, vague directions, malaria, or disbelief could stop me from taking it by the hair and dragging that bitch to fruition.

CHAPTER 30

My secret adventure was such a well-kept secret that even seasoned backpackers were confused about it. It became the subject of discussion during a float down an infamous river.

"That place is a myth, bro. It doesn't exist," said the Aussie boy, pimp-slapping a mosquito out of his face and scrunching his features into a billboard of annoyance.

"No, it's not. I know someone who's been there," the guy across the aisle responded. He sounded American, but I guessed he was Canadian. His blue tank top was just a plain, classic blue, all-wrong shirt that reminded me of third grade. He had to be Canadian.

"I've never heard of the place, and I studied up hard before I traveled here. It's bollocks," chimed in a third party, a girl with a British accent that sounded smart and refined.

Their little dispute tickled my fancy. Not only did it serve as needed entertainment during our three-day long slow float to Vietnam on the Mekong Delta, but it also pertained directly to me. The key was that they didn't know that. There was no need for them to know that, so I kept my mouth shut and glanced at the players.

The Canadian boy sat erect, like an out of place river gnome. The British chick slouched, seemingly unconcerned and worn out. The Aussie had his legs spread like his junk needed two seats, and he palmed his crotch, readjusting. The heat had probably glued his balls to his thighs. I grimaced at the thought.

They didn't know what they were talking about. Lips zipped, I mopped some sweat out from under my nose with my t-shirt, sat back, and enjoyed the debate.

"I swear it's real. It's a hotel or something. You stay there, in the middle of the jungle," the Canadian guy came again, dropping his voice an octave. The words came out in a semi-bark—assertive man bass.

"No way," said the Aussie.

"For real, it's REAL. I know it exists," Canadian boy argued.

"If it's real, then why didn't you go?" the British girl fired back.

"I...I just didn't have time," Canadian boy finished.

He folded in on himself. Boo hiss. Shame Street. His effort spiraled into a stinky pile of shitty storytelling that severely disappointed me.

The others loved it, though. They pounced on his tall tale like starving leopards. They bus stopped it hard, releasing a long and loud "pshhhhhhhh", similar to the sound a public bus makes when the hydraulics deflate and the doors open for departing passengers.

"Psshhhhhhhh, yeah right! What a crock of shit,"' laughed the Aussie. "Fuck off, mate."

"Good story. Now can you tell us the one about the three bears that own a hostel in Cambodia?" asked the British chick.

Canadian boy sat in silence, marinating in his infamy.

I smiled. I'm an occasional fan of low-level schadenfreude. He was smart to drop the conversation like a smelly carcass into the passing current. He was embarrassing himself, and since he couldn't back up his claim, his fabled location was destined to remain just that—a fable.

With the entertainment finished, the river drew me back. I took a deep breath that hinted of diesel, murk, and jungle funk. The droning of the ancient motor attached to our rickety slow boat was becoming part of my bones, and it kind of made me regret the decision my husband and I had made to not take our chances with the speedboat. Granted, the warnings about the speedboat had been pretty harsh.

Word on the street was that the Mekong Delta swallowed speedboats for a living, and if I get beat upside the head enough with a warning—I listen.

A random Spanish dude finalized the decision for us. He was the third person to shout about the danger of the speedboats, and he was living in Laos, so he knew. He said that the speedboat gossip was legit. The slow boat was worth the few days of travel that kept you alive, compared to the one that could kill you.

"Usually all the danger talk is *mierda*, but the speedboats are real spine snappers. A lot of people end up bloated at the bottom of the Mekong because of them," the Spaniard nodded nonchalantly.

The speedboats were about the size of a dingy and seated seven—very uncomfortably. They passed us three times during our slow boat ride and we glared at them as they sped by—a blur of humans squashed together into the boat like human meatballs, packed knees to tits.

Each speedboat had a car motor wired onto the back that whined a maxed-out screech as the Laos driver cranked it down the river like a meth head. The passengers wore pathetic helmets that one might wear at a second-grader's skate party, a sticker of *Dora the Explorer* on the side. If the speedboat hit a rock, it was game over. The helmet was a placebo— the Tinkertoy of safety games.

I watched them barrel by at fifty, maybe sixty miles an hour, and I found it interesting how so many people were willing to bet their lives on a stranger's ability to navigate what boulder sits here or what sunken log lurks there.

Successfully navigating the Mekong at high speeds was a memory game at best. The drivers bet on the premise that the river didn't shift, the water level didn't dip, and that the good grace of Lady Luck was on their side. If any of those things failed, they were having a high-speed collision that would end without airlift, 911, or even a simple truck ride to a hospital. That is, if they were still functioning enough to get fished out of the mud soup after their aquatic cartwheels.

The slow boat was fine with me.

It wasn't all that bad anyway. The slow boats carried passengers and freight. They were about ten feet wide and sometimes up to 150 feet long, with v-bottoms and open-air seating—spacious and sturdy.

The only thing that made me jealous of the speedboaters was my sore ass. Our slow boat had no padding on the seats, just rough wooden slats that were dimpled with years of weighty tailbones, luggage, and crates.

Rugged on the butt, our asses paid the highest price for the three-day journey from Laos to Vietnam. I constantly shifted from one throbbing cheek to the other. My coccyx was a pulsing nail that I balanced on through clenched teeth and tweaked muscles. I had to deal though, because it was a test of patience.

Slow-mo. Sluggish thuggish—the Mekong took its sweet time. We crawled down it and over, and over again, until I found myself treating the water like a liquid movie screen. Besides my book and conversation, it was my only entertainment—a liquid serpent winding its way through the Asian terrain.

Compared to America's heinous war stories that took place on this river, the Mekong was kind of a let down. I must say, it was an anticlimactic introduction to a heavy piece of history. It was lethargic and kind of boring.

In my head I thought that for sure the Mekong was a grade five, rev your adrenal gland kind of river, but no. It didn't even nibble at the nerves. Instead, it was just a sometimes wide, sometimes narrow, slow moving river. But, the longer I had a staring contest with it, the more I realized that I was wrong. This river was a hustler.

Underneath the surface was where the skeletons hid. The top gloss of terracotta and milk chocolate perfectly masked whirlpools, rip currents, and jagged rocks. If you fell out of the boat, you might disappear like Augustus Gloop into Willy Wonka's edible creek, never to be seen again.

Sweating buckets into the sticky atmosphere and letting my eyes relax into the passing tropical canopy of jade, olive, electric lime, and absinthe—I rested my head on my husband's shoulder.

I liked our slow boat.

I enjoyed the Mekong.

I loved the awkward conversation between Canadian tank-top boy and the others, because it bonded Gareth and I together through secrecy. Tank-top boy was on his own with his jungle jibba-jabba—that's what he got for looking like Richard Simmons on the Mekong. But actually, Canadian tank-top boy, who looked like his mom had dressed him and claimed a secret destination existed somewhere deep in the rainforest of Laos, wasn't such a dummy.

He was right.

His fabled adventure spot did exist, and it was very real.

Gareth and I had just come from there.

CHAPTER 31

The adventure started three months prior, on a cold day in Auckland, New Zealand. My newlywed husband, Gareth, and I were planning to leave for Southeast Asia in the next month—so it was a must that I visit Caroline first. Caroline is a friend who is very well traveled. And, during her gallivanting, she'd been somewhere I was dying to go.

From my warm spot on Caroline's couch, trekking through a steamy rain forest seemed galaxies away, but it was important to attack my adventure plan early. I usually don't make super solid plans when traveling, but this was different. For this, a plan was vital—Caroline's secret destination called for it.

"Here—this is where you cross the border. After that, just ask around for the office. You'll find someone who knows," said Caroline, tapping a slender finger on the map.

Her natural, round-filed nail bounced up and down on Chiang Kong, Thailand.

"That's it? We just have to find it?" I asked, concentrating on the heavily tattooed page of her *Lonely Planet*.

Penned loops, penciled underscores, and dog-eared corners proved that she had used the book like the veteran traveler she was. Where she was leading us wasn't actually in the book, but the map was useful.

"Yeah. It's all good. You'll figure it out," she replied, standing up and gliding back to the kitchen to refill her cup of tea.

I closed the guidebook and set it on my lap. Its weight was surprisingly substantial. I wouldn't take it with me—didn't need to. I'd memorized her instructions with the lust of a teenage girl memorizing the lip line of her first crush.

I understood how rare the opportunity was. Caroline was letting us in on a travel secret. At this point in time, there was no website for the destination. There was no write-up in any travel book, magazine, journal, pamphlet, notepad, or rolling paper. It was a ghost—legends of the jungle—and I would join the hauntings.

I zoned out for a second and stared through her living room window at the drab sky. I envisioned Leonardo DeCaprio in a scene from *The Beach* instead.

"I can't wait," I said to no one in particular, and stretched my legs out onto the ottoman.

"You'll love it. It's awesome—really amazing," Caroline yelled from the kitchen.

I heard the clink of spoon on glazed ceramic. She came back from the kitchen, not only with her tea, but also a sliced up chocolate Lamington.

"Nice. You're not just a busted face, eh?" I joked, reaching out and taking a Lamington before she could sit.

"Mmmm, that's right. So, you going?" she asked, plopping down next to me.

"Yer damn tootin'," I answered through a mouthful of cake.

XXX

Getting to the exact border crossing in Thailand wasn't easy. Not a lot of travelers went there, so English became scarce, which made asking questions very difficult.

We weren't sure if we were where we thought we were. Things got hectic and our secret destination started seeming unreachable. For a minute, Gareth and I were ready to throw in the towel.

Exhausted, biting at each other, and with achy muscles, we considered hitting the Hilton instead of the rain forest. I was never really going to do that, though. I may have threatened it, but I was full of shit.

So, instead of pushing forward with lackluster effort, I made a paradigm shift—told myself that nothing worth anything came easy. I reset my sight on the prize. After the secret destination became our sole focus again, the universe threw us a bone, as it always does. It's funny how doors start to open once you concentrate on a goal hard enough.

Out of nowhere, we met a first-time traveler from London named Craig. He'd heard of the same place we were headed and, just like us, he was trying to get there.

Imagine that.

We picked him up and together we became a trusty tripod. With our adventure powers combined, we trudged toward Laos.

It was still confusing, though. Tough going. For a minute, we weren't sure if the buses that we took were correct or if the roads we chose would go from bad to non-existent.

Jostled, weary, and confused, the three of us constantly compared notes in hopes of staying on track. We even went further than that and asked other travelers we bumped into about our destination, foregoing our secret for actually finding the damn place. But, they never knew what we were talking about.

Heads shook.

Confusion ruled.

We borrowed travel books, and they never had our destination listed. We asked locals if they'd heard of the place we were trying to reach—no one ever knew.

It was like we were asking for directions to Shrangri-La.

Then—somehow—our destination was close enough to spit on.

XXX

The day we arrived, rain was coming from every direction—sideways, up, down, and swirling. We were getting dumped on. Buckets and troughs. A grey blanket covered the Earth. I was fascinated by its ferocity, and since I was already wet, I didn't feel the need to seek shelter. I just stood in nature's shower, letting the sheets of wet bang down on me. I squinted against it, trying to focus across the river at the blurred forest line.

I stood alone, saturated but happy, on the shore of the Mekong Delta River waiting for Gareth and Craig. They'd left me in Thailand and crossed over into Laos because we needed money.

Their crossing of the Mekong was conditional. It was an escorted boat ride, escorted walk to the money exchange, and then an escorted trip back to where I stood. We'd accidently arrived at the Laos border without enough cash for the visa purchase—oops. So, border patrol kindly took the boys across the river in a rowboat to get cashed up in a tiny Laotian town.

Through the rain, I finally spotted the boys and border patrol re-boarding the wooden toy they'd used to cross the Mekong. They headed back my direction. The Thai patrolman worked the oars hard, his yellow rain poncho plastered against him like a second skin. There was no way that it was keeping him dry. Dry was out of the question for all involved.

"You get it?" I yelled through the pounding droplets as the boat skidded up the bank.

I grabbed the nose of the boat to steady it as they disembarked. The bow felt slick and warm.

"Yeah, come look," Gareth yelled back, grabbing my hand and pulling me toward the little shack that was used as a makeshift border-crossing office. Once inside, we shook off like wet dogs.

"Check this shit out," Gareth laughed, pulling a wad out of his pocket.

At the time, one hundred USD was worth over a million Kip (the currency of Laos). Gareth's cash exchanged had made us instant millionaires, and we laughed liked hyenas at the fat stack. Just like that, we were Jay-Z and Beyonce—cash money deep.

Gareth, Craig, and I threw down enough dough for our visas, loaded the same tiny rowboat with our Thai escorts, and fought the Mekong current into Laos.

The game was beginning.

Like a drooling wolf, I sniffed at the scent of our trail.

We were getting warmer...warmer...warmer...

"This place is wild," Craig muttered.

We plodded down the one-street, Laotian town. Unlike Thailand, Laos seemed deserted and dirt poor. Leaning shacks. Cracking concrete. Peeling paint.

The humid, post-downpour musk puffed from the mud, and I was happy the rain had stopped so we could actually have a good look for the store we were trying to locate. Oddly, the rain had stopped just as quickly as it had started, like someone had turned off the faucet.

We did as Caroline said and asked locals where to go. They lounged in doorsteps and glared at us skeptically. Finally, a few guttural grunts and crooked fingers led us to an unmarked storefront.

"Oh my God. This is it," I said to Gareth, squeezing his free hand as he pushed the door open. Inside was a basic room that housed one desk and a young, thin, white man that didn't even look up when we entered.

"Hi," I greeted him.

He finally raised his face, wearing slack features and bored eyes.

"Hi," I repeated. "We heard that this is where you sign up for the jungle stay," I smiled and removed my backpack from one shoulder, lowering it gently to the floor.

The man returned to his work and grumbled something. His hands shuffled papers. He chose one, scanned an E.T.-like finger down it, and then said something in Lao. A pretty girl appeared from the back room, answered him in the same language, and then turned and left.

"I have an opening for three, lucky you," he announced in a French accent.

"You're kidding? Ha!" Gareth burst.

We high-fived. The man turned and went out the same door the Asian girl had used. We quit celebrating and looked at each other for answers, confused about what was happening.

"Pippa has your paperwork. Pay her," his voice finally yelled from somewhere in the bowels of the store.

The Asian girl rushed back in. Their one-two-switcheroo was as smooth as her shiny hair that swung back and forth as she ran at us with a small stack of papers.

"Here—fill these out. Are you paying separate?" she asked in perfect English.

"Yes," Craig said stepping forward. "Do you have a pen?"

Pippa turned and left again—no explanation.

Gareth and I exchanged looks.

So far, things weren't what I had imagined.

Finishing the paperwork and getting on the way took about fifteen minutes, and after handing over our credit cards, we were hurried out of the office.

It was anticlimactic. For all of the hard traveling, confusion, and trials we'd faced to get there, I wanted a welcome of open arms. Instead, we were shoved into the adventure. I half expected a boot to the ass as the office door slammed shut behind me.

A dusty truck rumbled out front in the street. The doors were open and piles of backpacks were strapped to the roof.

"Get in," Frenchy snapped at us.

"Geez," Craig murmured swinging his backpack up to the rack on top of the truck. "Someone hasn't learned third-world time keeping."

When the Frenchman said he had room for three, what he meant was that we'd gotten very, very lucky. He just didn't tell us that until later.

It turned out that before we crossed the border into Laos, the trip had been full. Then three serendipitous spots came open literally minutes before we swung open the front door of Frenchy's storefront. We just so happened to walk in and take those spots fifteen minutes before the leaving bell.

Shazam!

Adventure fate.

In retrospect, the puzzle pieces concerning Frenchy's terseness and his girlfriend's rush came together to make a clear picture. They weren't rude—they were prepping to bounce. We'd barely made the cut.

Inside the truck was a motley crew of backpackers. I had no idea where they'd come from or how they'd heard about the secret place, but we didn't discuss it. We just greeted them, squeezed in, and sat back while the driver exchanged Lao words with Frenchy through his rolled down window.

Bunch of Lao words. More Lao words...

"Let's go," Frenchy finished, slapping his hand on our driver's window.

He turned and walked back to another Jeep that was idling behind us. Frenchy climbed into the driver's seat and shut the door. As a two-party caravan we pulled out of town, headed straight for destination unknown.

XXX

It took a minute to get away from the shacks, buildings, and proof of human existence, but eventually the walls and faces got fewer and fewer.

Laos was crazy. At one point, we passed a home that I thought was built on stilts. Turned out they weren't actually stilts—they were bombshells from an earlier war. I leaned forward and tapped the Laotian driver on the shoulder.

"Were those bombs that house was standing on?" I asked.

"Bombs. Yes," he answered, like it was a building material purchasable from Home Depot.

We wound deep into the hillside, at one point taking a road that looked freshly made the day before. Traffic disappeared until there were no other cars. No people on foot. We were alone except for the other Jeep trailing us, its roof laden with more faded backpacks and other gear that shouted international travel.

Behind us, Frenchy drove wearing his Aviators. I wished "Danger Zone" was playing to heighten the moment. So far, his shades were the best part about him, but I hoped my first impression was wrong, considering the fact that he was obviously part of the weekend. The whole class-A dickhead motif wasn't really working for me.

We twisted our way through gullies, peaks, and narrow passages between overhanging bush. As the woods got thicker our speed got thinner, dropping to a Sunday stroll to better manage the nature maze.

Then we hit jungle. The further we snuck into it the denser the shrub became, until we reached a river. It wasn't a wide river. It maxed out at maybe twenty feet across, but it flowed well. Ripples decorated the surface.

I guessed it was a deceitful river—the kind that's deeper than it is wide. It seemed to serve as a gateway into the real rain forest. On the other side of it, a narrow but deeply scarred and treacherous looking path led steeply into the guts of the jungle.

"What's this?" Gareth asked rhetorically.

"It's a sandwich," I answered.

Mumbles came from other travelers, but then all idle chat stopped as we rolled slowly toward the shoreline.

"Are we driving through this river?" a girl asked.

No answer.

I assumed we were headed across it, but at the same time I didn't know how we'd actually go about that. Plus, the road across the way looked like a no-go. But, a few seconds later I learned that some vehicles are built to blow your mind.

The Jeep, the kick-ass solider on wheels that turned out to be an all-terrain mobster, inched forward wearing steel balls, rolling like cold honey into the rushing water.

The nose went down, and my stomach followed it.

Within seconds the entire truck was in the middle of the river and completely submerged, except for about three inches on the top of the windows. Our new view was army green river water.

"Oh my God," I gagged to Gareth, digging my nails into his bare thigh.

He ripped his leg from my grip.

Squeals filled the interior, along with a few of those sounds people make when they're shitting their britches—the ones that later nobody admits to making.

Where my talons had been on Gareth's leg, tiny half-moons tattooed his muscle. I tried to focus on them instead of the fact that we were trapped in a car under water.

Trapped wasn't right, though.

We were driving underwater, moving forward somehow. I didn't understand.

Our knobby tires made traction on some sunken surface. The driver sat up in his seat, straining his neck to get eyeshot of the shore through the three inches of viewing room he had in the windshield. The massive engine snorkel breathed for all ten of us, belching hard as the Jeep finally revved its way up the opposite bank and onto the rainforest trail.

"Holy shit!" I spat out of my slack mouth.

I felt like I'd avoided a ninety mile-per-hour foul ball to the face by a last-minute duck. I think everybody did. We were all in shock. Gareth was grey and mute. Everyone else stared straight ahead, focused intently on our future.

It had to get easier. Otherwise, someone was going to blow a gasket this weekend.

XXX

Things didn't get easier, but they did get more interesting. After the river, new entertainment slid past our mud-streaked windows.

Wicked plants.

Contorted trees.

Explosions of color.

Sunrays broke the darkness in crooked beams of gold and I pressed my forehead against the jostling window to get a better look—to try to climb inside what I was seeing. The Jeep ride was becoming an acid trip.

We crawled up risky gradients that set off spinal fireworks in my back. We skidded up slippery embankments and tilted sideways at angles that threatened flipping, but somehow we didn't. We just kept going—working against gravity.

We drove on four wheels, and then two, and then back to four, but we never dropped to zero, even when the ground turned from packed mud to slushy muck. Drizzle lit the jungle into a sparkly mess. The vines and high-gloss leaves winked, soaked in glitter and goo.

I reclined into my seat. My adrenaline was drained. I took deep breaths and patted Gareth's leg.

"All good," he reassured me, patting my leg back and using his other hand to pass me a fresh bottle of water.

"Yeah, I know it's safe," I lied, taking it from him and swallowing a casual swig.

"Oh yeah?" Gareth asked, eyebrows touching the ceiling.

I must have still been pale.

"Totally copasetic," I lied again and turned my attention back to the window.

I knew I needed to pay attention with a smile and whistle. This was a moment more to relish than to sweat. This was the good stuff—sketchy—but good.

Back home, I'd have given up my left pinky finger to get out of bumper-to-bumper traffic and into a precarious jungle adventure, so I didn't want to be rude-olph the insolent-nosed reindeer and spend the entire Jeep trip biting my nails and whimpering into my husband's shoulder. That would be douchey.

So, I said into the window, "I know it's all good."

And this time, I said it with conviction.

I thought, *So what if we flip and slide to our deaths down the mountainside? It's way better than death by boredom or adventure-less existence, wearing my hamster-wheel sad face and mentally chanting, "ONE DAY I'LL DO GREAT THINGS. ONE DAY."*

"Village," the driver broke me out of my trance, pointing ahead of us on the road. "No photos, please."

The bumps, jumps, and curves flattened. We pulled out of thick jungle and into a clearing that humans clearly had called dibs on, dotted with small shacks and fire pits for outdoor cooking.

"Cameras for later!" our Laotian driver shouted, throwing the Jeep into park next to the biggest shack there.

He didn't have to remind us about manners though, the truck was full of respect. Respect for the machine that had somehow tackled a non-road. Respect for the driver. Respect for the jungle, the journey, the indigenous people—all of it and everyone.

We understood sacred. No one had to ask why they weren't allowed to pose awkwardly with an Laotian man, making bunny ears over his head while a friend photo-bombed in the back. We weren't those type of travelers anyway. This expedition wasn't tour bus status. We weren't Facebook vs. Six Flags—no Wal-Mart sponsor or Exxon pipeline fund.

This was real.

Backpacks on. Water bottles out. The heat curdling our organs.

"We'll go through a safety talk when we get to the top of the mountain," said Frenchy.

We gathered in a circle on the edge of the jungle line getting our prep spiel, and I was roaring to be let loose.

"Remember, no pictures with the locals. These are people, not tourist attractions. Save the camera for the treetops. This is about respect. If you want to help, you can donate money or goods at the end. Okay then...bug spray. Water. Let's hike."

And that was it. Our secret adventure had finally hit the GO button.

CHAPTER 32

Buzzing. Spindly insects. Soggy steps. Dankness. Bird alarms.

Red petals, yellow wings, cobalt blue exoskeletons.

Shadow shapes that made you wonder what creatures hid in the black pockets.

The jungle was more alive than I expected.

With every step the trail eased upward, eventually raising its incline from wheelchair ramp to waterpark slide, and it wasn't long before our bodies were slick with sweat.

Lungs stung.

Breathing came in scratchy gasps.

As a whole, our crew wasn't Olympic ready. Most wheezed and stumbled their way through the heat. I was in great shape though, thank God. My husband was a natural born ninja, so there was no worry there.

Despite the heavy conditions, we owned that hike. I'm built for equator weather—loincloth ready. The one hundred percent humidity and stifling heat created my perfect happy space.

"Think we can we go a little faster, maybe move up?" I asked Gareth quietly.

I was tired of walking on the heels of the chick in front of me, and she probably already wanted to stab me. Plus our third party, Craig, was tucked happily into the collection. He talked quietly with a short, fit girl. I was the perfect moment to get a little alone time with my husband.

"Yeah, let's do it," Gareth replied.

So, we took it up a notch—went around the outside—strode toward Frenchy, who sashayed at the front of the pack, plucking mindlessly at a flower he held between his long fingers.

Frenchy was Exercise Man—unbothered.

A sophisticated, hiking cyborg that had probably done this trail a million times. But, he had to keep stopping because his zombie herd needed attention. Every time he pulled over, his forehead wrinkled into a million speed bumps.

"Pfffffffff…" he mocked.

He propped his hand on his bony hip while he waited, not so patiently.

Gareth and I stuttered to a stop behind him.

"You guys go ahead," he said.

"Really? Is it a clear path the whole way up?" Gareth asked, tightening his pack straps and glancing up-trail.

"Yeah. Just stick to it until you get to a heavy, cable zip-line. Wait there. We'll get caught up….eventually," Frenchy sighed.

He stared down the trail at a couple that had pulled over mid-track and removed their shoes and socks. The male stared into the empty hole where his foot used to be, and then he sniffed it.

"Jeeeee-sus," Frenchy exhaled.

It was time for us to bust move.

"Ta," Gareth said, moving beyond the train wreck and nodding for me to follow.

Leaving the group was the best decision ever. Without them, we were able to fully absorb nature. Human noises were replaced with a jungle soundtrack—insect hubbub, bird squawks, and frond rustles.

Gareth powered up the umber pathway. Mud imprints squished into place with every flip-flopped step. Being a Kiwi, he refused any shoe except the flip-flop—a.k.a. the jandal. If he wasn't in jandals he wore no shoes at all.

That was Gareth. He was built for the outdoors and not for cubicles. He once told me that he thought he'd been born in the wrong era. His struggles were always twenty-first century based, and I believed him when he said that, if the apocalypse ever rained down and we had to survive on a newly primitive planet, I had no better man. It was among our concrete castles and paved empires that he shriveled—calculating mortgages, organizing dinners, and caring about labels went against his DNA.

But, here in his element, he was shining. The jungle made him uber-sexy, and as his strong legs pumped lean muscles that forced sweat beads onto his shirtless, tanned back, I found myself getting jungle horny.

I was just getting ready to tell him what a hottie he was and make some corny "me-Jane, you-Tarzan" comment when I saw it.

There, on the path about seven feet ahead and perched on a low-hanging branch, was a goddamn monkey.

XXX

I know monkeys.

I heart monkeys.

I'd seen monkeys in the wild before, but they were always in large numbers—trooped up.

That was one type of sighting I'd had, the fun sighting. The other was on guided tours where someone in a khaki-colored shirt and pith helmet would stop, point, and yell "monkey!" before whipping out a pair of oversized binoculars and scientifically describing the furry primate. That type of sighting was the sterile, nature experience. I'd also seen zoo monkeys, the worst type of sighting.

This furry guy didn't fall into any of those categories. We met him balls-deep in HIS jungle, up close and personal, where his squished-up monkey face mugged us down hard.

We were the interlopers. And, at only a few feet away, I could tell he wasn't just any monkey.

He looked like he'd just gotten a blowout at the salon and had a facial the night before. This monkey was dashing and marvelous. He was huggable and squeezable, with puffy caramel-colored fur and pink cheeks. And, like the polite monkey he was, full of etiquette and class, he just sat on the end of the branch staring at us. He didn't give away a nano-inch of muscle twitch.

My husband hadn't seen him yet. He was marching ahead like a professional trooper, and I wasn't about to let him ruin my Kodak moment.

"Gareth. Gaarreeethhhh...." I whisper shouted. "Heyyyyy! Pssssstttt!"

Gareth stopped and turned back to me slack jawed, "Wha?"

"T h e r e issss a m o n k a yyyy," I mouthed, pointing up the path in front of him.

I over exaggerated my movements, like a Disneyland animatronic in *Great Moments with Mr. Lincoln*. I was practically drooling happy juice. My cheeks burned from smiling so big and I felt like I might pee a little— just a squirt or two.

Gareth turned in slow motion to trace the invisible line from my fingertip into the distance.

"Ooooohhhhh," he said, still facing the furry critter. "Oh! Pretty boy."

Gareth slowly turned back to me grinning. Now we both were shitting ourselves with joy. The monkey just sat and stared, apparently way too cool to blow a load over a couple of humans. We were his paparazzi—annoying, featherless vultures hovering and making a big deal about his cuteness. He wasn't amused. Stone cold stare—a furry statue on a branch.

"You've got to get a picture," I hushed, trying to unzip the outer pocket of my backpack without scaring the monkey away.

"Pass me the camera," Gareth spoke gently.

I finger crawled into my pocket for what seemed like decades before I finally found my camera. Stealthy and foxlike, I pulled it out without the slightest disruption and took weightless magician steps toward Gareth. I cleanly passed the camera into his outstretched hand. The transaction was complete.

"K. Okay...eeeaaaassssyyy" I whispered, backing up.

I stopped and stood. Waited. No breath.

In the quiet, the spicy scent of damp wood and heated vegetation took over.

"Steady," I mouthed.

Gareth raised the camera to almost eye height. His hand was stable. His finger was ready on the button, but just before he reached picture-perfect level, he realized that the power wasn't on.

"Damn," I heard him mutter as he raised his other hand with the smoothness of a Tai Chi master up to the top of the camera where the ON button lived, switching his attention from monkey to camera for just a tiny second.

And that was all the monkey needed.

Little fuzzy nuts were no longer statuesque. Instead, he too was moving like a Tai Chi master, crouching lower and lower on his branch until he was in the perfect pounce position. His legs flexed into maximum jumping angle and his eyes slanted into horizontal lines, zeroed in on Gareth like he was a giant, greasy banana.

"Um..." was all I got out.

The monkey swan dived.

He was a sleek machine in the air. Even his fur looked superhero-ish.

Gareth, the poor guy, never saw it coming. His concentration was still on the camera, but he knew he'd missed his photo op when the monkey landed squarely on his face.

"Eeeeeeek!" Gareth screamed like a girl—not his finest moment.

He swatted and stumbled backwards off the path and into the bushes. The weed-whacking commotion lit up the jungle as he ripped through roots and tore through leaves. He was shredding in the name of fear.

"Shit! Sh-sh-sh-shit!" he stuttered, flailing and wind-milling his arms, attempting to regain his balance.

Meanwhile, back at witness central, I was cracking up and backing away from the scene, bent over in hysterics while trying to pay attention to the monkey's next move. I didn't want him to get any funny ideas or get offended at my amusement.

"Bahhhhhhhh! Hahahahahahah! That monkey velcroed himself to your face," I laughed.

"Fuck off!" Gareth yelled back.

He climbed out of the thick bush and I went to give him a helping hand. That's when, out of my peripheral vision, I saw a brown ball hopping toward me with its back arched. I SWEAR it was smiling. The monkey was all swagger.

"Gareth?" I choked, backing down the trail.

The quicker I backed up the faster that damn monkey bounced toward me.

I quit laughing—fun time was turning on me.

"Charlie!" a voice yelled from behind me.

I froze, my lungs immobile in a ballooned state.

Frenchy waltzed up and snapped his fingers, and the wild monkey became instantly not so wild. It scooted right past me and took two more steps before spring-boarding off Frenchy's knee up to his shoulder. He sat down like it was a La-Z-Boy recliner.

"Excellent," Frenchy said, patting the monkey like it had just finished a highly informative PowerPoint presentation.

Frenchy walked right past us. Normal. Nothing to see here.

The monkey chilled on his trapezius. Through his still perfect fur and puckered raspberry lips, he pulled back his upper lip and flashed a nice pair of teeth as he rode his human-limo right past us.

"Bastard," I hissed.

"Hey, why don't monkeys play cards in the jungle?" Gareth asked, moving next to me and with his recovered camera and pride.

"What?" I asked, still trying to process what had just happened.

"You don't understand the question?" Gareth asked.

"No, I understand the question. I don't understand the…never mind. Why? Why don't they play cards in the jungle?"

"Because of all the cheetahs."

"I'm sure," I said.

XXX

We caught up with Frenchy.

"Are there cheetahs in this jungle, and do you know that beast?" I asked him, pointing to the monkey that snuggled into his shoulder.

"Yes," he responded flatly.

We'd made it to the top of the mountain and to the zip-line—the beginning of it all. My senses were attached to light sockets—arm hair erect, pupils dilated, and nose huffing everything from grass blades to wisps of clouds that had fallen from the clear sky onto the side of the mountain. They cradled the scent of summer rain and I inhaled a massive bucket of it into my lungs. It was fresh—the kind of oxygen made for flawless sleeps and enhanced synapsis firing.

"This is it," Frenchy announced, unsnapping his backpack straps and waving an outstretched arm over the valley below us like Vanna White showing off the evening's final puzzle.

Monkey jumped off his shoulder and ran up a tree. A questionable cable ran from where we stood out over a deep valley of rain forest and into the far distance, ending at a tree house.

"Pretty much what you wanted, babe?" Gareth asked wrapping an arm around my waist.

My words caught in my throat. I was staring at my dream. It wasn't just a "rope course" or a "tree top adventure" like you read about these days. This was original. It was raw, rugged, you might die, but it would be totally worth it type of experience—a home built by Peter Pan's wild boys in Neverland.

Beyond our tree top homes, what we'd really paid for still awaited.

The *pièce de résistance* was yet to come.

The valley was ours. It stretched its green fingers out into the distance further than any reminders of urban life. No lights. No roads. It was pure jungle, and the lack of tourism attached to this experience was unbeatable.

The area was absent of colorful billboards, snazzy wiring, telephone posts reinforced by metal platforms, and other things you would expect with such an endeavor. Instead, our whole weekend among the trees was only identifiable through the pale faces of the group members.

The tour was that camouflaged.

For anyone who didn't know better, we would have appeared to be a bunch of idiots who had wandered into the wilderness unprepared and totally screwed. But with closer inspection, if you zoomed in real tight, you'd see the quiet harnesses, the black metal line spanning the tree-filled gulf, and finally, the ultimate tree house hidden in the canopies.

"Okay everybody. This is your harness and your hardhat. You clip this on like this. You keep that buckled like that. You move here, and then you..."

Frenchy's speech was well rehearsed and lacked the enthusiasm that radiated off our anxious bodies, but his information was thorough. He admitted that he'd made all the cabling himself. He'd built the tree houses. This was his shit—top to tail. I stared at him, somehow confident in his abilities.

He said he'd never had an accident out there and that his plan was to keep it that way. This guy, the way he held himself and everything about the way he lived, it screamed INTENTION. He just wasn't the type of human to not take stuff seriously, and even if he wanted to slack off a bit, his ego wouldn't allow it. This was his baby. His baby was safe. While we played with his baby, we would be safe too.

"Like I explained earlier, you've been put into groups—five to each house. You'll stay the first two nights in one house and then rotate to a new house. But remember, this is not YOUR house. These tree houses are all part of the experience. I welcome and encourage you to move around to each house during your time here. Zip over to the neighbors. Say hi. Be friendly and courteous. We'll go through the rest of the information once we get to the main house."

His pointer-finger stretched out toward the cloaked tree house on the other side of the valley. When the wind blew just right, you could catch a glimpse of the roof corner thatch jutting out of the bark.

While Frenchy talked some more about the gear, I glanced down the path we'd come from. The monkey was back. He sat disinterested in the middle of the dirt. His eyes, shiny black circles that darted side to side and up and down, finally met my gaze.

XXX

"Hi, asshole," I mouthed.

He read my thoughts. It was like he knew that I thought what he did earlier was funny but not really cool, because it was kind of a tool-bag move to make my husband look pussified during our honeymoon. So, to make up for it, monkey carefully made his way over to my leg and started touching it soft enough to lull me into a trance.

"Monkeyyyy," I mumbled through a melting smile. "You flirting?"

He rubbed deeper into my leg as if to say, "Guuurrrllll you know it's true."

And he was just warming up. Rico Suave seemed like he really wanted to make up for his earlier escape from Mannersville, so he transitioned from a little leg rubsy straight to jumping onto my shoulder and grooming me.

"Ah….ahhhhhhh…." I moaned, totally forgetting that maybe this was weird or that I had an audience.

I closed my eyes and drifted into a place where only tender, monkey fingers can take you. This monkey was the massage king. He was Scalp Master. Follicle Fondler. It felt sooooo damn good.

"He's finding bugs in your hair," Gareth commented from my left.

I jolted upright, planets for eyes. *Nothing to see here. No monkey massage happening.*

"What? Eh?" I asked.

"I said he's finding bugs in your hair. He's eating them too."

"WHAT? That's crazy," I argued.

I was confident that there were no bugs in my hair. Plus, if there were, I was totally cool with using this monkey to get them out.

"He's just giving me a rubdown. That's all," I said.

"Look," Gareth said, raising the camera to my face and pushing the play button so I could see the video he'd just taken.

So, while sitting there with Monkey on my head, I watched a video of him picking at my hair and eating pretend insects. In the video, Monkey concentrated hard on my scalp, separating each hair strand and bending closer to the follicle to get a real good look at my imaginary ticks and fleas. And then, his pupils would bulge and he'd snatch the invisible tiny bugs with his miniature flanges and gobble each imaginary one. He'd pop that little mouthful of nothingness straight between his teeth and chew away while he searched for his next fantasy victim. He was imaginary grooming me—it was a bonding mechanism.

I grinned. Monkey's tiny digits continued toiling away while Gareth returned the camera to his backpack. He was less impressed than I was, so I purposely moaned too loud, tilting my head back to give it that nice strangled-duck sound.

"Oooooh yeah baby, that's the stuff. I loooovvvee it. Ohhhh it's sooo damn good!"

I peeped at Gareth to check his reaction. His stare was the same one I give my mom when she tells me five times a year (like it's the first time she's ever told me) that she thinks eighteen wheeler trucks should have their own driving lane, "Just like in New Jersey! They need their own lane those trucks." She always says it in a mom voice and accentuates it with a wagging forefinger. Every time.

I shut my eyes to Gareth's threadbare, monkey-massage tolerance.

"You're just peanut butter and jealous. You wish you had a monkey eating nonexistent bugs off your scalp—hater. Ya know, this actually feels so good that I'd pay to have him eat crap off my skull every day after work if I could. Seriously. Don't dis it 'til you try it."

Gareth shrugged in disdain.

"That's not weird, babe. I'd pay a monkey to do lots of things for me if I knew where to hire one. I'd hire one to do my laundry, and bills, and…"

"Alright! Let's go." The shout from our guide interrupted his list of monkey chores.

Monkey knew the drill. He was gone before I could thank him for my Swedish kneading. His fuzzy hindquarters bounced into a bundle of overhanging ferns and disappeared. I waved a Queen's goodbye— fingers pressed together with a palm screwing in a light bulb.

"Tootles," I mouthed, missing him already.

I swiped at a bubble of gnats and stood up.

"Can I go first?" I asked, moving in front of Gareth.

"Sure, babe. Make sure you check everything," he encouraged.

"K."

I stepped squeaky tennis shoes onto the makeshift wooden platform and attached myself to the thick cable above my head. It felt oily, slimed with jungle condensation. I checked the leather straps, the loops, the wire, and metal—twice. A bird squawked from somewhere deep in the canopy saying, "Hey Tony, here goes another weird-ass flying human. So strange…"

XXX

I memorized the green trench before I launched.

This was soooooo not a touristy zip line you read about in *Travel Magazine*. It was Roald Dahl's version of zip lining—a hallucinogenic idea that turned into a cable adventure. It was the NoDoz face slap and Red Bull nightcap rope course gone wild—boobs out, tequila body shots, testosterone fistfights, slobber, and sweat.

We were canopy high, and the tallest trees were nearly 200 feet tall, but we were also draped over a valley. We were very high up, and I was familiar with heights.

I'd stood on the edge of the Grand Canyon many times. I'd jumped out of a plane. I'd leaned my head against the top floor window of many skyscrapers, and stayed that way until my nerves quit doing the jitterbug. As a child, I basically lived on the roof of our two-story house, sneaking onto its questionable shingles just for fun. And when you're only four feet tall, a twenty-foot drop seems like an abyss.

But this was none of that.

This rope course wasn't any chump. It was wet palm, eye twitch, better trust your gear high.

"Sit down in it first to check your weight," Gareth coached some more.

"Hey-soos Christo, Gareth. Sfine. Have you not been watching everyone else? They're very much alive," I pointed to the people who'd already zipped across the valley.

They were ants moving about in the tree house in the distance.

"I'm not scared for you. I just want you to be smart," he said.

"Oh. You're the good decision checker, eh? Well, where were you that time I signed up for adult circus school so I could learn to do a backflip off a wall?" I asked.

"Ha! That's right. What was your Chinese instructor's name?" he laughed.

"Shaux Hung," I said, letting my gear take my full weight.

"Shaux Hung. Didn't he say you were too big to do a backflip off the wall?" Gareth dug.

"Actually, he said, 'You too fat. Backflip no good for you. You do cartwheel.' I liked that guy," I said.

"I like him too—without ever meeting him," Gareth said.

I gave my harness a little test bounce and smiled at Gareth. He winked back.

"See you on the other side," Gareth assured, giving me a strange bro-pat on the back.

"Break on through to the other side!" I yelled as I stood and jumped off the platform.

Wind in face.

Passing smudges of emerald and chocolate below.

Smile stretched to the point of snapping.

Feet dangling.

Freedom. Happiness. Childhood dream come true.

Flying.

XXX

"Ahhhhh ahh ahh (snort) ahh haaa haaa (snort snort) haaaaa!" I was laughing like a drunken pig as I came in hot to the platform at the awaiting tree house.

"Haha! Welcome!" a European boy shared my amusement, leaning in to stop my forward progress.

I jerked to a halt in his able arms.

"Thanks."

"You're most welcome."

He helped me get settled, unhooking my gear and gesturing toward the living room to the right.

There, in the tree house living room, everything had changed. Our crew—our non-talkative, kind of boring, and ungainly crew was awestruck. The zip drugs had set in. Flying had changed us, because suspended above the jungle and hanging out in a tree like our primate friends do, we could see things. We had a creature's view of our next three days, and it was fucking on.

This tree house in the middle of a real rainforest in Laos made Swiss Family Robinson look like a kindergarten art project made of elbow macaroni and pipe cleaners. This tree house was called *Le Gibbon Project*, and it was dazzling.

Three wooden stories—floors, stairs, and railings, all oiled to a shine. A rainbow of silky cushions decorated homemade furniture. There were bookshelves, tables, and teapots with matching pink teacups. It was truly a home in the trees, not just a half-ass shelter for stupid tourists.

And now that I was actually getting to spend the weekend in a better version of my childhood fantasy, I thought my heart might explode into a billion juicy fragments of sublime happiness.

I was over the moon. Thankful to be alive. Thuper exthited (using my stoked lisp). We huddled on the couches and floor like a shrewdness of apes. Frenchy shared another dialogue while pouring steamy liquid out of a large teapot and into assorted cups. His tone was melodic and soothing, his pace a slow waltz. He'd changed too—he was friendly, happy.

I was entranced.

"These tree houses have been built with attention to not only safety, but also comfort. The toilets, although not plumbed, have porcelain seats. For sleeping, there are padded mats, linen mosquito nets, layered platforms for better viewing, dividers for privacy, and other bits and pieces to help make your visit a nice one."

He passed the cups around. Each smelled of jasmine and was warm to the touch. Pillows of steam floated around us.

"Are all the tree houses like this?" an Australian boy with messy black hair asked.

"This is the nicest, but all of them are great. The others are just smaller, hence why I said before our hike that you'd get to know each other well. There's no time schedule here or planned trips. You eat when you want. Just tell one of the workers when you're hungry. All the food is cooked down in the jungle, and then brought to you."

He patted the sleek railing, took a deep breath, and continued.

"The guides are here to take you on walks around the jungle too, if that's what you want to do. NO FIRE in any of the houses. If you smoke, you smoke on the ground and keep your butts in a baggy to hike out with. If you need a baggy, ask the guides. Zip back and forth between all the houses as much as you want," he said, pointing at the cables. "Consider all the houses as one. You're staying in all of them. No doors. No locks. Zip at will. Any questions?"

Heads shook.

"Great. Let's get you going then."

Frenchy reached into his pocket and produced a folded piece of notebook paper.

"Okay, rooms. Tree house one: Danny, Cameron, Casey, Michael, and Luke. Tree house two: Gareth, Shelby, Craig, Angelika, and Helene. Tree house three…"

As he named off sleeping arrangements, Gareth stood and helped me up. I stretched my arms toward the thatched roof.

"Yay!" I whooped, enjoying the warm sting of muscle pulling away from bone.

"And here we are," Craig announced, walking up to us with a face of pure delight.

"Are you Gareth and Shelby?" a tall blonde girl asked, joining us.

Her accent was thick German—her eyes the color of winter lake.

"Yeah. Are you Craig?" I asked, grinning.

She stared at me unblinking.

"Sorry, I was just trying to break the ice. You must be Helene or Angelika."

"No, I'm Craig," she said, still unblinking and rigid.

I grinned.

"Helene. That's Angelika," she continued, without giving any credit to her joke.

She thumbed toward a short, brown-haired girl struggling with a pack as big as she was. "We're heading to the house. You coming?"

Helene was totally German. Blunt steel.

"Sure," I shrugged, glancing at Gareth who was staring at Helene like he was contemplating whether she was a zit or an infected hair.

Helene turned and walked off to gather her bags. She was packed down like a donkey, and Gareth shook his head as her spindly legs bent under the weight.

"Silly German," he whispered. Instead of pronouncing it *Jerman* with a "juh" sound, he pronounced it *German* with a "guh" sound, exactly like it's written. "Why are some Germans so boring, serious, bleckity blah. Helene seems like she's as much fun as polio."

"She made a joke...kinda...I think. Don't worry. Our roommates aren't the headliner of this trip. The goods are yet to come," I said.

In our new five-some, we took turns hooking up to yet another zip line. Then, without looking back, we zipped away from the first tree house in search of ours. We slipped deep into the overhang, getting the jungle funk stuck in our nostrils.

We were foaming at the mouth with exploration anticipation and excitement for dusk. That was when we thought they might come—the stars of the show.

But, first things always come first, and my stomach was brewing up something wicked.

XXX

"Babe, I need to use the bathroom," I whispered to Gareth.

"It's right up there," he answered, pointing to a wooden partition about five steps away from where we were all gathered in our tree house.

"Well….um…"

I was nervous about my ability to survive my bathroom break in ladylike silence. New food plus foreign cigarettes was threatening to cause a Death Star explosion.

He noticed my hesitation and gave me a reassuring elbow bump.

"Just go," he whispered. "It's cool."

This was the beginning of us getting more acquainted with our tree mates. We were small talking, nice-to-meet-you stuff, and unpacking.

Our tree house was nice—smaller, like Frenchy had promised, and less Swiss Family Robinson, while still beautiful and intriguing.

It was circular. Our "living room" curved into a little half-moon space meant for sleeping and relaxing. The other part of the tree house was two-steps up from sleeping level. It hosted the bathroom—a simple box featuring a toilet seat that opened to nothing but jungle air and a view of other treetops that looked miniature from height. It was the world's longest drop and every toilet-trainer's nightmare. A toddler's small bottom would slip right through and leave the poor child falling, flipping head over heels to the ground far below.

Back on the sleeping level where we were hanging out, a big wooden lock box sat off to the side. In it were the mats and mosquito nets. The two German girls rummaged through it in silence. I assumed Helene was looking for the best one to claim as her own.

"Grab us some sleeping mats while I think things over," I told Gareth through clenched teeth.

I waited, slightly hunched over with folded arms and a glistening temple. The wheel of decision spun in my head—*should I blow these strangers out, or not?* My manners wanted to keep private things private, while my digestive system wanted to publically release a butt tornado.

Gareth returned to my side carrying two decent-looking mats.

"Babe, for the love of God! You look like you're trying to solve an algorithm. Just go. Let it all hang out. No one cares," he said, tossing the mats out of the walk-space and onto the ground by our backpacks.

It was apparent that when he said no one cared, he included only himself in the count. He wasn't heartless, but he was easily bored and perplexed by my bodily function embarrassment.

Gareth was the kind of guy who walked around naked without notice, pausing occasionally in front of reflective surfaces to inspect himself for anything out of place—spreading this, lifting that, squeezing bits and pieces. He didn't care if strangers watched in horror or if his grandma was going into shock convulsions on the couch. To him, bodies were hunks of meat that released things, carried around organs, and vacillated between being clean and dirty.

That was it. No blushing cheeks or apologies for organic process. It was all part of being human. End of.

I heard him deep sigh as he sauntered over to the railing. The minute barrier that kept us from tumbling forty meters to the ground consisted of slatted timber and nail.

He leaned on it, gave it a firm shake and satisfactory eyebrow lift, and then gazed out into the distance—the view was killer. I might have enjoyed it more if I wasn't viewing it through a salty curtain of perspiration.

I tiptoed to his side.

"I can't do it," I abdicated. "I just can't. It would be like having a bad case of machine gun farts in a library. I'm not ready to take that step with these people," I hissed.

"Well, let's go into the jungle. You can dig a hole," Gareth suggested.

"YES! I can hold it 'til we get down there."

"You going into the rain forest?" Helene barged into our conversation.

She stood ready—hands on hips, pursed lips, daypack on, and with the first twinkle in her eye since we'd met her.

"I'd like to join you, please."

The "please" seemed like an afterthought, but her excitement was palpable. We couldn't say no.

"Okay. Sounds fun," I fibbed.

Then everyone got excited. It was a commotion of daypack loading and DEET spraying. Five minutes later we were all zipping out of our tree house and over to the main house where the local guides hung out. From there we descended to the forest floor where I immediately asked the guide where I could relieve myself.

Once the pressure was gone, I could absorb the reality of the murky jungle we'd landed in. It was awesome. Dense jungle. Raw landscape.

However, it was also something else.

CHAPTER 33

"Above. Above," our Laotian guide boy ordered us as we walked up to yet another river.

He wore an old blue t-shirt and cargo pants. He looked like he was out for an afternoon stroll to the corner store. The boy demonstrated what he wanted us to do, transitioning between holding his arms above his head and pointing to our daypacks.

"I guess it gets deep in the middle," Gareth reasoned.

No one lifted their pack above their head—yet. No one even moved. We were too busy staring down at the gurgling river that divided us from the waterfall we wanted to get to. It was obvious though—if we wanted the storybook waterfall and rain forest swim hole on the other side, the river had to be crossed.

"It has to be safe," I murmured, more for my own convincing than anyone else's.

The river burped brown bubbles.

"Come. Above!" the guide yelled, getting impatient.

Then, he was done waiting.

He trudged into the river, pumping muscular legs through the swirling current. He didn't take daddy steps one might use to step over a fallen log or avoid concealed boulders. It was a smooth, forward trudge. A current fight.

I was the first one in, following his cue and sliding my feet into the river. I wanted to be close to him. I figured this was his stomping ground, so I wanted his confident footprints to be filled with my doubtful ones.

My tennis shoes disappeared underneath the surface—visibility naught. The water was maroon syrup. It reminded me of Oklahoma floods.

Almost mid-river and obeying orders late in the game, I yanked my sweaty arms from my Dickies backpack, struggling to get free. I'd converted the mini-backpack from book carrier to an all-terrain everything carrier. I was happy it was playing along, and I was glad that it was so easy to lift above my head like I'd been told, because the water jumped quickly from my ankles to my thighs, and then straight to my bust.

"Careful, babe," Gareth encouraged from right behind me.

I got the feeling that he was trailing me less for reasons of luck and more out of concern for my footing. I'd been known to klutz my way through situations, a banged elbow here and good head ramming there. Even with my better than average athleticism, depth perception has always escaped and continues to escape my repertoire. If there's a rock ledge, it will make out with my forehead. My toes are constantly enticed by any edge built to stub.

Actually though, things were great in the river. The water was the perfect reprieve—not cold, not warm, but baby bear temperature. It felt great, and I glanced behind me to see what everyone else was doing.

Since landing, climbing down out of the canopies and onto the jungle floor, our group had been working as a singular unit—a military company marching with semi-sloppy cadence and sharp curiosity through the steamy forest. After awhile, we shared hiking sway and direction choices—everyone selecting the same stone for footing or stopping to investigate the same flower, taking turns inhaling the petal perfume.

We were getting more used to each other's presence, and by the time we reached the river, we were a comfortable lot. Crossing was just one more thing we did in unison, each person a copycat of the next. Same bag wrestling. Craig and the girls took equally careful footsteps to submerge their legs into the flow.

I smiled at the girls and at Craig. They didn't even notice. Their eyes were glued to the ripples rushing past.

"Ahh…ahh," I squeaked, losing my footing. "Shit!"

Because I was so focused on everyone else, I didn't realize how strong the water had gotten. It was weird. Although it blobbed across the surface, it hurried below, and the heavy rush against my now three-fourths submerged body was toying with me.

Luckily, it wasn't flowing at a full sprint that would take me down river and spit me out over a cliff edge, but nonetheless, it wasn't messing around. It could lift me off my feet if it wanted. Just one strong nudge and WHOOSH.

"It's okay. Just hold still. Find your footing," Gareth said, grabbing ahold of my arm to steady me.

"Shit…um, guys be careful. The water is pretty strong here!" I yelled back behind me.

"I don't think I can…" Helene's voice trailed off.

Gareth and I stopped mid-river and looked back. She was all frail limbs and bulky backpack. Teetering. A baby learning to walk. It wasn't looking good.

"Gareth, go get her," I said.

Our guide was already on the other shore, but he re-entered the river, hurrying through the current to help Gareth with the wobbly girl. Then the rest of us continued through the water, silent but wrought with tension.

"Thank you, thank you," Helene acknowledged the guide and Gareth, letting the guide take her bag off her shaky arms so she could navigate the water better. She latched to Gareth's arm like he was a lifeboat.

"Whew! That was intense," I laughed, climbing onto the opposite bank with my daypack still above my head.

I shook my legs out and ran wet fingers over my sweaty brow.

"It was stronger than I imagined," Craig said, wringing out his shirt.

"That was crazy," Helene said, taking heavy steps out of the water, still clutching Gareth's arm. "I didn't think it would be moving that fast."

"Rivers are devious that way," Angelika added.

We regrouped and re-shouldered our packs. It was the first time I'd heard much out of Angelika, the quieter of the German duo. I liked her choice of words—"devious". I was impressed she knew the word "devious" in English.

Learning Spanish, I was always fascinated by what words I picked up and what words I didn't. Juggling Angelika's use of "devious" around in my mind, I wondered if I knew the same word in Spanish. A few lazy memory cells tried to find the answer, then rolled over and died. I didn't know it, but then I remembered that I did know the word for "Smurf" and I felt the urge to tell her.

Pitufo—Smurf in Spanish.

"Hey Angelika, what's the word for Smurf in German?" I asked.

"Smurf?" she asked awkwardly, like the word couldn't possibly be real in any language.

"Yeah, Smurf. You know, little blue guys? White hat. White pants. No shirt. I know you have them in Germany because I saw them. I was at a knick-knack store in Berlin and they had some figurines there."

"Knick-knack?"

"I'm totally destroying this conversation, eh? Conversation King Kong," I said, waving my arms above my head gorilla style.

She let a grin creep into the side of her mouth.

I was fairly certain that she didn't know what King Kong was either, but at this point I was smart enough not to dig. At least we were all talking, getting calm with each other's company.

"Smurf..." Angelika muttered, then said something in German to Helene.

We trekked forward, passing sprigs of fuzzy bushes and girthy tree trunks being strangled by vines. We walked in a rectangle formation—

Craig and the Laotian guide in the lead. Angelika and I held the middle, and Gareth and Helene tramped in back.

I was just thinking how cool it was to be sharing this with people who would become weekend family when Helene decided to go ahead and fully break the ice with a four hundred ton sledgehammer.

XXX

"Oh my God! Shit! What is it?" Helene screamed.

We stopped mid-hike, turning around to inspect the commotion. Helene was ripping her daypack off her body. She grunted and squealed against her rushed hands, finally flinging her pack into the dirt with a panicked scream.

"What's is it?" Angelika worried, moving cautiously toward her freaked out friend.

The rest of us were cemented in place.

Helene ripped at her shirt. "There's something on me! There's something…shit! What is it? Please! WHAT IS IT?!"

My stomach tightened.

Helene lifted her wet t-shirt to expose her bare back.

Attached to it were five black leeches—juicy, swollen with her blood.

"Holy shit!" said Gareth.

He rushed to her, ripping the fat worms from her skin. They vacuumed to her back, making her epidermis pull out from her skeleton in little triangles as he pulled each one free. A leftover pink and bleeding circle of suction remained. She was polka-dotted with suck spots.

"What is it? Tell me! What is it?" Helene screamed.

"Leeches," Gareth announced, removing a handful of bloodsuckers in one swoop.

"What? WHAT THE FUCK!"

Helene turned to face Gareth, her eyes spinning kaleidoscopes. She pulled her shorts down, mooning him. "Are there more? TELL ME!"

Gareth pulled two from her right butt cheek.

Then, no hesitation, she stripped buck-naked, ripping every black hump off her skin she could find, and there were a lot to find.

Instantaneously, our group began a reenactment of *Stand by Me*.

Bags flew.

Shirts arced through the air.

Shorts ripped off bodies and pig squeals seeped through grimaced mouths.

Three seconds later, the five of us stood—basically naked—in the middle of the jungle, pulling our butt cheeks apart and screaming at everyone to look at us—inspect us.

Our guide was still dressed. He'd casually rid his body of the segmented worms with calm fingers and a half smile, seemingly happy to watch us whiteys flip out and get nude.

We stared at each other. Panting and shaken. Vulnerable animals.

"Leeches," our guide said through a perma-grin.

CHAPTER 34

"That was insane," Craig laughed.

"I know! Helene, I'll never forget the look on your face! Fuck! You were flipping out!" Angelika joked.

"I don't even care. How was I supposed to be calm anyway? A worm was sucking blood out of my ass," Helene defended between mouthfuls of white rice.

"You weren't supposed to be calm. You handled it right. I'm just happy no one had one in a more private place, you know, like real *Stand by Me* stuff—the infamous tighty-whities leech," I added, wiping my hands on the square piece of burlap we'd each been given as a napkin.

"That's right! Oh man. I forgot about that movie. Have you guys seen it?" Gareth asked.

He reclined into a pillow he'd propped against the railing of our tree house. The plum sky and hunter green canopy back dropped his features. The jungle made him hotter. We exchanged smiles.

"Yes. That's a classic movie!" Craig laughed.

"Isn't that the one with the mean dog that bites balls?" asked Helene.

"Chopper—sick balls," I growled.

We all laughed, talked some more about our favorite classics, and drank cool water out of our bottles that had been kindly refilled by our guide.

Back in our tree home, we lounged on floor mats and enjoyed a nice dinner of spiced chicken, sticky rice, water spinach, and pineapple chunks. Ginger and garlic steam billowed from the circular bamboo dishes. The striking fragrance accentuated the pink tone that was swallowing the skyline.

As dusk set in, we exchanged stories that were more flesh and blood than plastic and facades.

Helene told us of her recent break up.

Craig admitted his travel faux pas of not putting his liquids in a sealed baggie when flying. When he got to Thailand, his economy-sized shampoo bottle meant to last him four months had exploded all over his clothes and electronics.

I talked to them about how I broke my leg sledding.

Angelika told us that she grew up in the deep country of Germany. Her parents never allowed her to watch television, or any screen for that matter. Never a movie, never a show—only books and music. She stuck to their strange rule like a good kid—never viewing anything, even when tempted by friends. But, when she became a rebellious pre-teen, she finally watched a cartoon for the first time in her life. She watched *Alice in Wonderland* at a friend's house, and it freaked her the fuck out.

"I don't know what the hell a Smurf is. I didn't want to tell you earlier about my non-existent relationship with television. TV still scares me. I'll admit it now, since you've seen my boobs and ass," she said.

We all discussed how we had found out about the secret adventure in the trees, considering it wasn't advertised. You had to be in the know. We'd all gotten there through close friends, and we all agreed to only pass the information on to someone who would fully appreciate it. It wasn't something to go around talking about haphazardly, for any old nimrod to take advantage of. We wanted to protect it.

We relaxed with full bellies. When the sky went a soft shade of purple, others joined our conversation—the jungle critters. Dusk made them less shy. Gareth found a walking stick insect that was longer than his hand. It was chilling out on the roof, minding its own business. We stared at it for fifteen minutes, gossiping about its size. A furry, part-opossum/part-squirrel looking thing scurried past our food box looking for leftovers.

And the air was full of pandemonium.

All of the insects in the jungle were going to bed at the same time, buzzing a chorus of "goodnight" that was so loud we eventually had to raise our voices just to hear each other's words. We waited with baited breath for them to calm down and for something else—this was the time of day we'd come for. Dusk was supposed to bring the heart of our adventure, but instead…nothing happened.

Light purple went to dark purple, and then to black. Then it was our bedtime.

"Goodnight, guys," I said from my pallet on the floor next to Gareth.

"Goodnight," said Craig.

"Sleep well," said Angelika.

"See everyone in the morning," said Helene.

Even though it was still hot outside, Gareth and I had acclimated enough to want the clean, thin sheet the tree house provided in the sleep kit. We spread it over our curled bodies. A giant mosquito net draped from the ceiling over our all five of us. Our group relaxed into sleep in our home in the sky.

It was one of the best sleeps of my life, and then right before dawn…they came.

XXX

"Wake up, babe!" Gareth pestered.

He was rocking me gently at first and then aggressively.

"What?" I croaked.

Parched throat. Muddled morning brain.

"Get up. They're here," he said in a hushed tone.

I shot up. It was still dark outside and I blinked against the haze. I could smell night jungle, clammy and steamy. I tried to help my eyes get going, rubbing the glue out of the corners and jostling the lids.

I blinked again—vision clearer.

That's when I realized I was wrong. It wasn't exactly dark outside. It was dark, but there was the tiniest amount of light breaking through the black—fuzzy sunrays and moon shadows all mixed together.

"Where's the camera?" Gareth asked, moving away from me.

His attention was focused over the banister.

"Shhhh," Helene hissed.

She, Craig, Gareth, and Angelika had lined up together opposite of where I sat, staring into distance.

"Did you hear that?" Helene asked.

And then we all heard it. They'd started.

At first it was a faraway howl. Then it moved into a closer, deep moan. The call sounded singular, but it changed quickly.

It swelled.

I leaned over and pulled my camera from my backpack, found my feet, and stood. I stumbled over to the others, passing the camera into Gareth's extended hand.

The noise grew.

Oooooooooooo-ew-ew-ew-ew. Wuhhhhhh-ew-ew. Ewwwwww-oooop.
Ooooooooooooo-wop-wop-wop. Burrrrrrrrrrrr-ew-ew.

Then we saw them—a family of gibbons.

At first they were black dots in the distant canopy that vanished just as quickly as they appeared, but then they got clearer—bigger. Their fur gained distinct edges. Their black eyes squinted, and with expansive arms gymnastically flexed, they flew from branch to branch, swinging straight for us.

"Oh my God. They're coming this way!" Angelika squealed.

And they were HUGE. We all instinctively stepped back as twenty or more apes encroached and finally enveloped our tree house. Their cries vibrated our eardrums as their muscular bodies swung past. They were right there…just feet from us. All of us in the dawn lit treetops.

That sound is forever burned into my brain. I want to describe the moment as extraterrestrial, a galactic echo of barks that I could only relate to a sci-fi movie, but that's not quite right. It was…animal orchestra—a raw medley of notes that came from a time before houses, roads, or electricity. Old growth music—a primate composition of the most guttural bass beat. It was sooooo loud, like surround sound at the movies. We couldn't hear anything but the screaming gibbons.

With shallow breathing and my heart banging a staccato onto my rib cage, I tried so hard to make the moment last, but it was too short. The great ones always are. It was there and then gone, probably just how it should be.

A couple of days later, we left the jungle smiling, thankful, and thrilled. The money we paid to stay in those tree houses, the Laotian rainforest, and the area the gibbons used as their highway / playground / neighborhood—that price was too low. Our gibbon adventure exploded expectations. What we experienced…it was as if we were part of their tree-dwelling family. *Le Gibbon Experience* was priceless.

Magical.

Secret.

Our magical, secret adventure.

*Note: The Laos Gibbon adventure is no longer a secret. It now has a website, write-ups, and all the information needed to visit. This is why I say hurry and find the adventures that still don't have these things—because they will. Soon, everything will be digitally available for booking.

PART VI

"There are more good people than bad people, and overall there's
more that's good in the world than there is that's bad.
We just need to hear about it. We just need to see it."
Tucker Elliot

Long-term Travel Possible Gain List

1. THAT story. The one that's too crazy to be true. The one that blows minds, even your own.
2. International work experience.
3. An island life.
4. New ways of thinking.
5. A movie-like adventure.
6. Unexpected friends and allies.
7.

Long-Term Travel Possible Loss List

1. Your naivety.
2. Confusion about what you really want to do with your work life.
3. Weight.
4. The urge to surrender to fear.
5. Disbelief in magic.
6. Suspicion of strangers.
7.

Stranger Engagement

CHAPTER 35

We all have tenders spots of vulnerability—some more than others. The point is that no one is immune to needing help.

Life is muddy.

Sometimes you don't have the right cleaning products, rags, or physical capability to wash the mess off your boots, but your friend might...or the lady down the block who you've never talked to.

Life's messes are varied. Maybe it was a heavy argument with a loved one that put you in need of a good listener. Maybe it was that one last egg your chocolate chip recipe called for that you didn't have in the fridge, or maybe your back tire flattened—and there you were in the middle of no man's land with your trunk spare bare.

From the mundane to the severe, human lives call for help over and over again. None of us have gotten to where we are without it, but there's something odd about that truth. The oddity is that, nowadays, it seems like people don't believe it. Each accomplishment and burden is first pinned to the individual. We do it on our own—each man to himself. Each state to its own borders. Our country is self-sufficient and able to survive solo, in most situations.

But it's just not true. Somebody always assists you at some point in your daily life, in your national life, and in your world existence. If you understand globalization and food sourcing, then you understand that the modern world depends on shared and accessible space. We work together—all the time—whether you realize it or not.

Humans are naturally linked, and we actually enjoy serving each other. It brings a deep, biological satisfaction.

We are compassionate creatures.

Most hearts are good.

Helping is instinctual.

But, the world we live in now does not serve instinct. It has been shaped into something quite different. Now, humans assume each other to be rough, deceitful, thieving, and dangerous—especially strangers.

How could we have forgotten the goodness? What caused this stain on the reputation of mankind?

Maybe it's the news, with its piles of negative information and Rolodex of scare tactics. It could be that, or maybe people don't know how to interact anymore because human exchanges have been replaced by virtual smiles, pokes, status updates, and check-ins. Text me, don't call me. Stare at your phone, not at the person across the table. Maybe it's that people get burned, shocked, and disappointed so many times that they eventually narrow their circle to only those who've passed the long-haul friendship test with minor to no offenses. It's emotionally safer that way.

It could be a comfort thing too. Daily activities get repeated with the same, comfortable group of people until anyone outside of the parameters starts looking funny. Outliers become worrisome, bothersome—up to no good and worth less than a glance. Maybe it's a mixture of all those things, or maybe it's none of them at all. I don't know.

I have no clue why a lot of people are so scared of strangers, but I do know that I'm right about those people being wrong. Most strangers are not scary, mean, or yucky. They're good.

When was the last time you knocked on your unknown neighbor's door and asked if he or she had a level you could borrow? Have you tripped and fallen down in a busy, public place lately? Ever asked the person behind you in line for a dollar when you came up short, or did you just walk away from your miscalculated grocery items? If you haven't engaged with strangers lately, then you wouldn't know that, most likely, they will help you.

For me, venturing into different cultures and is what eventually changed the way I look at humans. Because of travel, I cannot be swayed from my belief that we are decent.

I know we are.

We are flesh, muscle, bone—happiness, sadness, and a rainbow of other emotions.

You can trust your fellow human…most of the time.

Trust me.

CHAPTER 36

In Amurrica, you learn early to be wary of the mustached man in the white van, offering you delicately wrapped candies, because he's a stranger—the one who thinks the uses of duct tape drift more toward the human binding realm than the DIY home improvement world. Beware of Chester the Molester and his brother Sleezy Scott—"Here, whiff this and tell me if it smells like chloroform."

As a child, I wasn't suspicious of humans until I realized that I needed to be, which was basically around first grade, when everyone started telling me I had to be.

At about age six, adults started telling me that strangers wanted to steal me. It was imperative that I understood that these strange people, mostly men, did not want my Barbie or my new Miss Piggy flip-flops, or my bologna and Velveeta sandwich on Wonder Bread, or even a polite conversation about my pony named Rubber Ducky. No, they wanted me.

Even my friends swore that every car that crept by was most likely waiting for the correct moment to throw a giant child-catching net over the five of us that gathered for an impromptu game of Four Square.

So, if at first hesitant to believe the evilness of my fellow humans, I slowly accepted the fact of their wicked ways and steadily began believing that any man standing near a playground was one minute away from getting his penis out and poking it through the fence. I knew this because of the tidal wave of similar stranger-danger information circulating around me. Tons of people said to watch out for strangers.

Teachers told me, and my parents, and their friends, my friends, and the old lady behind the counter at *Woolworth's*, the dying drug store that had one of those old fashioned diners in the back.

"Run along, and watch out for strangers, ya here? They'll git-cha," she'd harass through wobbly dentures while handing me the best chocolate milkshake ever.

She'd waddle off in her pink uniform, waving a gnarled hook-of-a-hand goodbye, and continue her day as if she hadn't just joked about kidnapping. I thought her sense of humor sucked—riding in the trunk instead of the backseat is not fun or funny.

Then stranger-danger got confusing. People switched from being serious about it to joking, and then to wanting me to talk to strangers, and finally getting mad when I was timid to do so.

"Go ask him! Be polite. Just say, 'Excuse me sir, but do you have change for a dollar?'" my brother would urge.

I was getting stranger whiplash from wavering between being encouraged to go up and be civil, and then being told not speak to them at all. They'd tell me to run in the other direction yelling, "Help! This man is not my father!" if one ever got too close.

Why was it okay to chat with strangers if other adults were around, but not if I was alone? It was as if strangers grew fangs and an appetite for sautéed child brains if no other adults were within earshot. Otherwise, they just wanted to give you a push on the merry-go-round or hold a too-heavy door open for you.

It was all crooked. Then I started thinking.

Who do you trust, when and where? How does a stranger become a friend? Is there a friend-screening company that makes sure it's okay to talk to people? Are people only good when lots of people are watching?

My thirst for an answer became insatiable. As I got older, I realized the lesson of stranger-danger had leaked into adult corners.

Lock everything.

Don't jog after dark.

You might want to buy a gun.

Only crack your car window an inch if someone comes up, knocks on it, and wants to talk to you.

The woman at the market is lying about how much she can drop the price of her avocados.

Everyone is on the take.

Beware. Evil, sinister people are everywhere.

So, when I first decided to go overseas by myself I was nervous, but I didn't talk about my worries, and I never admitted them.

I just said, "I can figure it out," and, "It will be fine."

Those sentences were my mantras, and I believed them as strongly as I believe in the sun rising in the east. I knew there were reasons to be afraid of the journey I was embarking on, but somehow my youthful brain also knew that if I encouraged those thoughts—if I invested in them enough and placed all my chips onto one big, worry square marked "trip terrors"—I would never get on the plane.

So, I took deep breaths and repeated my mantras when asked if I was nervous or scared to travel the world alone.

No, I'm not scared. I'm excited. It will be fine. I'll figure it out. I'm excited.

But, those who questioned my travels were relentless. They sunk their ideals into my tender flesh, presumably looking for thin-walled veins to penetrate and bleed me dry of my courage.

"But, you don't know anyone there, right?" the person would asked, perplexed.

"No."

"So, how are you going to get a job?" the person would ask, more perplexed.

"I don't know, but I'll figure it out."

"Innn-terrr-resttt-ing. Where are you going to stay?" the person would ask, with a sneer creeping into the corner of her mouth.

"I don't know yet. I have a bed in a hostel dorm room for the first two nights."

"But, how are you going to get around?" the person would ask, with a full-blown grin—the kind reserved for idiots.

"Probably buses or walking. Maybe I'll get a car."

"Hmmm. Is it dangerous where you're going? Safety first," the person would say, faking concern.

"No, I don't think it's dangerous. I mean…yeah. It's probably dangerous in the wrong areas, just like here."

And that's when the person would purse dubious lips. My ideas were sour grapes to the palate. Too many *I don't knows*. It was as though I was telling them about the work visa I'd bought for Rape Town with a fully-inclusive murder package.

"Well, be careful. People are crazy out there," the person would say, ending the conversation on a low note.

I would sulk away, repeating my mantra in my head until it was a shriek.

I'm not scared. I'm excited. IT WILL BE FINE. I'LL FIGURE IT OUT. I'M EXCITED, NOT SCARED.

And I'd add, *fuck off parade-rainer*, as the final thought. I thought it gave a nice and needed ring.

XXX

With my American distrust strapped firmly to my back and my vulnerable, weak, little vagina and boobs leading me into sure demise, I cranked my survival instinct up to eleven.

I departed American soil, ready to conquer the mean streets of the world. The brass balls I'd developed growing up on Oklahoman red dirt would turn to steel and grow in circumference as soon as I landed in foreign territory. I just knew it.

I needed to be able to sniff out a meanie. They always wear an acid cloud that reeks of lies. I hoped my keen sniffer traveled with me.

I was pretty sure my time overseas promised to take me to Cambodia, Ecuador, and many other places where I thought striking up a conversation with good ole' what's his face would not be the same as having a chat in line for the ladies room at *Mulligans Bar and Grill*. And I had to keep in mind that this was a solo voyage. There would be no plopping down on Emily's couch to tell her about the pervert who

grabbed my tit on the subway, her buttery Chardonnay and warm
sheepskin blanket settling my tensions as much as her agreement that
BART (Bay Area rail service) can be whack.

I would be alone to deal with my problems. I would be a wolfette in
the wild.

I couldn't phone a friend, or Ghostbusters, or pop into a bar where
everybody knew my name. If I had a day that circled the drain and then
slid down the shitty emotions disposal, shredding my esteem into tiny
chunks of disgustingness, I would be the one left to pick myself up, rinse
off, and talk myself into having a do-over.

That was that.

So, I had to teach myself to read people and to listen to the little voice
in my stomach that told me if a situation was naughty or nice. And
beyond that, I told myself that it was time to be more independent than
ever. If I didn't trust blondie to watch my bag while I used the bathroom,
the girl from South Africa with the ruby painted lips, then I would have
to carry it down the bustling train station hall, my back muscles
screaming, and jam it into a space barely big enough for me to squat in. I
might even have to pee on it accidentally. Those are the breaks for
putting the most trust in the one person I could trust about ninety five
percent of the time—yours truly. I had to learn to work more De La Soul
style, with "Me Myself and I."

But once I started traveling, I found out something. It's a little secret
that many don't know. It is very important and powerful, something that
could change your life. Are you ready? Brace yourself...

XXX

People are people—no matter where on the planet.

There are friendlies, grumpies, liars, thieves, listeners, givers, horny
bastards, and a buffet of other personality hues, all of which may shift as
quickly as open ocean weather. But, most people are your average do-
gooders, whether they wear a turban, trucker hat, hibiscus flower behind
the ear, or have a full facial tattoo. We're all brains, organs, dumb luck,
and self-preservation. Where the rubber meets the road, almost all

humans just want to get through life without getting too hurt or dishing out too much hurt.

People are people, and they are good. People all around the world—complete strangers—are ready to drive you, feed you, house you, guide you, amuse you, and comfort you at no cost. All charity.

They do this because most beating hearts just want to pump their way to another day without hassle and sadness. Most want to feel good. It feels good to help, and that feeling is not restricted to the borders of the city you were born in, your mom's safe arms, or a moral and kind religious leader.

If you don't believe me, then sit back and consider the situation for a second. There are billions of us functioning on this planet. Therefore—every day—there are a billion ways that comprehensive harm could be committed to the masses. And yet, here we are—unharmed—going to work, having down time, pretty much able to move forward with our lives without serious threat.

Banks, gas, food, roads, building materials, and textiles—it's all happening. It continues.

This planet's inhabitants are awesome. They're full of joy and awe. Let me give you a couple of examples to get the party going.

There was a young boy in California who came from a family with low monetary means. He hung out at his dad's store every day during the summer. There, he was inspired to build an arcade out of cardboard. Because of the world being nice around him, allowing his space to not worry but instead create, he got L.A. famous. Some random dude who visited the store to pick up a car part saw the cardboard arcade. He was fascinated by the boy's creation and made a documentary on him. It set off a string of cardboard arcades across the country. Check it out: *Caine's Arcade.*

Another example was when San Francisco shut down its streets and transformed into a Gotham City crime scene for a child whose dying wish was to become Batman for a day. The Mayor, City Hall, television stations, actors, volunteers—tons of people pulled together to let this child dress as Batkid, pull up in the Bat Mobile, and run alongside Batman down a major street to a real bank that was being fake robbed by the Joker. There was live coverage of his dream come true.

The streets were lined with cheering people who'd left work to witness the city come together to pretend the Joker was putting everyone in peril and that their only hope was THIS ONE CHILD. Many cried while they clapped. I cried while I watched online.

That's the power of humans—golden hearts and joined hands. We are bonded in our frail existence.

Mind you, this doesn't mean I'm Pollyanna. People can suck. You will get jacked, hence why you lock your car, keep aware of those around you at night, especially if you're a girl walking alone, and take a million other safety precautions. I'm just saying, most don't want to torch you or to be torched in return.

I am a walking, breathing, happy example of this truth.

XXX

In the thirty-eight countries I've traveled to, only three things happened to me that made me feel vulnerable and/or made my skin crawl.

I'm going to reiterate. IN TEN YEARS OF TRAVELING, I'VE ONLY FELT TRULY AT RISK THREE TIMES.

THREE…in many years of globetrotting. That's not bad.

The rest of the awkward moments were average, run-of-the-mill scares. These were my most awkward moments overseas—

First, when I was eating dinner in a candle-lit, barely-standing shack on the shores of the Mekong Delta, a young boy with shaggy black hair and a smear of mud on his cheek tapped me on the shoulder and said in near-perfect English with a Laos accent, "I stole your camera off the back of your chair. Do you want to buy it back?"

I said, "Sure," put down my chopsticks, dug in my pocket, and handed him a crumpled ball of pink Kip that was the equivalent of about three dollars.

He accepted it and immediately returned my camera in perfect condition. He even hung it right back on my chair in the same place it had originally, and carelessly, been hanging. I moved it to my lap and finished my dinner without much more thought as to what had just happened.

I racked it up as a valuable lesson. From then on, I will never again hang anything on the back of my chair. Plus, I never carry things lazily on any part of my body, or set my possessions down on the bench beside me and turn the other way for a glance at a passing car.

Once bitten, twice shy.

Secondly, I was very stupid and went to some random guy's hut in the middle of the jungle in Cambodia. I didn't know where I was. I went there to buy weed.

I wanted to buy a dime bag, and he agreed to the amount while we discussed it on the street, but back at his shack, he wanted me to buy a pound.

I said, "No." He said, "Yes." Then he started threatening me in Cambodian.

I stood up to go. He blocked the door, and, thankfully, that's when his girlfriend came out of the back room and calmed the scene. I left with a dime bag and no harm done to me, because of that girl.

Thirdly, in a co-ed dorm room in Airlie Beach, Australia that slept four people—two girls and two boys—I had a guy jack off in the bunk below me. He was sloshed drunk. Buck-naked.

He shook our bunk bed like a seven on the Richter magnitude scale—obviously needing to punish his tequila penis to get any feeling out of it. Then, when he couldn't get his overcooked spaghetti noodle to do what he wanted, he stood up and breathed dumpster troll breath on me.

"Hey? Hey you up? Wanna help me?" he asked.

I froze, playing possum in the four a.m. dark.

His friend wasn't back from their party yet, so the room only had this guy, a random chick, and me in it. The chick was sleeping on the top bunk of the other bunk bed. It was across from where I slept.

The drunk dude swayed for a minute, then staggered over to her. Through slit eyes, I watched his flabby pancake ass wobble with each step.

"Hey? You awake?" he asked her, leaning on her bunk frame.

The chick didn't play opossum like I had. Instead, she shot out of bed and bolted to the bathroom, locking the door behind her. He was left swaying; holding his saggy balls with one hand and the girl's empty bed with his other.

That was my cue. I was hot on her heels, but I shot out the front door—straight to the night worker's desk.

When the worker and I returned to drag that asshole out of the room, he was passed out again in his bed. I swear his penis was two inches long. It looked like an old French fry. We couldn't punish him anymore than nature already had, but the worker tried. He dragged the drunk, still buck-naked dude out of our room by his hair and tossed him into the street. Then, the popo got called.

Shame on that freak. A plague on his micropenis.

Those three instances were my worst travel moments over ten years. Bad things were bound to happen. And there will always be bad moments that concern humans, because people can be naughty and some are evil. But for me, even when evil did poke its horns into my space, someone was always there to help. You're never really alone in your plight. Travelers—just like you—are everywhere. They get it. They will help you.

For instance, another time in Australia, but this time Byron Bay, I was staying at this funky hostel called Arts Factory. I was sleeping in the Pentagon, an all-girls dorm room. There were a lot of us in there, and one night at about four a.m., a dude came stumbling in and made a ruckus.

"What the," a girl mumbled in the dark. "Get off me!"

"Who's there?" another asked.

The lights came on. All of us sat up at the same time, suddenly fully awake.

The guy who'd entered our room was shirtless. He appeared to be in his twenties and he looked wired. He stood in the middle of the room, like a dog caught eating the foam out of pillow. Then, a chick with a strange accent shouted, "Who the fuck do you think you are?

From there... it was <u>ON</u>.

We were all from different corners of the world but acting as one, beastly weapon of war. We dove off bunks—swinging, punching, kicking. Some grabbed rocks or poles. Some had weapons they'd traveled with, just for occasions like this.

He got the bash...hard.

He was dragged out of our room, semi-conscious and bleeding, and dumped at the front desk like the sack of shit he was. He had no idea he'd walked into an MMA ring.

Sucks to suck.

So again, even though that boy could have caused some damage, he didn't get the chance to, because good prevailed. It was actually inspiring Wonder Woman stuff.

When bad things happen, the help of others usually fixes them. Sometimes it doesn't go down that way, but usually it does.

In poorer countries I've passed through, it seems the hectic situations usually arise due to possessions and/or money.

When people are poor, they are more likely to take what they don't have, what they can't afford, or what they can make money off of. As a backpacker carrying certain things of value, like electronics, you might be a target every once in a while.

The key is to be smart—don't flaunt the goods.

XXX

In the end, the stolen objects are just things. Things can be replaced. Hide them to be safe. Lock them up. Try to protect what's yours as much as possible, but when someone wants it, give it up. It's not worth a fight or even a frown.

For example, let's take an American idiot overseas.

In Colombia, Monica, Cam, and I went to a beach called Playa Blanca. It was very rustic. Cows cruised the sand. Vast fields of weeds and the occasional shed spread out from the shore.

Our hostel was a four-walled concrete block with cut outs for windows and bunk beds for sleeping. That was it on this beach, and although we were used to rugged and raw, this place just didn't feel right. We decided that one night there would be enough. Good thing too, because the beach location got weirder as the day and night progressed.

"Hi," the young chick said, extending a bandaged forearm in Cam's direction.

She was alone, the only other backpacker on the beach, so it seemed. She mumbled a name that I didn't catch, but her inflection bounced off my eardrum and raised a flag. The accent was American, no doubt— kind of eighties valley girl.

This was rare. I was stoked. I hurried up and inundated her with a barrage of typical questions.

"Hi! Where you from? Where've you been traveling? What brought you here?"

But, instead of listening to her answers, I was drawn to her bandage. It was stained a shade of yellow-green along the meaty inside of her forearm. A blob of crimson in the shape of Texas saturated the area just below the crease of her elbow.

"Your bandage needs changing," I said, skipping the formalities.

"Oh, yeah," she replied, stealing a sideways look at her wrap as though it were a cotton glove she always wore to the beach. "I'm just tired of changing it. I've done it three times already this morning."

"Three times? Since what time this morning?" I asked, arching my eyebrows.

"I don't know, probably three times in the last two hours or so," she said, darting beady pupils toward the surf.

Whaaaaaa?

"Look, I'm not a doctor. I don't know a lot about anything, but I'm pretty sure if you're changing a fresh cotton wrap that's quite dense bout every thirty minutes—and it's still weeping colors similar to baby poo—then something ain't right."

"Yeah, my friend is surprised I came out here at all, but you know, I want to keep traveling. Seeing stuff."

She used her good arm to toss her hair off her tanned shoulder.

I rolled my eyes. I couldn't help myself.

"Can I see it?" I asked.

The young American girl, blonde-haired and blue-eyed, unwrapped the wrecked forearm. It smiled a monstrous grin at me. A Frankenstein line of stainless steel sutures ran vertically from her wrist to elbow. It gurgled infection.

"What the hell?" I moaned, cupping a hand over my nose and mouth.

XXX

Turned out American Girl had been stabbed in Santa Marta, Colombia. But, it also turned out that American Girl had done everything she could to ensure her stabbing.

1. She'd gone out to a music festival with a guy she didn't know to an area of town she'd never been.
2. She drank heavily into the witching hours.
3. She eventually drank herself blind, until everything shut down and any good sense she started with disappeared.

When she left the bar blind with drunkenness, the streets were empty and the crowd that was so happily enjoying the concert was gone. All that was left was sludge, both the inanimate and living kind.

So, a very wasted, very blonde, very foreign Miss America stumbled out of the bar and into the four a.m. shadowed street, with her purse conspicuously draped across her perky tits and her stumbling feet advertising her vulnerability.

She said she had only walked a few yards before she was fronted. A crew of thugs, both male and female, surrounded her. It was dirty time.

A dude told her to hand over her purse.

She said, "No."

A girl responded to Miss America's insolence by producing a butcher knife, stabbing it into Miss American's forearm, and ripping the knife downwards toward her wrist. *DING*—you got ganked.

I guess Miss America really wanted to keep her purse. Must have been the runway hit of the season or something. So, as Miss America is telling me this, I'm starting to feel her room temperature travel I.Q.

"Stab wound. This is a STAB wound, and now you're here leaking on some random beach filled with cows and no antibiotics? What the fuck are you thinking? Has your cheese slid off your cracker? You knittin' with one needle? Slip into the gene pool while the lifeguard wasn't watching?" I asked.

I was a hemisphere away from feeling the need to sugar coat my feelings on the situation. I rambled, letting my anger lead the way.

"I mean, I'll take one for the team with the best of 'em—ride out a flu with Vitamin C and eat ninety percent of the food I drop on the ground without ever putting into play the two-second rule, but you've been stabbed. STABBED! Right there. That slimy line that looks like it might start talking in tongues. That's your nasty wound," I said, pointing to her suture like a second grader identifying the grossest insect in the bug collection.

Miss America glanced at her cut like it was a rug burn.

"Well, I went back to the States to get it fixed. It was kind of big deal...actually. Made headline news back home," she smiled—very proud moment.

"I don't care if you went to NASA to get it fixed, it's not doing well now. You stay in this heat with these flies and your nursing skills, and your little story will have a sequel. It will be about you getting phantom pains in your ex-arm area. I mean, I'm sure the salt water will help, but I think you're past natural remedies—you need some main-vein pharmaceutical shit, quick like. You need to go twenty-first century on that mug," I said shaking my head.

"Yeah, maybe you're right."

That was the first time I saw her look nervous during our beach heart-to-heart—deservingly nervous.

She left the island that afternoon, leaving the three of us with the reminder that when someone wants to jack you, let them, especially in a foreign country. You can replace your camera, but not your shredded brachioradialus muscle.

Yes, I've had my stuff stolen, but no, I've never been threatened like that. Usually you're safe, but if you behave like a dumb and exposed traveler, you may get treated like one. Sign up for trouble, and you'll most likely find it. The key is to not get your pen out when someone asks, "Do you want to participate in my heroine and AK-47 smuggling experiment? Just put your signature right here (pointing to crotch)."

Be smart.

Proceed with caution, as you would back home, and amazing things can happen, like, for instance, meeting good strangers.

CHAPTER 37

Quite the opposite of encountering fiends, I've mostly only met super heroes, class-A acts, angels, and comrades overseas. I've had the most tremendous times with strangers, and I've hung out in some shadows, lurking, and cutting jokes with shape shifters. No one ever tried to harm me, intimidate me, or do anything but help.

People are fantastic.

For example, I've had a street full of Spaniards assist me with finding an apartment address that was blowing my mind.

I'd just arrived in Bilbao with zero Spanish in my lexicon, and a street name and number that I'd repeatedly looked for to no avail, squinting and mumbling at the misleading wad of paper.

The place I was trying to find was invisible.

It was dusk and I was exhausted, lost, and getting to that frustration stage that threatens tears. I finally built up the courage to ask an old woman in English if she could help, knowing that she wouldn't have a clue what I said. But it was the best I could do.

I had no other hope. Homesickness blanketed me.

"Ma'am, can you please help me? I can't find this address. Please," I begged.

Heat rose in my cheeks.

She studied the sweaty scrap of paper in my trembling hand and finally said, "No existe," and shook her head.

That Spanish I understood. My address didn't exist—I was screwed.

I was about to collapse onto the ground in forfeit, bawl, and then try a game of charades with her—s l e e p o n c o u c h p l e a s e. But, before I could start, she rattled off more Spanish to a man wearing a beret sitting on a bench across from us. He stood and scurried over to help. They talked, and then he yelled up to a window where a young girl was flapping a dusty towel in the breeze.

"Un momento," she replied, before appearing like a sorcerer in our circle.

Then she yelled to a teenager who was playing with a soccer ball a few feet away. The boy got a man involved who was taking a walk with his daughter. It was a communication trail of falling dominoes, and within minutes the whole street was full of helpers chattering like search and rescue dolphins, pulling me up and down alleyways to locate my hidden destination. They'd materialized from shops, arched doorways, cars, and mopeds.

They swirled around me, laughing and hugging a protective welcome, knowing damn well that I didn't understand a word, but also not judging my ineptness. At least twenty people happily lent me a caring hand in that time of need, without me really asking.

Turned out, the building name had been changed, something only locals would have known during a time long before Internet searches and smart phones. Together they found the address, and I got settled into my new home.

Although the Spaniards are the only group example I have of people coming to my aid, there have been many singular souls who I, and my travel friends, owe a hefty dose of gratitude.

XXX

In Peru, my friends and I had made our way to a small beach town up north called Mancora. It was the first time I'd experienced desert beach— the blue waters licking the edge of a barren town dotted with cacti and spindly trees that burned a rich brown.

When we first arrived, we walked the dirt road searching for a hostel—dust wafting under our flip-flops. I craned my neck toward the

sky to see if it offered another color besides the sand tint that draped
everything.

"What the hell?" I asked Deirdre. "Is that a dog?"

I pointed to the top of a leaning telephone pole where a giant, shaggy
dog sat. Its head was concealed from view. The ancient, wooden pole
swayed in the wind, but the mutt seemed unbothered.

"Odd. I'm not sure," Deirdre replied, squinting into the sun.

"How the hell did it get up there? Its fur looks oily, and I think…"

I didn't have to finish my thought.

At the same time, we both saw the blood red head of the huge vulture
emerge from its tucked position. Seeing us, the fiend took flight.

"Gross! Holy shit! That was like a cartoon! I've never seen anything
like that," I gagged.

"Fuck that. I'm not sure what to think about all that," said Deirdre.

We walked conjoined-twin-style the rest of the way, flip-flopping
faster, until finally veering into a driveway that promised hammocks. It
had pictures of them painted on a crooked sign.

What we found at this particular hostel was hammock paradise—at
least twenty were strung head to foot in square patterns that stretched
over the property. It was perfect for our plan to not use our legs over the
following days.

On the first night there, Danny noticed something by his foot.

We were a group of seven at that point, and as the sun sank into the
ocean we all assumed our positions in the center hammock spiralgram.
We could all talk and hammock at the same time, which equaled travel
success.

"What the hell?" Danny interrupted our casual conversation with his
sharp British concern. "Did you see that thing move by my daddy toe?"

"Did you just call your papa toe your daddy toe?" I asked.

"Dude! They're scorpions!" Cam spat.

Fourteen bare feet simultaneously shot into the air.

I lost interest in the daddy vs. papa toe debate as the curved stingers of hundreds of skittering arachnids transformed the sand into a churning mural of desert nightlife.

Can I get a FUCK THAT?

We wriggled and squirmed in repugnance, unsure how to escape back to the room without hover boards. But, we were damn certain we were changing hostels the next day. We made our unanimous decision while individually coiled in the fetal position within each of our swinging hammocks, discussing our future with verve.

"Let's go somewhere with grass, not sand," said Mon.

"Yeah! Somewhere with no snakes, or vultures, or those worms from *Dune*," I said

"The movie with Kevin Bacon?" Deirdre asked.

"Kevin Bacon—jump back!" I said.

The next day after some solid searching, we finally found the hostel we wanted. It didn't have vultures, scorpions, or anything unordinary, except for Mr. Pistola—as we named him.

XXX

This guy, this guard of guards, wore a gun on his hip and frown on his face. His job was to watch the grounds, but he quickly became more than just a watcher.

His ridged face that had seen too much desert sun folded and gathered in pockets of friendliness the more we became regulars in his world. He went from Peruvian ruffian to smiling gun-toter. He even laughed when we called him Señor Pistola, a.k.a. Mr. Pistol.

He didn't speak a lick of English, so I started chatting in Spanish with him about little things, Mancora things. They were the kind of conversations you should have while traveling, and with the help of those chats, our new home became inspiring. However, there was one major problem.

One of my friends is an animal adorer. Her bleeding heart had no right traveling to the backwoods of South America without a blind fold and an iPod looping "Happy" by Pharrell in her earphones, because every scrawny dog, mangy cat, and squawking bird hopping on a splintered leg ripped her soul open.

And there just happened to be a four-legged setback across the street from our hostel.

She was fixated on a certain dog, leash, and shack situation. She didn't realize her mission to save the animal world was an impossible feat.

In some countries, the safety of animals is about as concerning as Rosie O'Donnell's career. And, in many countries animals are treated with kicks, starvation, disregard, or to serve a bigger purpose, such as dinner or brunch. They're not like the shiny animals of the USA.

I've seen a pigdog that had a snout and oinked, but also had doggy paws and a straight, wagging tail. I've seen live kittens in a restaurant listed on the menu, with their cage photo beside the dish number. I've seen people who couldn't feed themselves or their children, so when a puppy came a beggin', it had a snowflake's chance in hell of living. It was food for the humans—understandably so. The definition of humane blurs between borders the same as a passport stamp in steamy weather.

So, for my sanity, I learned to think differently. I realized that there are many different strokes for all the different folks of the world, and who am I to force my beliefs down their throat?

Cute animals aren't always beloved pets. I like animals, but I have learned to tune them out when needed, just like when Michael Bolton is playing on the radio or when my boyfriend asks me to scoot over in bed.

But, for my friend Emily, her battle was just starting. On the third day at our new and wonderful hostel, Emily woke in hysterics.

"I can't take it! I can't go another night hearing that dog whine! I can't! We have to do something!" she cried, face swollen with pet-loving anguish.

Her un-slept hours had obviously been spent in torment. She paced the room. Deirdre, Monica, and I watched, unsure how to interrupt. Emily owned the stage, as most unhinged women do.

"What do you want to do?" I asked between her sobs.

"What do you mean by *do something*?" Deirdre stretched the question out.

"That dog across the street tied to the empty shack! He's been there since we got here! His ribs are poking through his knotted fur! I can't take it," she slobbered, running twitchy fingers through her tear-soaked hair.

She crumpled into her pillow. It muffled her sobs.

The dog probably did bark all night, but I wouldn't have known. Again, my mute button was fully installed by this point, so I wasn't quite sure if the canine had been howling, or if a giraffe had been screaming, or if a Liger had given birth in our bathroom. Anything was possible, so I chose my words carefully.

"The dog's bark, or his…wails…I understand they're bothering you, but we can't do anything, babe. This isn't like home. These people live in poverty—as do the animals," I said.

"Plus, we don't know why that dog is tied to that shack. It might be there to guard what's inside. If we untie him, we don't know what hornet's nest we're shaking, even if it is a good, totally sensible deed," said Monica.

"There's probably no vet around. Even if there were, we'd be helping a stolen dog," Deirdre reasoned.

"Let's stick to our monkeys and our circus," I added.

"No one's coming for him! He'll die tied up. Ignored. Alone," Emily sobbed.

Her voice was barely audible from her dejected position on the bed, but her back still arched and fell in sad spasms. It said everything we needed to hear.

And so it went.

We had to do something.

XXX

We walked as a team down to Señor Pistola, and this man, this guy who had probably never thought about saving an animal before in his life, talked in a gentle, hushed voice with us. He listened—arms crossed, wrinkles deepening, losing his Peruvian poker face.

He agreed that the dog had been there a long time, but he didn't offer an opinion on whether or not that owner would return. I finished translating our spiel and he froze—the thinking cowboy—John Wayne weighing out his next move at the saloon.

Finally he asked what we wanted to do—"¿Qué quiere hacer?"

And when I said set him free—"Liberalo"—Señor Pistola went stern.

This dog was not his concern…but we were. This was serious.

Under the protection of the next night's crescent moon, Señor Pistola helped us set up a CIA team. He arranged a cut-and-run with the assistance of another hostel owner who agreed to take the dog in once we set his raggedy butt free. When Emily severed the rope that had burned a bloody slit into the dog's skinny neck, I swear the dog said *thank you* in Spanish dog talk.

A couple of nights later, Señor Pistola helped us take an injured kitten to a supposed veterinarian that lived an hour away in a town the size of my daddy toe.

He was becoming Yosemite Savior Sam—Señor Save the Whales.

We loved him for it. He helped us, and he didn't have to. It was outside of his natural flow, and yet he stepped up for us. He was good— we just had to ask.

The good people list goes on to such an extent that this whole book could be about the magnificent strangers I've met on the road. People are kind and helpful, but they're also hilarious and intriguing.

XXX

Many strangers have put an unexpected smile on my face, like the random Aboriginal man I passed on a lone street in Darwin who glanced at me and said, "Baby got front."

I was shocked—not at his comment or witty tit-for-ass replacement, but that Sir Mix-A-lot made it all the way to the outback of Australia.

There was also the time that I interviewed for a nanny position in New Zealand. The job was for two toddlers, both one and a half years old. The mothers sprayed me with questions for about forty-five minutes, as any good mother would, and should, do. They were cool about it though. Their friendly manner was only outweighed by the warmth and beauty of the home I'd been invited to interview in—cups of tea, spectacular view.

Seated around a natural wood breakfast table, I was relaxed. I was on a roll with my answers. The moms wore receiving smiles and nods of approval.

"And so, where do you stand in terms of punishing or correcting our children when they're naughty?" asked the mom with thick brown hair and dark green eyes.

I paused.

"I'm not sure what you're asking," I answered. I believe in correcting your own kids in whatever way you feel is best, but when it comes to OPCs (other peoples' children), I've always stuck to the rule that I can advise them to be nice. If that's not working, I can only do what the parents have told me to do. Punishment is not non-family member territory, unless you're the school or the law.

Mother number two jumped in.

"You know, like if they're being bad. How would you punish them if they're breaking the rules?" she said, crossing her arms and leaning back in her chair.

"I'd put them in the oven," I answered.

Straight face. Sip of my tea. Full eye contact.

"On what temperature?" green eyes asked.

Straight face. Sip of her tea. Full eye contact.

XXX

People have made me smile and laugh around the globe way more than they have made me frown or cry, or even get nervous. But, it was the willingness to accept me and assist me that really put a lump in my throat. Such lovely souls everywhere.

In Panama, a hostel worker who'd been dropped on his head a million times as a baby gave my friends and I directions to a liquor store. It was night. We were very drunk.

He said, "Take a left on the first street. When you pop out at the top, there's a liquor store."

We thanked him and followed his directions. We hesitated to continue following his directions though, once we arrived at the street he told us to walk up. It was blacked-out, full of shapes that looked like they might be booths by day and double as homes by night.

Confused and functioning on vodka cells, we started up the street. We laughed and joked, making quite a ruckus. A few feet into our stroll, we started noticing things in the dark—the whites of peoples' eyes.

Things lurked in the shadows.

I spotted a face half-lit by candle flicker, and as soon as I saw it, it shrunk backwards into the dark. We kept walking, but quieted our voices. Finally we saw the faint glow of a street lamp up ahead, and we jogged a bit to reach its burn just as a couple of men appeared in a doorframe to our left—staying carefully cloaked by the gloom.

We ran past the men, and when we popped out into the light of the street above, a woman carrying groceries on the opposite sidewalk froze. We froze too—a Panamanian standoff.

A pregnant second ticked by.

"¿Vienen de allí?" she asked loudly, her voice strained with fret—*did you come from there?*

"Sí, de allí." I pointed to the alley—*yes, from there.*

The men slunk back from the doorframe I pointed to.

"Venga!" she yelled—*COME!*

"Come on guys," I signaled to my friends to follow my sprint across the empty road to where she stood, groceries gripped by white knuckles.

When we reached her, she got within inches of my face, and with the care of a scolding sister, she explained that the place we'd just come from was the street people in Panama City go to get murdered in. She said we should not be anywhere near there, and she insisted that she escort us to the shop we were looking for to make sure we were safe. Great soul. She may have saved our lives.

Later and further north in Bocas Del Toro, Panama, we started partying at a hostel called Aqua Lounge. It was the perfect party palace, a hostel built on a deck that stretched into the cobalt Caribbean Ocean.

The swimming pool was a hole cut out in the deck that went straight into the sea, and you could use a high dive off the top of the bunkroom to do a gorilla bomb into the warm, turquoise water if one felt the need. The hostel also had a floating trampoline, swings, jet skis, and at night while you slept, the Caribbean Ocean splashed up between the dock slats, tickling your bare feet to remind you how great life can be.

That hostel also had Speedy, a semi-fixture of the place. He was a young party boy from Costa Rica. He sold weed to make enough pocket change to taxi, bus, and boat his way down to Bocas every two months to surf, drink, and smoke.

We started calling him Speedy, because when he talked he sounded exactly like Speedy Gonzalez. It was as though he went to school at Warner Brothers Academy.

"Heeeeeeey mahn. Do you waaaaaaaant to stay weeth meeeeeeee at my house eeeen Costa Reeeeee-ca?" he asked us, two days before we were set to leave Panama.

Turned out, Speedy's dad owned a string of ice cream stores throughout Central America and a fat holiday house in the gated community of a ritzy beach town.

Our answer was, "Duh."

We stayed with him for the rest of the week and even went to a music festival with his friends, something we never would have known about if we hadn't met him, accepted his generous offer, and listened to his indigenous opinion on what we should do while in Costa Rica.

But, my absolute two favorite strangers I've come across overseas were in France and New Zealand.

These people displayed remarkable human kindness that I will never forget.

I'll tell you about the New Zealand man later.

For now, we transport to the French Alps during a snowy December.

CHAPTER 38

When I lived in Europe, some friends and I were invited by a girl named Liz to stay at her cousin's/aunt's/brother's château in the French Alps. It took me half a second to say, "YES."

After arriving at the log cabin in the town of La Clusaz, we kissed cheeks with our French hosts and offloaded our backpacks in the snug home, our bones defrosting against the warm flames of a log fire that smelled of pine and winter memories.

The cabin was adorable—the carpentry detailed and the furnishings thoughtful. We poured Merlot, exchanged pleasantries, and then decided that it would be fun to make our way back into town to take a look around before nightfall. Liz wrote the address of the château down on a piece of paper and gave it to Jon. One of the nice Frenchmen offered to drive us. Minutes later, we—the Frenchman, Jon, Ethan, and I—wound down snowy roads into the charming Alpine town.

On the main road in town, the Frenchman dropped us off and offered in broken English, "Taxi. House," before driving away, beeping a pleasant goodbye.

His exhaust pipe burped tiny white balloons into the crisp air that smelled of pine. I looked around and was instantly smitten.

Crafted chocolates. Quaint cafés. Delightful shops with architecture that reminded me of fairytales I'd read as a child—gingerbread-ish.

"We should get some groceries for the next few days," Ethan mentioned, strolling past a window decorated with lace curtains and wicker baskets full of fluffy breads. The pink tinge of dusk settled around us and added an extra layer of enchantment to the resort atmosphere.

"Yes. Great idea. This place is unreal," I replied, my breath billowing out of my mouth in dragon bursts of white smoke.

We popped into the supermarché, grabbed a few boxes of random goodies, and went back into the street to flag a taxi. One rolled up to our booted feet within seconds. Its headlights glared through the dusk turned dark, stars beginning to sprout overhead.

"Merci," Jon said, swinging the backseat door open.

We piled in.

Without getting out the piece of paper with the name of the street on it, Jon spouted, "Keem-een dez Eb-ooo-liss, noo-mare-row quatre sept doo, see il voo play."

It was a pronunciation slaughterhouse.

The driver scowled, adjusted his furry hat, and hit the gas with a grunt. He must have understood, because he drove us back up, up, up the snowy road from which we'd descended hours earlier. A tinny radio chirped in French through cheap speakers. Outside, snow began to fall harder.

"See, told you guys I was good at French," Jon bragged.

"You took French your senior year of high school from a half-dead man in Arkansas. You admitted earlier that you don't remember a damn word. All you did just now was poorly memorize and regurgitate the information off one little piece of paper in your pocket. Now you're claiming language savant status? Player, please..." said Ethan.

I didn't add my two Francs to the argument. Instead, I gazed out the windshield into the black night and thick snowflakes that hit the heated window, disintegrating on contact. We snaked up the mountain for many minutes. It seemed longer than our original trip, and just when I started to speak up, we turned onto our street.

Up ahead, our château wore a fresh, snow beanie. Our taxi crawled to a stop at the top of the driveway. The driver rambled French at the windshield instead of at us.

"What is he saying?" Jon asked.

"Oh, I thought you had this. Here, let me help. He says, 'After the party it's the hotel lobby,'" Ethan quipped.

"Whatever, dude," said Jon, leaning toward the driver. "Um...here, sir. Yes. Thank you."

He offered a wad of French money, holding it over the seat and fanning it in the driver's view. The driver snatched it out of Jon's hand.

"Au revoir," the driver grumbled.

We'd barely clamored out of his taxi before the driver threw the car in drive and busted a tight U-turn, plowing back down the mountain. In the rush to get out of his way, I'd dropped our cardboard box full of pastas, fruits, vegetables, cheese, crackers, and butter. The fresh groceries spilled into the snow, adding color to the stark white pallet.

"Shit," I huffed. "Can you help me, please?"

Ethan bent and helped me gather the white-dusted zucchinis and tomatoes while Jon stared at the chateau.

"Looks like everyone went to bed early," he said, scratching his head.

The walkway was obscured by long shadows. A dim glow from an upstairs window was the only light source. I looked around—the whole street was blacked out.

"Maybe they over poured the wine," I guessed, trudging toward the front door, snow crunching loudly under my boots. Ethan and Jon followed. Their footsteps seemed even louder than mine. The noise carried further than it should have. Life was eerily quiet on the mountaintop.

Ethan paused—food box gripped lovingly between his long arms.

"Wait. It wasn't like this before."

"What do you mean?" asked Jon.

"I mean, our chateau had that weird shaped light and a curved walkway, not this straight one. Get the address out," Ethan barked.

"Are you sure?" Jon asked.

"I'm sure. Get the fucking address out," Ethan demanded. His words dissolved into the cold night air, a white plume of worry. I looked around and shook my head.

"You're right. This isn't the house," I whispered.

XXX

Ethan was damn right. He was so right that it turned out we weren't on the correct street or even in the right neighborhood. We'd been dropped off in outer space—the street abandoned of all living things. Every house was lacking occupants, the darkness inside mimicking the night sky and sinking pits in our stomachs.

No cars.

No answers to knocks.

Then, as though mocking us, the snow started coming down so hard that all we could do was stand on the ridge behind the row of empty homes and try to find a reference point. We could barely make out dots of light below.

"That's not far. We can take this back ridge," suggested Jon.

"I guess. It'll be a major shortcut to taking the road. And those lights have to be it. It has to be the right road. The drive up here was the same one we took to get into town. We're not far," Ethan chattered through banging teeth.

The cold hugged us tight.

"Alright then. Let's tap it from the backside. Let's get to those lights," I said.

We started our decline, groceries still in hand. But, we quickly realized something. Just like any hike on the backside of any mountain, it was more than we'd bargained for.

Everyone lost it.

We all slipped, fell, tumbled, rolled, and luckily the only thing that got hurt was our groceries. The brand new and yummy looking food was lost in the white blanket of winter, the cardboard boxes long ago tipped and treaded on by all three of us. Tomatoes were abandoned to snowy graves, gifts for the lucky rabbits of spring. A jar of jam was left to be double-preserved by the harsh freeze.

For some reason, I started to find it all really comical. I liked watching everyone do accidental cartwheels down the hill, including myself. At one point, I fell so hard that I rolled four times, washing machine style, before stopping. When I finally stopped and found my feet, I looked myself over and saw to my delight that my new outfit was identical to the Michelin Man. That's when I peed my pants from laughing. It felt warm and nice, then cold and wrong. I laughed more.

"This isn't funny," Ethan snapped.

At this point he'd given up on walking. He was sliding down the hill on his butt, foregoing his feet for the much quicker and colder way to reach our destination.

"Quit laughing," he snapped again.

Jon glared at me.

"I don't think it's funny," I laughed and snorted into the cold.

I looked up the mountainside from where we'd just come. I could see the massive stick of butter we'd bought jutting out of the white. I wanted that stick of butter. I wanted to carry it as a wand and wave it at the boys to lighten their moods or maybe piss them off more. I'd say things like, *this is serious, boys. We have only a little margarine for error. Butter make every decision count.* It would be our midnight hike talisman.

I chuckled at the punnies, trying not to let the boys hear my self-amusement. It didn't work.

"STOP fucking laughing, Shelby," Jon grizzled.

He never talked to me that way. Our threesome was becoming unstable.

"Okay, okay. Jeez," I muttered. "Everything is fine."

Then I laughed again. I knew I had to get it together or they were going to bury me in a drift, but the scene was so ridiculous. I wasn't sure I could. Plus, there was a part of me that knew things were getting dire. I suppose that was the part causing the laughter. I'm peculiar that way.

We hiked/fell further down the mountain and the lights got closer. Then, the lights were super close, and instead of getting excited, we all deflated. The lights illuminated our mistake. They weren't house lights at all—they were lights attached to energy poles and other things that made the world go around. They weren't going to help us get safe.

I stopped laughing.

XXX

"Guys, let's stop and think," I suggested.

"Yeah, we need to think," Ethan agreed.

He dropped to the snowy floor and balled himself into a globe shape. He was shuddering. I was sure his ass was crystalized from his butt-sled technique.

"The best thing to do now is go back to where we started," said Jon.

"I agree. We should stick to what we know. We need to go back up there. Follow our footsteps," I said.

The movie *The Shining* flashed before my eyes—frozen Jack Nicholson smiling at the end.

My throat constricted, and I don't know why, but I raised a forefinger and said in a scratchy groan, "Redrum."

"What the fuck?! DO NOT say Redrum right now. What's wrong with you? FREAK! You're freaking me out!" Ethan yelled from his balled position on the ground.

"Oh come on, Ethan! If we were lost in a giant hedge maze at the Overlook Hotel while wearing bad seventies sweaters then fine, my comment should freak you out. But we're in the French Alps!"

I waved my arms around at the scenery. Snow dust floated off my jacket.

"We can always hike back up and break into one of those homes. We'll live. Stop being so dramatic," I chided.

"At least we don't have to worry about bears," Jon intervened. "They'll be snoozing, if France has any that is. Hey, did you know hibernating bears make butt plugs for themselves before passing out for the winter?"

His comment was a great conversational curve ball. He even used an upbeat tone to enhance the mood change. I played along, knowing he must have smelled Ethan nearing a panic attack.

"I actually did know that. I don't know why I know about bear butt plugs, but I do. There's a special name for it, like Tupperware or something," I said.

"Tupperware! You think the scientific name for a bear's homemade rectal plug is Tupperware? I'm going to die surrounded by idiots," Ethan shouted.

He stared at me with flame eyes—dual laser beams that bored a hate-hole through my forehead. Then he flopped onto his back, legs spread eagle. Resignation pose.

"Tappen. It's a damn tappen," he said toward the sky.

Jon and I looked at each other, then to Ethan, then back to each other, and up the hill we'd just slid down.

All enthusiasm was gone.

I filled my lungs with cold air and blew out hard.

"Well…Tupperware keeps things dry and safe too," I said, because I had nothing better to add.

We needed to quit discussing bear butt plugs and climb. Playtime was over. I crossed my red-throbbing fingers we'd get home…or at least to a place that felt like a Tupperware container.

XXX

"We have to break in," I said.

After a tough and long climb, we were back on the street where we'd started. It was completely abandoned. We were completely exhausted.

"Those doors aren't made of paper mache. They're like lumberjack shit, carved from some great-grandfather's favorite oak tree using a shank and some elbow grease. They're not budging without a battering ram," Ethan said, giving a gentle kick to the snow stack that gathered at his feet.

We stood at the front door of the house we'd mistaken as our own. Before we tried to kick its front door in, we'd rapped on the doors of others, trying to find one that contained humans. No luck. No one was around.

"We can always find a window to break, but once we get inside we need to find firewood and hope that the water is turned on. I guess we can melt snow if the water is a no-go," said Jon.

"Whatever we do, we can't stay out here much longer. I'm losing feeling in my phalanges," I said.

"Phalanges. Anatomy 101 biznatch," Ethan said, looking like he wanted to high-five me, but his fat glove was stuffed so far in his pocket that his shoulder just kind of raised and then re-settled.

We were still trying to keep things lighthearted. We needed to. But beyond that, we needed to find people.

"Let's get going—locate some humans," said Jon.

He cupped his hands around his mouth and sent a steam shot out from between his gloved fingers.

"Let's at least go to the end of the road and see if we can find another road with houses, and hopefully people in those houses. If we can't, then we'll come back here and do some serious breaking and entering. Do you still have the en-en-en-energy to hike?" I asked both of them, my teeth drumming together in tiny, rhythmic clicks.

"Yeah. Let's do it," Ethan coughed.

"Let's hurry. I'm c-c-c-c-c-cold," said Jon.

We tramped.

We complained.

It was freezing—dangerously cold.

We had almost given up when a house full of lights shone on the horizon. It was an A-frame full of yellow glow and noise—the blessed noise of conversation and laughter. It seeped through the rafters the closer we got.

Rescue-energy made us to run down the driveway.

Knock. Knock.

Nothing...

BANG. BANG. BANG.

The door flew open.

CHAPTER 39

"Bonjour," a tiny man in a knitted reindeer sweater greeted us.

A green turtleneck hugged the bottom of his chin. His smile almost touched his earlobes. A wine glass tilted in his right hand, the merlot reclining on the rim like a lady in waiting.

"Oh my God. Thank God. Hi. We're lost. We need some help, please. Can we use your telephone?" I rambled.

The tiny man stared at me.

"Bonjour," he said again.

"Bonjour," I parroted.

"Can we please come in?" Jon asked from behind me.

"Bonjour," the man continued, taking an unyielding swig of his wine, the kind of gulp usually kept for beer bongs or shots.

It left behind a burgundy mustache on his shiny upper lip. He widened his smile to circus proportions, wrapping it around the back of his head. We smiled back. Smiling contest.

"Bonjour," the man whispered this time, giggling a little, eyes glossed with wine buzz.

"He doesn't speak English," Ethan said through his teeth.

Ethan was smiling a third-grade class photo type of smile—teeth touching together tip to tip. Everybody still smiling. Smile Fest.

"¿Habla español, señor? Estamos perdidos. Necistamos ayuda, por favor,"—*Do you speak English? We're lost. We need help, please,* I tried in Spanish.

I'd found with French people that sometimes they were hesitant to speak to me if I didn't know French. In fact, they rolled their eyes and cussed as they walked away, especially if I'd asked them my question in English.

But, I'd also found that if I asked my question in Spanish after I asked in English, they were receptive. It was like I was allowed to shed my dumb American label if I could prove that I spoke anything besides ranch dressing and baseball. But this time, the Spanish didn't work. The jolly elf just smiled some more and slurred, "Oui," at us and, "Bonjour," yet again.

"Can we come inside? We're cold," I tried again, this time making the international sign for cold, wrapping my arms around myself and shivering.

"Ah, oui! Entrez!"

Jolly Elf took me gently by the shoulders and pulled me into the entryway. A million shoes were lined up next to a decorative entrance table. I looked down at the elf's feet. He was wearing knitted socks covered in snowflake patterns.

I did some more smiling and then bent to untie my snow-encased boots, hoping I was wearing something more appealing than my usual hole and stain combo.

The house smelled of Christmas tree, warm bread, herb chicken, and sugared cherries. I watched Jon and Ethan take giant whiffs as they crossed the threshold. We hadn't just been saved—we'd been saved by Santa's helper and Julia Child.

"Entrez," he nodded to Jon and Ethan, still smiling and drinking while we unbooted.

In the background the living room hummed with voices. Jolly Elf kept talking to us in French that we couldn't understand.

"Frenchity French French. More French. Frenchama Frenchle Frencheroo."

Trolling my memory for any French, I came up with nearly nil.

Baguette. Crepe. Menage á trois. Encore.

I figured if I put those words together in that order, we'd get kicked out of Jolly Elf's home, so I zipped it. Thank goodness for gestures. Miming makes the world go 'round.

Through waves of hands, splayed fingers, and a few little curtsies like you see in the old Renaissance movies, Jolly Elf led us into the living room where about fifteen family members sat around a giant dinner table. It was covered with steamy vegetable platters, casserole dishes, breads, cheeses, and wine...bottles and bottles of wine.

"Bonjour!"

"Bienvenu!"

"Faites comme chez vous!"

"Nous sommes juste en train de diner!"

Various people told us various things in French, and we nodded like we got it.

The friendly household didn't seem bothered by the loss of translation. They never stood up, acted rattled, slowed their dining, or seemed bothered or surprised by our appearance mid-meal. Quite the contrary, they never missed a dinner beat.

They continued eating, drinking, cheering, laughing, and discussing things to such a level that conversation overlapped, French sentences pinging off each other and bouncing onto the floor.

One younger man in the crew did know some English, as he was the only one who seemed to notice us. When I say he knew English, I mean he knew two things: snowboard and Monica Lewinsky. He said both of these things with an accompanied demonstration. While everyone else ignored him and ate and drank with gusto, he stood up periodically to act out snowboarding.

He swayed; waving arms around in the air and accidentally bumping the dinner table with his crotch just enough to give the wine glasses a shudder and send the rest of the family into fits of rapid fire French.

"Snowboarding!" he'd yell.

And for Monica Lewinsky, he would stand and yell, "Mone-eek-uh Loo-een-skee!"

He'd pretend to wear a dress, point at an imaginary stain, and then put on a look of shock followed by coyness. After, he'd laugh like Woody Woodpecker and sit down to return to his roast and potatoes. He'd repeat this display of English vocabulary every few seconds.

"Snowboard!"

Jumping up. Crotch hitting table. Glasses clinking. French complaints. Sitting down for a second, then…

"Mone-eek-uh Loo-een-skee!"

Jumping up. Crotch hitting table. Glasses clinking. French complaints. Pointing to imaginary stain on dress.

I found it mesmerizing. His family barely noticed.

XXX

"We have an address," Jon told Jolly Elf, pulling the crumpled piece of paper out of his pocket.

Jolly Elf took it, swayed a little while he read it, and then walked over to a chunky, black phone that sat on a bookshelf. These were the days of landlines. Everyone hollered at Jolly Elf from the table as he picked up the receiver. He bellowed back, wine glass in dialing hand while he punched grey numbers with a heavy middle finger. He used his wine glass as an earmuff, pressing it against his ear. Only a few seconds ticked off before someone on the other line picked up.

"Allo… (French. French. French. More French)," said Jolly Elf.

He was so jovial. He grinned and signaled me over with new verve, passing me the receiver. Its bulky weight was heavy in my hand.

"Allo? Bonjour?" I asked, pressing it against my ear.

A thick, French accent speaking in English responded.

"Hello. Hello there. I am a friend of Simon. He does not speak English. He asked that I help you. What are you doing there?"

"Oh, awesome. Yeah, see we're…"

And I told him our story. I tried to make it sound as innocent and non-dumbass as possible, and he sat patiently listening until the end of the crooked tale.

"All we need is a ride or to get a taxi. We have the address. If that doesn't work, maybe we can call the States and get the phone number for the château. I think they have a phone. Well, actually, I'm not sure if they do or not. Maybe a ride is best," I said.

"Uh-huh. Could you please put Simon back on the phone?" the man asked.

"Sure. Simon?" I said, extending the phone toward the waiting elf.

His wine mustache had turned a deeper shade of maroon.

"Oui! Simon!" he said, pointing to the reindeer on his chest and taking the phone from me.

"Oui. Oui. Ah…oui. Hmmmmm. Hmmmm. Ha! Oui. Hmmmmmm…hmmmm. Oui," Simon said to his friend on the line.

While he talked on the phone, Ethan, Jon, and I exchanged embarrassed glances. The family clinked and clanged behind us—glasses kissing, silver cutlery bumping porcelain plates. I felt stupid for being so stupid. We should have checked the address before we got out of the taxi, but better yet, we should have actually given the taxi driver the address instead of letting Ethan try and translate it in French. He meant well, but the road to blizzard hell and (thankfully) Simon's house was paved with good intentions.

"Oui. Oui," Simon seemed to be wrapping up the conversation, but instead of hanging up, he held out the phone to me again and nodded.

I took it. "Hello?"

"Yes, hello again. Simon says he will drive you to your street."

"Oh my gosh. That is so kind, so great! Thank you. Thank you for your help. Please tell Simon he rocks!" I almost yelled into the phone.

"Okay, goodbye now."

"Goodbye."

"Mone-eek-uh Loo-een-skee!" the boy shouted from behind us.

Outside, the sky was dumping on Le Clusaz, France.

XXX

Simon abandoned the wine. He headed our way with a man from the dinner table and started bundling up in winter gear. Dinner was finished. Most of the food and drink devoured. The family lounged about the house, purring in French about things I imagined being childhood memories. The fire in the living room popped and spit embers toward the iron mesh that protected the burning fragments from the shiny wood flooring. Ethan, Jon, and I re-buttoned our coats and tightened the strings on our hats.

When Simon finally swung open the front door, a blast of winter storm barged its way into the house. He and his friend trekked straight into it, hunched over in defiance. We followed their boot trail.

A heap of snow buried the car. Together we freed it, wiping jacketed arms over the windows and hood, trembling in the frigid wind. The snow came away easy like salt grains that had been dropped from the clouds, instead of frozen water. With the windows cleared, we all dove inside.

"Okay," Simon said, once the car was started and we were all safely seated like packed sardines.

"Final leg," Ethan mumbled into my shoulder.

We backed out of the driveway, tire chains grinding into the packed snow.

We drove.

We searched.

The men shot French at each other like BB gun pellets.

Tension was rising, along with the temperature in the car as our insulated bodies rubbed against each other with each winding turn.

We twisted through the Alps, and on one particularly hairy bend, Simon lost control of the car.

We swung left.

We swerved right.

He fought to get control, but it was useless.

We went into spins.

We completed three full circles—hairy three-sixties on an iced mountain road.

I held my breath the whole time, pretty sure it would be my last French Alp visit.

SLAM!

Luckily Simon's car spun into the mountainside instead of down the cliffside. The rocks stopped our careening.

Simon and his friend filled the car with colorful French, the kind we Americans refer to when pardoning ourselves. In the backseat, the three of us were stunned into silence.

Not-So-Jolly Elf put the car in park, took a deep breath, and then threw the car into reverse and got the hell out of dodge. He was on a fucking mission.

XXX

About thirty minutes later, we arrived on our street.

Jon, Ethan, and I said thank you probably too many times. We offered money and our first-born children, but Simon and his friend refused. We finally got out of the car. We were at the right house. We heard Liz's laugh through the walls.

"Honestly, thank you," I said, one last time before shutting the door.

That was the first view I got of the rear end of the car. It was dented badly, taillight busted. Our mountainside run-in had eaten his car. I knocked on the fogged driver's window. Simon cracked it, his feathery eyelashes flapping against the wind.

"Please, look," I said, beckoning him to get out of the car.

Simon climbed out. With chubby snowflakes collecting on his head, he stared at the rear end of his car. The new valley that was creased into the bumper area stared back at him.

Simon's expression was deadpan.

I felt horrible, and finally I got the courage to break the silence.

"We owe you money. I'm sorry," I said, talking to him like he magically learned English in the past thirty seconds.

"Money. We owe you," I said like Yoda, making counting movements with the gloved fingers of my left hand and using my right to point at the deep indention in the tail end of his Euro car.

Simon finally acknowledged me, taking a break from staring at his mangled car. He looked me in the eye. Then, he hugged me—a good, warm hug.

"No. Okay," he said, smiling again.

CHAPTER 40

Strangers have not only enriched my life, but they've helped keep it on track, even pushing me in new directions that I didn't know I needed to be heading. When traveling, engaging with strangers is part of the game. You learn again to be open-minded, just like you were as a toddler—unashamed or scared to walk up to someone and say, "Hi."

I don't have a method for judging character, like a college friend's dad who liked to pick up hitchhikers. He wouldn't let them in the car until they sang a song. The song the hitchhiker chose and the way he sang it supposedly predicted if he was going to try to slit my friend's dad's throat or sit coolly in the passenger seat telling nomadic tales.

For me, I don't have anything as sophisticated as his method to judge a first impression, but I kind of want one. I wish I based character on whether or not someone can do the Chewbacca noise, or if they prefer chocolate or vanilla ice cream.

I must say, I don't trust people who have an aversion to lip balm, and winkers never get my vote. That's about it.

Otherwise, I listen to my gut. Usually, my gut says people are nice. Don't fear them or the atmosphere they've helped create. Embrace it. If they offer help, take it. If they want to show you areas of their beautiful country, go. If they want to house and feed you, accept. Then, give back.

We are good animals.

We are a good world.

PART VII

"Home is where you feel at home and are treated well."
Dalai Lama

Long-term Travel Possible Gain List

1. THAT story. The one that's too crazy to be true. The one that blows minds, even your own.
2. International work experience.
3. An island life.
4. New ways of thinking.
5. A movie-like adventure.
6. Unexpected friends and allies.
7. A new home.

Long-Term Travel Possible Loss List

1. Your naivety.
2. Confusion about what you really want to do with your work life.
3. Weight.
4. The urge to surrender to fear.
5. Disbelief in magic.
6. Suspicion of strangers.
7. Single status.

Home Away From Home

CHAPTER 41

Homesickness is a real thing. Home might be a person, a bed, a city, or a culture, but regardless of the title, homesickness is a very real emptiness. It can be more potent than a flu that comes out both ends.

For some, homesickness fades with time. For others, it amplifies until they jump on the next flight out. For me, I don't really suffer from it. I get the home-sniffles maybe...sometimes...rarely.

I know my pattern too well to get homesick.

For the first five months in a new place I'm really discombobulated. My emotions go up, down, and do a backspin mid-dance floor. Any opinions formed during that time period are write-offs. It's too disorienting.

About six months in, I get my head wrapped around things. I know the good places to eat. I've met some people. The streets make sense, and I don't have to stare at the local currency for ages before paying.

After twelve months in a new place, I'm in the game. That's about the time I can trust my feelings. I've been there long enough to pass some judgments and give a thumbs-up or down to certain aspects of the set up.

I've mostly liked the countries I lived in. Some I loved, but even as much fun as I was having moving around the planet, I'd always planned on going "home" to the States at some point. I knew this because there were always things that weighed on my mind while overseas—comparisons or missing entities.

I'd miss weird things from the USA, like ghetto macaroni and cheese, the boxed Kraft with florescent yellow, powder cheese. I'd want to go out dancing where people were proud to vertically hump each other, pelvic thrust on top of the bar, or get in a line and perform the same dance steps with the precision of a dance corp.

I hadn't found a perfect overseas match yet—not that I was looking for one. I just noted that I wouldn't/couldn't live in these places forever.

The closest I ever got to bonding with a new location was when I lived in Spain. It was a rough start, admittedly. I stumbled through the tricky streets and language like an abandoned four-year-old, but after about eight months into Bilbao, I finally came right. It was around then that the language had had enough time to penetrate my grey matter, creep into my dreams, and roll off my tongue. I could even eavesdrop, so things got real good. Add a local boyfriend to the mix, and Spain became a carnival. But still, there were things that felt like square pegs to my round holes. Sometimes the antiquated side of the city got to me.

For example, I didn't want to have to purchase a *bombona* of gas every week just so I could take a hot shower, and then be out of luck the next week when it ran empty.

Bombonas were propane tanks, cumbersome, janky little things that were a boil on my Bilbao butt. When your *bombona* ran dry, forget about getting a quick replacement. Your shower would have to wait a day, maybe three, maybe more. The *bombona* man was on strike more than he was at work. It was a greasy, hair-pulling occurrence.

I preferred climbing into the shower, twisting the knob to the red area, and then sinking into a steamy waterfall of goodness. Fuck struggling with my towel while I dragged a heavy metal gas tank around the kitchen, hurrying to attach plastic tentacles to its head before my nipples froze and fell off.

And then there was the cost of living, lack of jobs, and limited space thing.

My Spanish boyfriend, Carlos, lived with his parents at age twenty-five, and so did his thirty-year-old sister…and their grandmother, and their cousin, and their Uncle's sister's husband's daughter.

This was normal.

They were middle class. The same family pile was stacked in most apartments, because housing is stupid expensive there. That's what happens when things are finite. Only so much land means only so many houses and so many owners.

High demand + low supply = champagne at diamond cost.

That's the equation they're born into. My twenty-something Spanish friends accepted their fates with half smiles and eye rolls. Life never claimed to be fair, so drink wine and be merry.

They knew they would probably never own property. They kept their fingers crossed on inheriting, but they would probably only rent and/or share any space they could find for the rest of their lives. To make ends meet, they'd take any scarce job they could while endeavoring to find one that matched their passion and paycheck dreams of six digits or more.

I didn't talk about my options. It would have been a fly in their Kalimotxo.

The miles of land back in Oklahoma that were not only affordable, but ripe for the picking, stayed un-discussed. On the red dirt where I was born and raised, I could build what I wanted, start a business pretty easily, and own a slew of toys if it blew my hair back. It wasn't that hard. Oklahoma is stupid affordable.

Most of the states are fairly easy living. I'm not saying everyone in the U.S.A. has an easy life. They don't. People starve here. They're wronged. There is blocked access to a better life—burnt out lamps on the street that is supposed to be paved with American success stories.

I'm just saying that, compared to some countries around the globe that could have hosted your birth, you should thank your lucky stars and stripes if you're American. As an American, you are spoiled rotten. Being born USD approved—you've already won the lottery. You have rights in a wealthy country. That is that.

It took living overseas for me to really understand the benefits of my birthplace. I had to experience other ways of living to miss the one I'd been brought into in, same as anything else. I know sweet is better than bitter, because I've had both on my tongue.

Plus, it was that whole absence thing. The blind man knows the value of sight once it goes. Take something away and you'll know how you really feel about it. Humans, eh.

Traveling really helped me. It made me realize my good fortune—my white girl, fluent in English, middle class, option-filled, college-educated, big-tittied luck. I also further understood why I wasn't able to picture myself living in these places I'd traveled to/lived in for a while…no matter how much I loved them.

I was keenly aware of the fact that, although I adored Spain, it limited my choices. Options mean freedom. Freedom is nice. The United States offered me a few more options. So to me, America always had a just a bit more glitz on it, and trading that in to live somewhere else was going to take a lot of persuading.

I hadn't found that mix of modern and rugged, complex and simplified, that works for me. Again…not that it was my goal. I wanted to live overseas long-term. I wasn't looking to immigrate to a new land, but big things always happen when you're not looking.

CHAPTER 42

Australia was the first country I lived in that was exotic, while also cutting edge, affordable, and doable. It was closer to piquing my interest in making a home away from home, but it turned out to blow hot and cold in the same breath.

I'd purchased an Australian holiday work visa through one of the handful of visa companies that do that kind of thing. For one price, they took care of my visa paperwork, my flight, my first night stay in a hostel in Sydney, and offered help with finding a job. They even offered a tour of the city on the first day. It was a pretty cushy introduction to leaving the USA solo for the first time ever.

Their promise of help was supposed to make me and other travelers feel good, like we had someone to hold hands with and give us a nuzzle if needed. I never called them for a shoulder to cry on, but I did visit their office on day three in Sydney for some advice, only to be brushed off and herded to a computer.

Google was their answer to all questions. The visa they'd offered me was a hunting pass for a job, and the help they offered me in trapping that job turned out to be little more than a finger point in the direction of the playing field. It was my first lesson to not believe everything you read or are told, not only in the USA but also everywhere on Earth— never ever, no matter how respectable and highly regarded.

This company's lack of follow-through started around eight a.m. on a sunny December morning. The welcome party wasn't exactly what they'd described, but oh well. Not the end of the world. After going through the regular airport rigmarole, I stepped outside into the big city—cars on the wrong side of street. The air smelled clean with only a tinge of acid. Noise of familiar clinks and clacks of hustle and bustle, but so far, nothing seemed shocking.

One thing was weird though—the sun. I stretched my arms toward it and inhaled, shook off the flight dust. The intensity of the rays sent my eyes into spasms. The sun is different there. My shades barely took the edge off.

"Hello," a guy with blonde hair, nice teeth, and an awesome Australian accent walked up with his hand extended. "I'm Grant. I'm with Work Oz. Welcome to Australia."

"Hi," I said, offering mine back. "Super stoked to be here."

We shook. Tight grips. I recognized the emblem on his t-shirt. It matched the one on the sunglass case they'd supplied me when I'd signed up. I'd used it to hold my weed.

"Long flight, eh?" he asked studying my features.

My limbs were liquid. My brain was baby food.

"Yeah. I'm pretty worn out."

"No worries. I'll just collect the others then we'll head to the hostel. You'll have a bit of time to relax before the city tour."

"Cool."

"Jet lag is a nasty. It's worse going the other direction, mate. Just wait until you head home," he said, looking beyond me into the airport crowd. "The bus is over there. Go relax," he instructed, pointing toward a van parked on the curb.

He walked off.

"Okay. Thanks!" I said to his back.

He flicked a mini-wave of acknowledgment over his shoulder.

I poured another gulp of Southern Hemisphere oxygen into my lungs.

Australia.

Vegemite sandwich.

XXX

The van was filled with other backpackers.

"You gonna find a job here?" I asked a short boy who'd announced he was from Washington.

"Yeah, but I have family here. They should set me up."

He clicked his tongue against his teeth, slung a wiry arm over the adjacent headrest, and crossed his legs.

"How about you?" I questioned a hippie girl wrapped around herself in the back row.

"I don't know yet. I'm gonna take my time. Figure it out," she lulled.

She seemed preoccupied, or maybe on NyQuil. Maybe both. The window held her gaze.

No one seemed to be in as much of a hurry or worry as I was. I needed to get into downtown quick-like. I needed to be employed yesterday, and I had no idea what I was doing. I didn't know anyone in Sydney, Darwin, or any spot on the continent. I was on a blind date with Australia, with only enough money to get me through about one month of my yearlong plan. I stifled the shrapnel of nervous sentences threatening to explode out of my mouth.

"That sounds like a good plan. Take it slow," I replied to the hippie girl.

Deep breath.

It's fine.

I was glad to be wearing sunglasses.

In downtown Sydney, our hostel looked like an old office building. Rows of tinted glass, separated floors of concrete. We were hustled into rooms and mixed with other backpackers who were also fresh off the boat. I was in an all-girl dorm room that slept ten. The walls were lined with bunk beds and the space smelled of apple shampoo. I chose the only bed that was left, the top bunk of a bed closest to the windowed wall.

"Hi, mind if I take this?" I asked the girl on the bottom bed who was about a quarter way into *The Kite Runner* by Khaled Hosseini.

"Of course not. It's all you," she replied.

Nice smile. British accent.

"How long ya been in Sydney?" I asked, dropping my pack at the end of the bedframe.

"Just over a month now. I just got here."

A month = just got there. Her travel calculations weren't following any mathematics I knew.

"You here to work or just travel?" I asked.

"I'm here to live and work, but Sydney is hard. Every traveler wants to be here, so it makes holiday work scarce. I've met people that have been looking for a job almost a year. Crazy," she laughed and moved her green eyes back to her book.

"Crazy," I nervous laughed back.

I used the ladder on the side of our bunk bed to climb up into my new life. It reminded me of childhood sleepovers and the thought brought another pang of panic. Home was literally an ocean away, and I was currently on the bottom of the globe.

I needed to collect my thoughts.

Up top, I reclined onto the lumpy pillow provided by the hostel and mentally thumbed through my qualms.

Was Sydney really jobless for foreigners? Why was this chick so relaxed about not finding work? One month? She'd been here ONE MONTH? What the shit?

Instead of thinking myself into a sinkhole, I decided to nut up and ask the hard questions. It was the first lesson I'd taught myself on not being afraid or embarrassed to figure stuff out. If I didn't do it, no one would do it for me.

I dangled my head upside down off the bed and stared at her. I could feel my eyes filling with blood. I thought of Donger in *Sixteen Candles*— "Wassa happenin' hot stuff?"

"Hey, mind if I ask you something?" I asked.

"Not at all," she said, laying her book down on her chest.

"How are you not worried about not finding a job? Do you not have to work?"

"Oh, I'm on the Pound. We're almost four to one on the Australian dollar. My money goes a long way here."

Her smile stretched a kilometer.

"Oh, okay. Thanks."

I pulled myself back up onto my pillow.

Damn. No more yanky my wanky. The Donger needs works.

I wanted a more inspiring reason for her calmness, like a crystal ball hidden in her backpack that promised a café position next Tuesday.

It will be okay. I will be great. It will be the best.

I chanted myself into a shallow nap. Half an hour later, I was awakened by the tough truth.

XXX

A girl I didn't recognize shook me awake.

"You with Work Oz?" she asked.

"Yeah," I slobbered.

"There's a guy outside who wanted me to tell you your tour van is leaving."

"Shit. Thanks."

I ripped myself awake, hustled out of the room and out to the waiting van. It was time to meet Sydney—kiss cheeks with what would be my new world for the next few months.

The city was great. New, funky architecture. Unidentifiable trees with gnarled bark. Funny, little cars driving on the left side of the road. The sexy Australian accent of our tour guide. So far, I liked it.

We were provided lunch during our tour—a paper sack filled with a sandwich, chips, and a drink. We dined picnic style on a bluff overlooking the city beach, Bondi Beach. It was perfect. We chatted, but the conversation waned with each bite and chew. Our guide took advantage of the gap.

"So, Sydney can be a tough city for a few reasons, but there are some animals, insects, and reptiles you need to be aware of while you live in Australia. No matter where you travel or live, just keep in mind—our wildlife can kill you."

His approach was blasé. We listened to his death list while trying to be as cool about it as his delivery. The top ten deadliest of everything was in Australia.

Salt water crocs and death rolls.

Box jellyfish with killer venom.

A blue-ringed octopus that's only the size of golf ball, but a better killer than Jeffrey Dahmer. There's no antivenom for its sting, so if you get hit, you're a goner.

The Inland Taipan Snake—its kiss is worse than all other snakes in the world, and it's a master of disguise, so good luck spotting it until it's too late.

More snakes.

Then spiders.

A stingray or two.

Oh, then the Great White Sharks that like to swim up to Bondi Beach, the exact beach I was staring at. The city put in a net to try to keep them out, but sometimes it keeps them in, *hahahahahaha!*

My favorite tale was that of the funnel-web spiders. They're city spiders, but all thick with sexy tarantula features. They like to pretend they're human and live in homes with air conditioning and cable television, or tucked away under the sun visor in your car. If they bite you, you have about fifteen minutes to get to a hospital.

Interesting news.

Although what our tour guide was telling us was surprising, it didn't freak me out. Not finding a job freaked me out more.

The job market was my main concern, while I stared down at the surfers taking full advantage of their lunch break. I zoned out on the warning speech. The words went right through me...or so I thought. I'd find out later that my subconscious was recording every syllable and secretly shitting itself.

XXX

That night back at the hostel, life was all good in the hood. The chicks in my dorm room and I chatted about backpacker stuff, the energy that pulsed through Sydney, and what our future plans held.

As the yawns grew louder, I told my fellow backpackers goodnight and climbed onto my top bunk, one of the six bunk beds scattered throughout the room.

Each pair of bunk beds was pressed up against the perimeter of the room, leaving one big hole in the center for walking, mingling, or doing whatever twelve girls who don't know each other do when assigned to a room together—which is get naked, pillow fight, and then clean the leftover caramel off each other's nipples with tongue lashes. You know—girl stuff.

I fluffed my pillow as best I could and curled up in the fetal position under my scratchy blanket. As far from home as I was, I was delighted to find that my body didn't act like it. Without effort and within seconds I dropped off into blissful sleep. I was rocked into dreamland and held tight by the capable arms of my new adventure.

Part of my ease was probably down to exhaustion, but I'll account the rest to being in an all-female dorm room. All girls meant less whiffs of butt bouquet and armpits that smell like they'd been cooking taco burgers all day. Plus, chicks usually have daintier sleeping habits. Some guys really like to suck the paint off the walls, snoring like demons and somehow staying comatose through the night.

For whatever reason, most girls don't do that.

We are quieter, softer creatures. We may pee a bed or four, but we don't imitate Shrek when we sleep.

The group of girls in this room didn't disappoint. We were all unobtrusive, respectful, and magically went to sleep at the same time. This is something that almost never happens. It was awesome, and at about two a.m. I ruined it all.

XXX

In the wee hours of morning while everyone fell deep into REM—including me—I suddenly sprang from my bed and Spider-Manned my way across the line of windows. In seconds, I had gone from prone position to hands suction-cupped against the wall. Then I jumped down to the window ledge where I walked / crawled / screamed my way along each glass panel in an attempt to find a way out.

I frantically fumbled at the locks.

I screamed about encroaching arachnids.

I am a sleepwalker.

Thank goodness I'm not good at figuring out the finer details of mechanisms in my sleep, like locks or doorknobs, because in this case, if I had been successful, my payoff would have been a swan dive from four stories up. The sidewalk would have broken my fall, along with every bone in my body. That would have been an excellent way to start my year overseas, but that didn't happen.

Instead, I woke up crouched and breathing heavy with one hand scratching uselessly at the slick glass and the other jiggling a metal handle.

In my half-asleep, half-lucid state I'd realized that the lights were on.

As my brain fog lifted further, I realized I wasn't in my bed. I was pressed against a window.

Hmmmmmm....

I twisted my head to look behind me, and that's when I realized the entire room of girls was awake too.

All twelve of them had left their beds and were gathered at the OTHER end of the room—as far away from me as they could get without actually sprinting into the hallway. Every pair of eyes looked rabid. Some mouths were torn back in that "horror face" you see in old black and white movies where some chick just had a vampire show her his fangs. Others just looked plain pissed off but pale, caught somewhere between *I think I'm gonna have to stab this bitch* and *I think I'm gonna have a panic attack.*

I stared at them.

They stared at me.

"Oh. Hey, guys," I finally said. "I was just having a dream."

Speech of the year, I think.

Then, I casually climbed down from the windowsill and used my same adept mountaineering skills to get back onto my top bunk. I fell asleep as soon as my head hit the pillow and slept like a baby.

I awoke at nine a.m., refreshed and ready to figure out my new life in Sydney. I would find a good job, damn it. The sun streamed in the windows. I had the whole room to myself. Everyone had already vacated, probably jumpstarting their morning. I took my time getting up, taking advantage of the privacy and leisure time. I went through the motions of getting ready in turtle mode.

Slow, hot shower.

Relaxing towel and lotion session.

Mindless blow-drying of the hair. A few outfit test runs.

I settled on a denim mini-skirt and black tank top. I looked cute. Ready. Able.

I finally made my way down to the breakfast/kitchen area where I saw a group of girls from my room hanging out, munching on cereal, and talking. I sauntered up to their table—all sunshine and roses.

"Hey y'all. So, are any of you going to the Work Oz office today to ask about jobs or anything?" I beamed, trying on my cordial, Oklahoma manners.

Nothing. Not a damn tweet. No crickets. No breeze. Bitchfest 2001. Apparently, acting like you forgot your meds, spazzing hard, threatening spider death, and following it up with a yawn and the world's best sleep isn't kosher.

That's how I ended up NOT at their table. I went and sat with the loner hippie chick that hadn't been in my room. Turned out, she was from the Bay Area. Also turned out, she'd sold her eggs straight out of her ovaries to get overseas. She wasn't in a hurry to get a job, because they'd paid pretty well for her eggs.

"I'm going to Melbourne today," she told me through sideways bites of Muesli and peaches.

"Me too," I improvised.

I wasn't going to Melbourne until right then. I'd obviously made the wrong name for myself in Sydney. It was time to taint my name in a new place. Melbourne sounded good enough, and this chick who was willing to have a surgery that removed her future children from her belly to have some good times in Australia seemed pretty driven. I figured she'd help me keep my eye on the prize.

CHAPTER 43

Melbourne was colder than it should have been. Winter just wouldn't let go. The city was actually having its coldest summer in history, and I trudged through its stinging wind every day, determined to find work and make my time there cheerful.

I found out that the nasty rumors about holiday workers were true. There were loads of backpackers with working holiday visas and only limited holiday jobs, the kind of shift work or monthly gigs that paid decent and had managers who didn't mind new faces clocking in every day.

I was desperate to find work, because I had to. Due to my slim bank account, it was GO WORK or GO HOME. My loaded ego wouldn't allow the latter. There was no way in hell I was boarding a plane with my tail tucked between my thighs, so I walked the streets like a starving wolf, asking if anyone needed help, and little by little the jobs popped up their scrawny heads.

I scrubbed toilets with my Bachelor's Degree. I washed dishes with my bilingual, managerial, and leadership qualifications. And, while I got paid doing those things, I kept looking for a job that paid better, one that I semi-liked.

It finally came in the form of a café position—the job that I landed pretending to be the world's best barista. That job helped things a lot, but it couldn't help everything.

Things were weird in Melbourne. The cold was freezing everyone's personality, and I'd been threatened to get beat up three times on the train to work by partiers who'd taken their lurking hours from two a.m. to four a.m., and then stretched their filthy talons into business hours.

"What the fuck you lookin' at, bitch?" a sweaty girl with black hole eyes yelled at me across the train.

I had been staring at her and her friends. Six a.m. vampires are difficult to ignore.

I turned away from her snarl. I was getting used to the riff-raff and intimidations—sick of the status quo. Fuck her. If she wanted to fight, I would.

A girl that I knew had been jumped outside of a bar, her face beat into purple lumps of mushy flesh. A group of us took turns bringing her cups of tea, food, and anything else she needed for two weeks after the incident. She stayed in bed the whole time. Books. Sleep. Pee breaks. And after about fourteen days, she looked less like the Elephant Man and more publicly presentable.

"What really happened?" I finally asked.

"I said something smart to them," she admitted through blows on her steaming chamomile.

"Still, four on one is bullshit," I replied, taking a good look at her still swollen cheekbone.

"Ummmm," she hummed, sipping at her drink.

"Ya know, last week a fight broke out on the tram I was on. An old man called a group of teenagers a bunch of niggers. They looked Aborigine. They said some stuff back. He said some more horrible stuff, and then a young business man grabbed the old dude by the throat and threw him off the tram into the street."

"That's good," she said, daintily setting her tea on the side table.

"Yeah, it was. The week before that I watched a girl give a blow job to a guy on the train right in front of me. That wasn't so good."

"What? Was everyone watching?"

"Yeah, I mean, everyone in the car was. It was just those two, me, and some other random guy. It was late. Almost midnight. I thought something like that might be a turn on, but it felt awkward and wrong. The couple seemed looped out. It was just...yucky."

"Mmmmm," she said returning to her tea with a shiver. "Hey, you notice all the black lights in the public bathrooms?"

"Yeah. It's odd, like walking into a bathroom rave," I said.

"I heard they're meant to stop heroine users from shooting up. Can't find a vein in that light."

"Huh," I grunted, feeling suddenly dirty.

And so it went like that in Melbourne. Lots of druggies. People, kind of rude. Me, overworked. Threats to steal my purse if I didn't get off a payphone. Name calling on the train. A businesswoman calling me a stupid American when I pronounced the word niche like "nitch" instead of "neesh". Cold summer. Anger radiating off the pavement.

I constantly counted the calendar dates until the day arrived that I could quit my job and travel around the rest of Australia. I'd come to Australia knowing I would work for three months and travel for a fourth, hitting the east coast and into the famous outback to see and do my dreams.

Great Barrier Reef. Kangaroos. Waterfalls. Uluru.

I would not spend a dime of my savings, because I'd worked my ass off at the café and saved enough to do whatever I wanted for one month. I had a five thousand dollar budget for four weeks of playtime—not bad, but my psyche was paying for it. I was exhausted, energized only by the few, thin rays of sunlight that broke grey clouds and did a pathetic job of warming my tired heart.

Two things kept me going during that time.

One was my excitement for the bright side of Australia—the awesome side. I couldn't wait to get out of the cities and into nature. I would swim the beaches. I would sail the ocean. I would dive the reef, hike the outback, and sleep under the stars. It would be a cultural awakening.

The second thing that kept me going was odd. It was related to a gift I have—one I was born with. I don't know how to explain it exactly, but sometimes I know stuff. I'm not really sure what causes it. Whatever the reason, I just sometimes have a feeling…and that feeling comes true.

In Melbourne, I had that feeling. I knew something great was coming, and I knew what it was.

XXX

The first time it pinged on my radar was in St. Kilda—an art-funky part of Melbourne. I was eating Thai food with an Irish girl. She pulled out some travel photos from her purse during dessert.

"Wow, where is this?" I asked, thumbing a photo of a fern-lined river with the clearest, most turquoise water.

"New Zealand," she answered.

The feeling hit. My gut made an electric checkmark somewhere in my psyche.

A week later, another photo brought the feeling again.

"This is the biggest bungee jump in the world?" I asked a Canadian guy who had become a regular at my café.

He'd brought in photographs of his travels, and his prized possession was this New Zealand pic.

"Yup. The whole country is full of crazy shit to do. It's the EXTREME capital of the world. I loved it. I had no idea it was going to be like that. I actually like it better than here, and my whole goal was to get to Australia," he said, using care to return the photo to his man bag.

My gut screamed at me. Checkmark number two.

And from there it just kept happening.

Someone would tell me about New Zealand, or show me something from New Zealand, or I'd walk past a travel poster of it, and my soul talked to me. It was really strange, because I had a work visa for New Zealand that I didn't mean to have. I'd only gotten it because Work Oz said that I could stay overseas longer if I got a work visa for New Zealand as well as Australia. I'd gotten the work visa for New Zealand only weeks before leaving for Australia. A quick phone conversation led to the paperwork.

"Where is New Zealand?" I asked the Work Oz woman.

"It's a small country southeast of Australia. People really like it. They speak English, so you won't have to work your way through learning a new language."

"Well, sweet. I'll pay for a work visa there too, so I can be away longer."

"Great," she said.

I could hear the tapping of computer buttons in the background. The deal was done.

"Great," I repeated.

I didn't even check to see where it was on a map. I didn't know a damn thing about it, and neither did anyone I knew. Mind you, at this time there was no *Lord of the Rings*. Not many Americans knew about New Zealand prior to that movie. I'd even been asked if I could drive there from Australia, taking some bridge that connected one country to the other. I told them I didn't know—maybe there was a bridge…could be. Dunno. I was really pleased about my accidental New Zealand work visa, even though I didn't know diddlysquat about the country.

When I finally quit my job and worked my way around Australia, I had an awesome time. It was beautiful, wonderful, amazing, and inspiring, but again… New Zealand wouldn't leave me alone.

More conversations.

More photos.

Books.

By then I was positive. Something was going to happen there—something fucking fantastic, something much better than the ass whooping threats of Melbourne and the centipede bite to the neck I got in the outback. The bite was blistered, bubbling in the shape of a melting arrow. My first reaction to it was *yikes*. My second was, *I wonder what insects they have in New Zealand. Probably friendly ones that wear top hats.*

XXX

I was right. The insects in New Zealand wear top hats. Everything there is friendly. As a matter of fact, there is nothing there—on land anyway—to even cause the flap of a nervous eyelid. No snakes. No killer spiders. No bears or big cats. Nothing bigger than a deer. Just furry, happy things and chirpy birds.

I learned that fun fact while on the plane, and when I landed in New Zealand, I started my time there by having a long phone conversation with a Kiwi woman.

Standing in the dead Auckland Airport at half past midnight, I was somehow feeling chatty. The Work New Zealand person who was supposed to pick me up from the airport no-showed. He was not only my ride, but also my connection to my one-night-free hostel stay in Auckland, hence the phone call—I wanted my free stuff.

But, instead of just talking about the lack of a driver, I ended up asking about glaciers, explaining Oklahoma armadillos, and mimicking my dad's hick accent for about fifteen minutes—"Worsh your clothes on Mon-dee, and all y'all come over on Tues-dee for supper."

I blabbed about the plural of *y'all*—*all y'all*—and other southern phrases, like *get-er-done*, and how my dad compares everything to a bear.

It's colder than a bear. It's bigger than a bear. It's better than a bear. It's dryer than a bear. It's cheaper than a bear.

"His bear sayings go on and on," I told her. "In my dad's mind, it really doesn't matter what you compare a bear to, because it all works as long as you add 'you bet' at the end. Like, *longer than a bear, you bet!*"

"Uh-huh," the older woman responded, apparently staying on track with my redneck story. "So, you're an American?"

"Yes, I'm American. Amurrrrrr-ican!" I added, because things were already out of hand on my end.

I twisted the metal phone cord and stared at the ceiling.

"Murrica," I muttered.

"Hmmm, well that's more interesting than a bear."

I laughed.

"I might have a job for you. Can you come by tomorrow to talk? You are looking for a job, yes?" she asked.

I was shocked into toy soldier pose.

"YES. Yes I can come by tomorrow, and yes I am looking for work. YES!"

I gaped at the silver buttons on the phone. This was no Australia. *Au contraire mon frère.* My gut did not lie. Within freakin' seconds of being in New Zealand, I got a job—a real fucking cool one. IN YO FACE, Melbourne!

My job was to fly around New Zealand to all the colleges, universities, and tertiary schools to promote the reverse of the exact work visa I was on. I worked with Work Experience USA. They send Kiwis to work at ski resorts in the United States during our winter season. My task was to find the Kiwis who would want to work at Winter Park, Vail, Aspen, etc.

Granted, I hadn't planned on staying in Auckland. That part of the deal wasn't so great. I couldn't really complain, but I was still a little bummed. New Zealand is all about the untouched bits—the glorious, prehistoric, unscathed nature. And here I was, staying in a city of two million people, when I don't even really like cities. Sucker move. But it worked out, and when I say it worked out, I mean everything fell perfectly into place for my liking and benefit, just like I was Bugs Bunny.

I magically found a cheap room for rent in a house located in one of the most upper crust neighborhoods of Auckland—St. Heliers. The city beach was at the bottom of the road. My job was located less than five blocks away. The bus stop was at the edge of my lawn and it connected me to the entire city. BOOM BITCH!

And my job, well it turned out to be pretty damn sparkly. It took me to Queenstown, Wanaka, Dunedin, Nelson, Wellington, Christchurch, Hawks Bay, and a handful of other outstanding locations that most tourists want to visit. I went all over the North and South Islands of New Zealand—for free.

I worked with a cool Kiwi girl, and, of course, the older woman I'd talked to on the phone. I lived with Kiwis. And I was really getting into the Kiwi way of life, when one day I noticed the Kiwi girl who lived in my house, Emma, talking shit to one of the Kiwi guys who lived there too—we called him Peroxide.

Their argument sparked my interest, because Peroxide was a genuine asshole— a dick munch who bleached his hair snowy white, wore tight leather pants, and marched around the house spitting orders, complaints, and threats.

"You left food bits on the bench again and I'm fucking tired of it, ya nasty beast," he hissed at Emma, flinging his gym guns around the room.

"Please, crumb control. The kitchen is clean. It's you that's the problem. That peroxide is mutating your brain," Emma yawned.

Leaving him to fume, she sashayed out of the kitchen and into her room with gazelle grace, closing the door behind her with a smooth click.

She was right. The kitchen was clean. He was mentally awkward.

"Cunt!" he yelled at the cupboard, then turned his wrath toward me. "Well…what are you looking at?" he grumbled.

I glared back at him. Hand on hip. Words ready, but locked into a holding pattern until further provoked.

He huffed a flat, "Ignoramuses," and ran a finger over the clean countertop before exiting stage left. His leathered thighs squeaked tiny goodbyes in his wake.

I knocked on Emma's door.

"Come in." Her voice squeezed through the wood.

I pushed the door open and stood in the doorway.

"Wanna castrate our roommate next week? We can see a movie or something after," I suggested.

It was the first time I'd asked her to hang out. Before that, we'd only spoken in passing niceties. *Hi. Hey. How's it?*

"Sure. Got any dull scissors or a butter knife? Actually, let's just twist it off," she said.

"Sounds good. That won't take long. I'm sure it's the size of a baby fist," I answered.

Emma nodded, smiled.

That's when I knew she and I would eventually run this dude out of the house and take over the kingdom.

About a month later, that's exactly what we did.

Along the way she introduced me to her friends, and after that my New Zealand life exploded. I developed an awesome crew. We ran deep. My blood started smelling Kiwi-ish, and shit got crazier and funnier.

XXX

People sell a place. You could be in the middle of the most beautiful, striking, breathtaking destination in the galaxy, but if you finish taking a photo and the local behind you says, "Fuck off, ugly," it might become lackluster. If five minutes later a local woman busts your lip open, and that same evening an old man tells you to go home and never come back, you probably will. There will be no bragging about your vacation or recommendations to your friends. Screw that place.

But, contrarily, if a place is only kind of pretty—a few trees, some ho-hum hills—but the people are awesome, you'll have a great time. You'll want to go back. You'll tell your friends to run, not walk, in that direction.

That's how New Zealand is, but with the added spectacular scenery.

The people are fantabulous, and don't even get me started on the topography of that country. It's a nature lover's wet dream. For me, it's the ultimate great people/nature combo.

So, the people—Kiwis are really laid back, but not pushovers or lacking in zest. They're the quiet riot type. They're kind too. They tell the bus drivers thank you and have more conversations than altercations. They actually invest in each other and people in general, or at least that's what I've witnessed.

I'll give you an example from when my job took me down to a small town on the South Island. It was about thirty minutes outside of Wanaka, which was a bigger, very popular town.

I got a room at a boutique hotel. My room was simple, a kitchenette with dated décor. The owner was really nice. He was an older man, maybe in his late fifties. He and his wife had started the boutique as their retirement project.

I ordered breakfast from him every morning and he'd deliver it on a wooden tray. Oatmeal. Orange slices and apple chunks. Pot of tea. Sugar cubes. Fresh cut morning glory in a little white vase.

I'd walk over to the office to place my breakfast order, have a chat with him and his wife, then glide back over to my place to wait for the delicious delivery.

"They warming up to you?" the woman asked me about my Work Experience USA audience through coral pink lips.

It was my last morning there. The hills slept in the window view. I leaned on the reception desk and stretched my legs.

"I think so. I think they liked my spiel," I told her.

"If they don't, the wife and I can rough 'em up. Teach 'em some manners," the man joked. "Same brekkie as yesterday?"

"Yes, please. It's a beautiful morning," I said.

"It is. You going down to Wanaka later? Going to have some fun and enjoy the spring weather?" the man asked.

"Oh, no. I didn't rent a car. I'm fine here. I'll just hang out and read."

"That sounds nice and relaxing," said the woman.

I thanked them and went back to my room. Twenty minutes later, the man came in carrying the wooden tray with the breakfast goodies, but with one little addition.

Oatmeal. Orange slices and apple chunks. Pot of tea. Sugar cubes. Fresh cut morning glory in a little white vase. A set of car keys.

"You left your keys," I told the man, pointing to the set.

"No, I didn't. They're for you. The wife and I discussed it, and we want you to go have a good time. Take our car. You're too young to be staying home and reading on a weekend like this. Go down to Wanaka. Let loose a little," he said.

He nodded and turned to leave.

"Wait," I grabbed the key ring and walked to him. "Thank you so much. This is one of the most generous things anyone has ever offered me, but I can't—not because I don't want to, but because I'll want to party if I go down there. I can't be drinking and driving."

He scratched his chin.

"True. I didn't think about that. Well, let me talk to the missus. I'll be right back."

He left. I held the keys in my hand, thinking how trustworthy and awesome these two people were. Five minutes later, he returned to my room, a smile on his kind face.

"My wife and I both agree it's a bad idea for you to drink and drive, but we both think you should still go. We think you should hitchhike down there."

"What? Hitchhike?"

"Do you hitchhike?" he asked in the same way you might ask someone if he or she plays croquet.

"I've gotten rides from strangers. I wouldn't say I hitchhike, though. Is it safe to do that here? In Australia I heard…"

He waved me off before I could finish.

"This isn't Australia, love. The fruit stand is where everyone goes to hitch rides. I'll take you over there, get you going."

And he did. At the fruit stand, a married couple—both professors—drove me down to Wanaka, and gave me ripe grapes and a juicy peach to munch on while we talked about everything from crows to rollercoasters.

In Wanaka, I danced and partied my ass off—had an amazing time. The boutique couple was right. I wasn't meant to be at home reading on a Saturday night.

CHAPTER 44

Most Kiwis are like that. Generous. Thoughtful. Ready to enjoy life and make sure you do too.

The longer I lived in Auckland, the more I bonded with my Kiwi friends and life. I extended my three-month work visa to six, and then onward. There wasn't an inch of flesh on my bones that wanted to be anywhere but there.

My friends and I went to concerts. We swam the beaches. We boated. We rented baches (Kiwi vacation homes) in remote and outstanding locations. We played in the parks. We gathered at each other's houses for dinner and board games. We did all of it without a ton of money or means.

We saved. We worked and played hard. We worked together to make magic happen—and oh, how enchanting it was.

These Kiwis and me, we were cut from the same cloth, although raised on opposite halves of the planet. We shared our sense of humor, positive outlook, happiness level, and purpose. The people I met there made me feel comfortable. They cared about my soul, not my shirt, car, career, or un-flat stomach. They are a people of substance.

My friends, my Kiwi mates, we were destined to be friends. I'll go ahead and call it fate. I dare say we were meant to meet, linked by destiny and cosmic rules, because we are duplicate souls. They are fragments of my whole—ingredients to the recipe of my existence that, if left out, would have indisputably dulled my finished product.

They accepted me like I'd always been there, like I was a slice of their childhood memories. They swooped me up and broadened my belief system. I became a better person, and the cherry on top of this love sundae was that they also cracked me up.

Kiwis are hilarious. Witty. Sharp shooters.

In my opinion, they have the closest sense of humor to Americans, even though a lot of people think we only like pies to the face and fart jokes. Believe me, Kiwis and Americans mesh well. One warm-ish January day taught me just how connected I was to my Kiwi friends.

XXX

Three years prior, I'd started hosting a day of games called the Drunken Olympics.

This was something I'd dreamed up while living in London and feeling particularly lazy. I wanted to get friends together for a day of physical games in the park, not board games in the living room like we usually did. But, the only way I thought that could happen was if I enticed everyone with spiked drinks, so I combined the two—drinking and sporting. I figured we could compete in a way that lazy, drunk, uncoordinated people could enjoy, yet still excel.

The answer was a day full of things like the slow bicycle race, where you see just how long it can take you to ride a bike four feet without putting your feet down.

We had the three-legged race. A belching contest. Egg toss. Backwards sprint, and some other weird events. My London fun went so well that I took it back with me to New Zealand. There, the event grew. The obstacles got more intricate. It was starting to have a pretty good following.

On this fourth year of my Drunken Olympics party and the warm-ish January day in New Zealand, things were really poppin'. It was the best Drunken Olympics to date, because Deirdre had a friend who owned a prop shop.

Cindy's prop shop was a heavenly warehouse filled with all the random things a set designer or party planner might need—a wall of ghetto boxes, shelves of snow globes, hallways of big wheels, boxes of '60s lamp shades, stuffed beavers, old fashioned cash registers. You name it. Cindy had just what we needed, and we needed some weird shit for these Olympics.

For the Fourth Annual Drunken Olympics, which was to be held at 2:00 p.m. in a park down the street from my friend Tracy's house, I needed plastic starfish, ice chests, life jackets, and some award pedestals.

Cindy's prop shop did have the plastic sea creatures, life jackets, ice chests, and other bits and pieces, but she didn't have three different sizes of pedestals for the award ceremonies. Bummed out, I searched for replacements.

"The only thing I have that comes in three different sizes and shapes is chairs. They're wheelchairs. There's a tall, antique one that barely rolls (to use for 3rd place), an average hospital wheelchair (2nd place), and a shorter, fancy, sport wheelchair with angled wheels (1st place)," she told me.

"That'll do," I said. "Plus, they'll come in handy if someone gets hurt. I mean…we will be drinking to excess."

We were set. The day came. We competed and drank hard. As the day progressed, the Fourth Annual Drunken Olympics was a huge hit. It went so well that we partied into the late day and transferred from the park back to Tracy's house to keep the fun wheel turning.

We danced. We disputed earlier awards and bragged about nonexistent athletic prowess. We held the awards ceremony in the living room, using the wheelchairs instead of pedestals. When the awards were over, instead of moving the wheelchairs off to the side, we ended up experimenting with them. I tried popping some wheelies, and pretty soon I was feeling confident. At midnight, I was feeling so self-assured that I decided one last race was in order, but lack of proper protection gear was threatening to keep it from happening.

"Please. Plllleeeaaaassseee!" I wailed to Jade from my second place wheelchair, while wearing my red, white, and blue headband that matched my Miss America Pageant t-shirt.

"Dude, you're going to get hurt. Trust me. It's not that I don't want you to do this. I totally want you to, but I think you need a helmet," she replied, looking at our other girlfriends for confirmation.

They stood in a circle around me, holding beers and wearing heavy grins. Tribe Called Quest played in the background. Some of the girls nodded "yes" to my idea. Others shook their heads, "No."

"She'll be fine, mate," Amy added.

"Ahhhh yeah…ahhhh…nah. Get her a helmet. Safety first, Simpson," Deirdre said.

"But that's the whole problem, I don't have any helmets," Tracy slurred.

I tried to pop a wheelie unsuccessfully. It was a mini-hop instead.

"Come on!" I growled at Tracy, rolling back and forth. "Are you making Damon wear a helmet?"

Jade thought for a minute. "Um, yeah…even though I don't think he needs it."

"What?! I have the coordination of a mountain goat!" I yelled.

I tried to pop and lock again, this time almost tipping over backwards. I spun the wheels hard to fling the footholds back to the ground. They pounded out a deep BANG against the floor.

"Uh-huh," Jade said.

I slumped in defeat. Then, a light bulb came on in my attic.

"How about we duct tape pillows to our heads?" I asked.

"Okay," Jade agreed.

"I'll get the gear," Tracy yelled as she stumbled out of the room.

XXX

So, with a bed pillow wrapped around my head and strategically fixed in place by duct tape, I was fully ready. I looked like a B version of Dark Helmet in *Spaceballs* and so did Damon. He was forced into the same pillow helmet. Fair.

We lined up at the top of Tracey's very steep driveway. The concrete was dark, except for the bottom third which was illuminated by a sphere of peachy streetlight. The partygoers gathered in its roundness.

The driveway was actually quite a bit steeper than I had planned on it being. My new secret plan was to finish the race in one piece, maybe try to keep my speed to an embarrassing crawl. My mouth has a bad habit of writing checks that my body can't cash.

"On my GO…" Jade yelled up the hill. "GO!"

Damon was out—long gone past a distance I could catch up to. Since he was out of my reach, I decided to make my way to the bottom the same way a new skier would, traversing in nice, neat lines.

"Easy does it," I talked myself through it, enjoying my leisurely style.

My friends were already making fun of me by the time I reached the finish line.

"Hey grandma, nice lines!"

"You suck, Simpson!"

"All talk, no roll."

I slugged over the finish line, immune to their taunts and beaming from underneath my pillow helmet.

"Guys, I may have lost, but I really think I have some great control over this chair," I said.

And I did. So did Damon. We rolled around getting better and better until Jade had the fifth best idea ever. She and her sister-in-law, Anna, rummaged around in her car trunk.

"Yup," was all she said before getting back in her car, starting it up, and reversing toward Damon and me.

I stood and began folding up the wheelchair for transporting purposes.

"Nah, nah, nah, nah," Jade corrected me through her open window. "Nah mate, we're gonna pull you. Anna is getting a rope."

"I don't understand," I said, walking up and leaning into Jade's window.

My pillow helmet bumped against the sides, refusing me total entry.

"I thought you were giving us a ride somewhere," I said.

"I am. I'm giving you a ride around the block. Get behind the car," she instructed.

I turned and looked at Damon. He shrugged and rolled into position behind the car. Anna threw a rope out of the open hatch to him, keeping hold to the opposite end.

"Take that Damon," she demanded. "Shelby, here. This one is for you."

Another thin rope flew out of the hatch and landed a couple of feet away from Damon. I obeyed, settled back into my wheelchair, rolled next to Damon, and took ahold of the rope.

"Ready?" Jade yelled.

"I guess," I yelled back.

I tightened my grip around the rope, preparing for a rapid lift off, but Jade was sensible about her whack idea. We rolled forward at a comfortable pace. It was pretty sweet.

Once we were doing well, she picked up the speed a bit—not high speed, just enough to have a little fun. Anna had the ropes wrapped twice around the headrests to take some of the pressure off her grip. She clutched the ends and smiled back at us periodically. With the ropes stretched to full length, Damon and I had plenty of room for maneuvering.

"All good?" Anna yelled to us through the open hatch.

"Sweet as!" Damon yelled. "This is really nice," he said to me, like he was trying out a new wake board.

We rolled steady—starting to get a bit cocky, taking a few turns slalom style.

"Damon, check this out," I said.

I swung hard left like you would if you were water skiing behind a boat, letting my rope go slack and then waiting for the moment when it caught, whipping me back toward the wake, or in this case, Damon and the middle of the road.

"Nice!" Damon laughed.

He popped some wheelies, did some big turns.

"Woooo!" I yelled.

Wind through my pillow.

Duct tape stretched tight under my chin grin.

We cruised behind her car at low, but fun speed. Looking over at Damon with his pink pillow helmet and towrope I thought, *huh. Who'd a thunk it? Me and the Kiwis—freaks of a feather freak together.*

XXX

I had a blast in New Zealand. I had a great life, an awesome job, even more awesome hobbies, and the most awesome friends. I also had the kind of outdoor adventures National Geographic writes about. I was surrounded by fascinating landscape, and it was all in my backyard.

Glaciers. Rain forests. Sand dunes. Black sand beaches. Cave systems. Manicured hills. Jagged mountains. Hot springs. Volcanic lakes. Winding rivers. Clean oceans. All of it less than a few hours away.

After work, on the weekends, during holidays…I explored. It was easy to fall in love with New Zealand, and even more so when I fell in love with a boy.

CHAPTER 45

I think a lot of girls fantasize about exotic love. I know Fabio is a rancid example, but you know what I'm talking about. It's the idea of some cut up, rough but smooth, sophisticated at the table and uncouth in the bedroom, foreign type. He fixes cars using a sparrow's feather and some seaweed, and has a history of wrestling sharks. He's offered to take you to his family's castle in Vienna and Switzerland for Christmas, but only after he finishes his PhD in Physics—first things first.

Because I started traveling at twenty-four and planned on doing it for quite a while, I thought I'd probably meet someone who wasn't American. I didn't plan on it, but it was a distinct possibility. I wanted my kids to pronounce things weird.

I met my future husband at a friend's house in Auckland, the first time I traveled/lived there. He came sliding in the room like Kramer from *Seinfeld* and told a story about how a friend's dog's fleas ate a trail from his toe to scalp, then u-turned, flossed, and started back down.

He'd slept on my friend's couch a few nights before. That's where the attack happened, I think. I didn't catch all the details of the story, because I was mesmerized. He looked like a Calvin Klein model, did commercials sometimes, and was a builder the rest of the time. Well-spoken. Funny. Kind. Painfully unaware of his hotness.

We started hanging out, and I knew I was in trouble the day he got in the shower with me after a big night of partying. We'd watched the sun come up and didn't head home until mid-morning. A shower and soft bed were exactly what we needed. It wasn't our first time showering together, but it was just the first time I felt a love pang in my chest.

"Gareth, is the water alright?" I asked.

"Yeah. It's great. This is exactly what I needed," he said, sudsing up.

"Everything else cool?" I continued my line of questioning, helping scrub his back.

"Yeah. Why? You need more room?" he asked, running big hands through his wet hair.

"No. Do you?"

I poured shampoo into my hand.

"No," he said.

"Are sure you can tell?" I probed just a little deeper.

"What do you mean?" he asked, stopping the cleaning process.

"I mean, I didn't know if you could tell if you have enough room. Surely it's hard to see through those dark shades."

He'd unknowingly worn his sunglasses into the shower, too tired and comfortable with his eye gear to realize they weren't actually part of his face.

We laughed for thirty minutes.

About four years after meeting, we married. I was almost thirty. He was just over thirty. After the wedding we moved around for a bit, hence the stories in Asia and England. Whenever Gareth and I were away from New Zealand, I missed it. It felt like the place I'd been born—no longer a foreign country. It was home.

We eventually made our way back to New Zealand to set up shop.

The USA became a faint memory. I no longer pictured myself anywhere but New Zealand. I knew where I wanted to live as we got older, what our house would look like near the beach, how my job would turn out, and our babies. My life was Kiwi from there on out.

I don't know how to express how lovely it feels to have a profound love for a country other than the one you were born into. There are no words, only feelings—warm, tear-producing, content feelings. New

Zealand lives in me as much as Oklahoma. We are now and forever together—my sweat, tears, and joy seeping into both soils.

I did leave, though, not because I eventually got homesick, but because Gareth and I went our separate ways. I needed my mom during that time. I came back to America.

Now, I go back to New Zealand annually. I plan on buying a home there someday and splitting my life in half, performing a flip-flop game of six months in the Northern Hemisphere and six months in the Southern. I miss my lifestyle over there—my thought process. I long for my friends, and they miss me too. They always ask me when I'm coming home, not visiting, but returning to where I belong. It feels unbelievably good to hear that.

Because of traveling, I now have options wayyyyy beyond what I would have had if I'd never left American borders. On the other side of the globe, I have a destination that is home. I am welcome there at any time. I am loved there at any moment.

You will be loved too.

Go.

Find.

Be awakened.

New, and even old, feelings await you.

Thank you for reading *Good Globe*. The stories told within these pages are entirely true and as accurate as a memory addled by time, euphoria, and vodka will allow.

I am extremely humbled and honored to share my travels with you, and I sincerely hope that you have gained something from this book. Whether it is a decision to finally explore this good, gargantuan globe or maybe just a willingness to overcome a personal obstacle in your life, I hope this book has left you with a desire to pursue something more than what you already have.

Please subscribe to my mailing list to get all the latest news about upcoming books, including my next scandalous book, *Bad Boudoir*. Subscribe and feel free to contact me at shelbysimpson.com. I would love to hear from you.

Again, thank you for taking this journey with me. And don't be afraid to start your own.

Shelby Simpson